The ID CaseBook

Case Studies in Instructional Design

Third Edition

Peggy A. Ertmer
Purdue University

James Quinn
Oakland University

PEARSON
Merrill
Prentice Hall

Upper Saddle River, New Jersey
Columbus, Ohio

To my parents, Marcy and Leo, and my seven incredible sisters.

PE

To Dolly Parton

JQ

Library of Congress Cataloging-in-Publication Data

Ertmer, Peggy A.
   The ID casebook: Case Studies in instructional design/Peggy A. Ertmer, James Quinn.—3rd ed.
     p. cm.
   Includes bibliographical references.
   ISBN 0-13-171705-7
   1. Instructional systems—Design—Case studies. I. Quinn, James, - II. Title. III. Title: Instructional design casebook.
   LB1028.38.E78 2007
   371.3—dc22   2006046212

Vice President and Executive Publisher: Jeffery W. Johnston
Executive Editor: Debra A. Stollenwerk
Senior Editorial Assistant: Mary Morrill
Assistant Development Editor: Elisa Rogers
Production Editor: Kris Roach
Production Coordination: Carlisle Publishing Services
Design Coordinator: Diane C. Lorenzo

Cover Designer: Jeff Vanik
Cover Image: Corbis
Production Manager: Susan Hannahs
Director of Marketing: David Gesell
Senior Marketing Manager: Darcy Betts Prybella
Marketing Coordinator: Brian Mounts

This book was set in Times by Carlisle Communications, Ltd. It was printed and bound by R. R. Donnelley & Sons Company. The cover was printed by R. R. Donnelley & Sons Company.

Pearson Prentice Hall™ is a trademark of Pearson Education, Inc.
Pearson® is a registered trademark of Pearson plc
Prentice Hall® is a registered trademark of Pearson Education, Inc.
Merrill® is a registered trademark of Pearson Education, Inc.

Pearson Education Ltd.
Pearson Education Singapore Pte. Ltd.
Pearson Education Canada, Ltd.
Pearson Education—Japan

Pearson Education Australia Pty. Limited
Pearson Education North Asia Ltd.
Pearson Educatión de Mexico, S.A. de C.V.
Pearson Education Malaysia Pte. Ltd.

10 9 8 7 6 5 4
ISBN: 0-13-171705-7

Foreword

I will never forget the first time that I used true case-based instruction in an advanced instructional theory seminar that I taught annually. I say "true" because I had, for a number of years, provided case scenarios for students to analyze and discuss. These were brief descriptions of problems that I assumed were based on actual events, but they could also have been imaginary—constructed to illustrate a particular principle or theory that was useful in making instructional design decisions. The scenarios laid out a problem, provided a minimal amount of descriptive information about the context and nature of the problem, and then directed students to brainstorm solutions. My usual strategy was to have students work on these scenarios in small groups and then discuss their solutions as a class. Most of the time, this worked quite well (or so I thought, anyway). Students generated many creative ideas, and we had lively discussions about how those ideas might work in practice. From my own experience on instructional design projects, I was able to temper the discussions with a dose of reality.

As instructive and fun as these sessions were, however, they did not expose students very well to the uncertain, ill-structured, and often ambiguous nature of instructional design that occurs in most real situations. I wanted students to experience what it feels like to engage in solving complex, ill-structured problems where they could better understand the consequences of whatever assumptions and decisions they made during the problem-solving process. Not surprisingly, this thinking on my part was influenced by recent work on constructivism and situated learning that was appearing in the research and theoretical literature at the time.

So, collaborating with a couple of students who were interested in case-based methods, we overhauled my course and added case-based problem solving as an instructional strategy. The course was designed so that students would learn *about* case-based instruction at the same time they were actually *experiencing* it. A few weeks after the term began, however, I had a full-scale revolt on my hands. Students complained that I wasn't teaching them, that they didn't know what to do, and that they were afraid they would fail to meet expectations that were about as clear as mud to them. Interestingly, I was experiencing similar trepidations as the instructor. I felt unskilled at guiding students through complex problem solving and I was as uncomfortable as they were with our different roles within the class. I expected more autonomy from them as learners but found it difficult to relinquish my role as authority or expert. It was easier to lapse into the mode of telling them the solution than it was to exhort them to struggle through the problem-solving process. Almost to the end of the semester, I remained unsure that the results would be satisfactory (i.e., that we would all get through the course without killing each other *and* would have actually learned something of consequence).

The story has a happy ending. We did survive. The students produced a quality of work that exceeded my expectations (and theirs, too, I believe). We all learned a tremendous amount, and there was a sense of satisfaction from the experience that is hard to describe.

The theoretical and empirical evidence favoring case-based instruction is compelling, but it was the experience of using it myself that made me a believer. Ertmer and Quinn make the point that students are often unfamiliar with, and apprehensive about, using case studies in instruction, and they provide useful suggestions and strategies in Part I to help students approach case learning. I think it is just as important for instructors to prepare themselves to teach using case studies. Teaching this way is outside the comfort zone for many of us, and we can inadvertently sabotage the very things we are trying to accomplish. Just as students get better and become more confident with practice in case learning, so do instructors. Instructors, as well as students, should adopt a reflective stance, keep an open mind, question assumptions, and reflect on the case-learning experience. Finally, as Ertmer and Quinn encourage, enjoy yourselves. This can be a fun and memorable learning experience.

Marcy P. Driscoll

Preface

More than twenty five years ago, Ken Silber (1981) proposed that in order for instructional designers to learn and apply specific instructional design (ID) skills, they needed to acquire essential, underlying cognitive strategies. According to Silber, these underlying cognitive strategies comprised fundamental problem-solving processes; to be successful, ID professionals needed to master the application of these problem-solving processes as well as specific ID skills. Since that time, a plethora of ID models have been developed (Gustafson & Branch, 2002) and the nature of ID has been widely discussed (Rowland, 1993; Spector, 2001). In addition, a significant amount of research and discussion has taken place regarding the core competencies of ID professionals (Richey, Fields, & Foxon, 2001; Tennyson, 2001) as well as the appropriate academic preparation of instructional designers (Bannan-Ritland, 2001; Winn, 1997). Still, we find ourselves in agreement with Ken: ID is, at its core, a problem-solving process and one for which students must develop and apply higher-order thinking skills.

Given our view of ID as a complex, ill-structured domain of knowledge, we recognize that professional ID competence requires more than technical expertise. Although some design situations may involve well-structured and clearly defined problems that will benefit from a straightforward application of a set of technical procedures, many more situations are ill-structured and poorly defined. In addition to the necessary technical skills and knowledge, such situations depend on the artistry and skill of ID professionals to operate creatively and effectively in ambiguous, uncertain, and open-ended contexts.

Yet, given the constraints of time and other resources, how does an instructor teach the technical skills that are prerequisites for ID practice while still conveying the complexity and ill-structured nature of ID? We believe, as do many others, that the case teaching approach used in this book has the potential to situate the learning of technical ID skills within authentic contexts.

There are probably as many definitions of case-based instruction as there are ways of implementing it. In this text, we use an approach to case studies that is based on the business school model—that is, case studies are problem-centered descriptions of design situations, developed from the actual experiences of instructional designers. Furthermore, the cases in this book are designed to be dilemma-oriented; each case ends before the solution is clear. Students are expected to evaluate the available evidence, to make reasonable assumptions as necessary, to judge alternative interpretations and actions, and in this process, to experience the uncertainty that commonly accompanies design decisions. In particular, we hope that by analyzing the cases presented in this book, students will learn how to identify ID problems and subproblems; recognize the importance of context in resolving such problems; and develop, justify, and test alternative plans for resolving ID problems.

Organization

The ID CaseBook is divided into two process parts. In Part I, The Case-Learning Process: Strategies and Reflections, we provide students with suggestions and strategies for how to approach learning from case-based instruction. Although it is our experience that students are typically excited about using case studies in instruction, they often are a little apprehensive as well, perhaps because of their unfamiliarity with this approach. We have found that by providing helpful suggestions upfront, students' initial concerns are considerably lessened.

Part II includes 32 cases situated in a variety of educational and business contexts. Case titles are categorized by audience/context and arranged alphabetically by title. In addition, the matrix on the inside front and back covers allows readers to see, at a glance, the variety of content areas addressed by the cases. This matrix will help instructors, particularly, select cases that are most appropriate to their students' needs. (Note: *The Instructor's Manual* provides additional information about the issues and subissues addressed in each case.)

Features of the Third Edition

The third edition of *The ID CaseBook* consists of 32 instructional design case studies, representing 9 new cases as well as 23 of your favorite cases from the previous editions. In general, the new cases in the book are longer and more complex than many of the earlier cases. Together, these new and "returning" cases provide students with wonderful opportunities to examine a variety of demanding situations involving a wide range of contents, contexts, and audiences. For example, several new cases are situated in international contexts and deal with diverse audiences (e.g., military personnel, English language learners, hospital personnel, and gay and bisexual men). We have also increased the number of cases dealing with issues related to learning objects, assessment, and the design and evaluation of online instruction.

As in the previous two editions, each case consists of a case narrative and a set of questions designed to invoke ID practice. The *case narrative* includes relevant background information for the case such as the problem context, key players, available resources, and existing constraints. In addition, each case includes *relevant data* presented in a variety of forms and formats. There are also two sets of discussion questions at the end of each case to stimulate students' thinking and to provide a focus for class discussion. The first set of questions—Preliminary Analysis Questions—asks students to identify and discuss issues from the case, to consider the issues from multiple perspectives, to develop a plan of action to resolve problems, and/or to specify possible consequences resulting from their recommended plan. The second set of questions—Implications for ID Practice—requires students to think more broadly about the issues presented in the case from the point of view of ID theory and practice.

As requested by previous reviewers and adopters of the book, we have reorganized the text to make it easier to identify and select relevant cases for your students. You will notice, first of all, that each case title now includes a subtitle that reflects the content of the case or the context in which it occurs. Sometimes these subtitles also provide information about the specific issues in the cases without giving away any of the more subtle details of, or solutions for, the cases.

Perhaps even more helpful to instructors than the addition of case subtitles, however, is the new organization of the text. Cases are now combined into sections, with each section representing the specific context in which that group of cases occurs. For example, the first section of the case studies contains eight cases that are situated in K–12 environments, followed by a section containing nine post-secondary cases. The third section includes 14 cases situated in a corporate or manufacturing environment, while the last section contains one case situated in a military context. This organization helps you identify which cases are most relevant to your needs. As noted earlier, a matrix (included on the inside front and back covers) pulls all of this information together, making it easy to determine which cases are appropriate for your students.

Finally, we have expanded Part I, The Case-Learning Process: Strategies and Reflections, to introduce readers to learning from cases and to provide guidance on selecting strategies for completing case analyses.

Ancillaries

The *Instructor's Manual* for this book is available online through the Prentice Hall website. To access it, go to **http://www.prenhall.com,** click on the Instructor Support button, and then go to the Download Supplements section. Here you will be able to log in or complete a onetime registration for a user name and password. If you have any questions regarding this process or the materials available online, please contact your local Prentice Hall sales representative. The *Instructor's Manual* includes:

Case Matrix: A summary matrix (also found on located on the inside front and back covers of the textbook) that allows instructors to see, at a glance, the particular issues and subissues of each case:

Teaching Suggestions: Ideas for instructors regarding the different ways the cases can be used with different levels of students;

Case Overview: A brief description of the case, including the "big idea" students should glean from the case;

Case Objectives: The specific focus of the case (the supporting concepts/principles learners should use in analyzing the case issues); the knowledge, skills, and/or attitudes students should gain from their case analyses and discussions; and

Debriefing Guidelines: Suggestions from the case authors regarding how to think about the case.

It is our hope that the combined features of *The ID CaseBook* and the *Instructor's Manual* will provide both students and instructors with a challenging and rewarding learning experience. We continue to view this whole venture as a work-in-progress. If you or your students have suggestions for future editions, we'd love to hear from you! Our e-mail addresses are **pertmer@purdue.edu** and **quinn@oakland.edu**.

Acknowledgments

Throughout this endeavor we have benefited from the support, advice, and encouragement of a number of individuals, including the contributing authors, supportive colleagues, patient family members, insightful students, meticulous secretaries, an outstanding editor, and thoughtful reviewers. Without the contributions of all of these people, this book would not have been possible.

First, we would like to thank all the authors who contributed to this volume. We're sure that you will agree that this edition includes the works of some of the best minds in our field. We have enjoyed working with all of them, for they have made our work interesting, enjoyable, and relatively painless. We firmly believe that each author has added something unique to the text and sincerely appreciate the time they all gave to develop and revise their cases. For your information, we have provided a brief biography of each author in the "About the Authors" section.

Our current and past students continue to be influential in shaping many of the details of the text, particularly in making suggestions for how to think about the case-learning process. We are also grateful to our colleagues who were willing to pilot the cases in their courses and to provide valuable formative feedback that improved numerous aspects of the cases.

In addition, we would like to thank our editor, Debbie Stollenwerk, and the production staff at Merrill/Prentice Hall and Carlisle Publishing Services. Debbie and her team have worked with us throughout the process to produce what we hope will be an excellent and useful third edition. We were also assisted in the design and development process by the insights and suggestions from a number of reviewers, including David L. Breithaupt, Boise State University; Carrie Dale, Baker College of Flint; Mary Engstrom, University of South Dakota; Patricia L. Hardré, University of Oklahoma; Kendall Hartley, University of Nevada, Las Vegas; William Milheim, Penn State University, Great Valley; and Susan Santo, University of South Dakota.

References

Bannan-Ritland, B. (2001). Teaching instructional design: An action learning approach. *Performance Improvement Quarterly, 14*(2), 37–52.

Gustafson, K. L., & Branch, R. M. (2002). *Survey of instructional development models.* Syracuse, NY: ERIC Clearinghouse on Information and Technology.

Richey, R., Fields, D., & Foxon, M. (2001). *Instructional design competencies: The standards* (3rd ed.). Syracuse, NY: ERIC Clearinghouse on Information and Technology.

Rowland, G. (1993). Designing and instructional design. *Educational Technology Research and Development, 41*(1), 79–91.

Silber, K. H. (1981). Applying Piaget's stages of intellectual development and Guildford's structure of intellect model to training instructional developers. *Journal of Instructional Development, 4*(3), 33–40.

Spector, J. M. (2001). A philosophy of instructional design for the 21st century? *Journal of Structural Learning and Intelligent Systems, 14,* 307–318.

Tennyson, R. D. (2001). Defining core competencies of an instructional technologist. *Computers in Human Behavior, 17,* 355–361.

Winn, W. (1997). Advantages of a theory-based curriculum in instructional technology. *Educational Technology, 37*(1), 34–41.

Teacher Preparation Classroom

See a demo at
www.prenhall.com/teacherprep/demo

Your Class. Their Careers. Our Future. Will your students be prepared?

We invite you to explore our new, innovative and engaging website and all that it has to offer you, your course, and tomorrow's educators! Organized around the major courses pre-service teachers take, the Teacher Preparation site provides media, student/teacher artifacts, strategies, research articles, and other resources to equip your students with the quality tools needed to excel in their courses and prepare them for their first classroom.

This ultimate on-line education resource is available at no cost, when packaged with a Merrill text, and will provide you and your students access to:

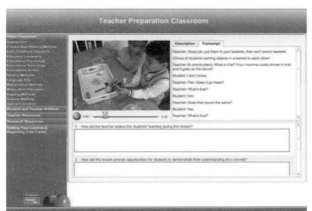

Online Video Library. More than 150 video clips—each tied to a course topic and framed by learning goals and Praxis-type questions—capture real teachers and students working in real classrooms, as well as in-depth interviews with both students and educators.

Student and Teacher Artifacts. More than 200 student and teacher classroom artifacts—each tied to a course topic and framed by learning goals and application questions—provide a wealth of materials and experiences to help make your study to become a professional teacher more concrete and hands-on.

Research Articles. Over 500 articles from ASCD's renowned journal *Educational Leadership*. The site also includes Research Navigator, a searchable database of additional educational journals.

Teaching Strategies. Over 500 strategies and lesson plans for you to use when you become a practicing professional.

Licensure and Career Tools. Resources devoted to helping you pass your licensure exam; learn standards, law, and public policies; plan a teaching portfolio; and succeed in your first year of teaching.

How to ORDER *Teacher Prep* for you and your students:

For students to receive a *Teacher Prep* Access Code with this text, instructors **must** provide a special value pack ISBN number on their textbook order form. To receive this special ISBN, please email **Merrill.marketing@pearsoned.com** and provide the following information:
- Name and Affiliation
- Author/Title/Edition of Merrill text

Upon ordering *Teacher Prep* for their students, instructors will be given a lifetime *Teacher Prep* Access Code.

About the Authors

Peggy A. Ertmer is Associate Professor of Educational Technology at Purdue University. She continues to love teaching with case studies and is currently exploring the connection between case-based learning and the development of ID expertise. Peg actively mentors both students and peers, including pre- and in-service teachers, in the use of case-based and problem-based learning (PBL) pedagogy, technology tools, and self-regulated learning skills.

James Quinn is Associate Professor in the Department of Human Resource Development at Oakland University. He has been coordinator of the Master of Training and Development program for several years and teaches courses in instructional design and evaluation. His primary research interests are in the graduate education and professional development of instructional designers.

Sue Bennett is Senior Lecturer in the Faculty of Education and Deputy Director of the Centre for Research in Interactive Learning Environments at the University of Wollongong, Australia. She teaches within the Information Technology in Education and Training program and is the coordinator of international initiatives within this area. Sue has extensive experience in the design, development, and evaluation of multimedia and online instructional materials.

Jeannie Brush is Senior Training Associate at Eli Lilly and Company in Indianapolis, Indiana. Her educational interests include the development of CBTs, scenario-based training, formative evaluation, and instructor certification.

Thomas Brush is Associate Professor of Instructional Systems Technology at Indiana University, Bloomington. His research interests involve the development, implementation, and evaluation of technology-enhanced environments to support inquiry-based learning in K–12 settings. He also teaches classes focusing on effective methods for integrating technology into K–12 classrooms.

Katherine S. Cennamo is Associate Professor of Instructional Design and Technology at Virginia Tech. She has over 20 years of experience in the design and development of instructional materials for corporate, non-profit, and academic organizations. Her teaching and research focuses on the application of learning theories to the design of technology-based learning materials, instructional video, and the preparation of instructional designers.

Lauren Clark is Associate Dean for Research at the University of Colorado at Denver and Health Sciences Center School of Nursing, where she teaches public health nursing and qualitative research. She conducts research related to cultural aspects of childhood obesity in Latino families. By using sound instructional design principles, she shares her enthusiasm for research in her teaching.

Nada Dabbagh is Associate Professor of Instructional Design and Technology at George Mason University. Her research interests include task structuring in e-learning environments, problem generation and representation in hypermedia learning environments, and supporting self-regulation in distributed learning environments. She has published numerous journal articles and book chapters in each of these areas and most recently the text *Online Learning: Concepts, Strategies, and Application* (Merrill/Prentice Hall, 2005) co-authored with Brenda Bannan-Ritland.

Melissa J. Dark is Associate Professor in the College of Technology at Purdue University. Melissa has worked on several STEM (science, technology, engineering, and mathematics) curriculum and instructional projects with industry, government, and higher education. She has experience in needs assessment, instructional design, development, and evaluation of education in STEM disciplines including traditional, face-to-face education, as well video, CD-ROM, and Internet-delivered courses.

Kara Dawson is Associate Professor in the School of Teaching and Learning at the University of Florida. Her research intersects the fields of educational technology and teacher education. She serves as program coordinator for Educational Technology and co-coordinator of an online Masters and Ed.S. program in teaching, learning, and facilitating change with educational technology.

Walter Dick is Professor Emeritus of Instructional Systems at Florida State University. His major interests are instructional design and evaluation. He is the co-author of the widely used text *The Systematic Design of Instruction*. Walter currently lives with his wife in Pennsylvania and Alabama.

Aaron Doering is Assistant Professor in Learning Technologies within the Department of Curriculum and Instruction at the University of Minnesota. Aaron teaches and researches the development of distance learning and spatial learning environments. His most recent research focuses on adventure learning environments and the integration of geographic information systems into K–12 classrooms.

Stephen Dundis is Associate Professor in the Human Resource Development Program at Northeastern Illinois University. He teaches courses in instructional design, needs assessment, and computer-based instruction at both the graduate and undergraduate levels. His research interests include design issues in online learning/support, virtual collaboration and problem solving, and case- and apprenticeship-based instructional strategies.

Joanna C. Dunlap is Associate Professor in the School of Education and Human Development at the University of Colorado at Denver and Health Sciences Center. Her teaching and research interests focus on the use of situated learning and social constructivist approaches to enhance learners' development and experiences, faculty development, and the design of online courses and programs.

Gary Elsbernd has more than 15 years of experience in the field of performance technology and performance-centered design and holds a master's degree in Instructional and Performance Technology from Boise State University. Gary designs user interfaces for a major insurance company in Kansas City and lives in Topeka, Kansas, with his wife and three children.

Teresa Franklin is Associate Professor in Instructional Technology at Ohio University. She has worked extensively with instructional design issues involving technology integration in K–12 curriculum development—especially in the areas of science education, teacher professional development, and online learning environments. Her recent work includes research on emerging technologies (handhelds, tablets, and gaming) in K–12 science, mathematics, and technology literacy classrooms.

Michael M. Grant, an Assistant Professor of Instructional Design and Technology at the University of Memphis, earned his Ph.D. in Instructional Technology from The University of Georgia. His research examines the design of technology-enhanced learning environments and learner characteristics. In 2005, he was selected for the Young Researcher Award by the Special Interest Group for Instructional Technology (SIGIT) of the American Educational Research Association.

Barry Harper is the Dean of the Faculty of Education and Director of the Education Media Laboratory at the University of Wollongong, Australia. He is on the editorial board of international journals and a member of the organizing committee of key international conferences in educational technology. His areas of research interest include cognitive strategies and instructional processes in education and training, collaborative learning in networked environments, learning designs, and learning objects.

John G. Hedberg is Millennium Innovations Chair of ICT and Education at Macquarie University in Sydney, Australia, and is Director of the Macquarie ICT Innovations Centre. He was previously professor of learning sciences and technologies at Nanyang Technological University, Singapore. He has worked on several ID projects in Australia. His most recent book is *Evaluating Interactive Learning Systems,* co-authored with Thomas Reeves.

Ronni Hendel-Giller lives in Los Angeles and serves as the Vice President of Automotive Operations for Maritz Learning. Ronni began her career as an instructional designer and has worked in a variety of roles, including facilitator and human performance consultant. Ronni holds a Bachelor of Arts from Hebrew University of Jerusalem and a Master of Science in Instructional and Performance Technology from Boise State University.

Janette R. Hill is Associate Professor of Instructional Technology at the University of Georgia. She teaches graduate-level courses in the areas of instructional design, research, and online learning. Her research areas include community building in virtual environments, the use of information technologies for purposes of learning, and effective strategies for online learning.

Simon Hooper is Associate Professor in Curriculum and Instruction at the University of Minnesota. He is interested in new media and his research focuses on understanding how technology can support teaching and learning. He studies the software development process and develops applications that take advantage of contemporary technologies.

Carol S. Kamin is Associate Professor of Pediatrics and the Director of Educational Research and Development at the University of Colorado School of Medicine. She is also the Director of the Project LIVE consortium, which develops multimedia cases for problem-based learning. Her research interests focus on understanding the role of media and technology and its effect on learning.

Mable B. Kinzie is Associate Professor at the University of Virginia. She specializes in user-centered instructional design, incorporating needs assessment, and rapid prototyping. She has designed numerous products for adult/life-long learning, e-learning, K–12 education, and consumer/public health, and has authored over 35 publications. She has received awards as professor, scholar, and instructional designer, and finds it's impossible to have too much fun.

Ann Kovalchick is Executive Director of Innovative Technology Services and Design at Tulane University, where she leads the integration of information and communication technologies to support user services, teaching and learning, and application development for administrative services. She has a Ph.D. in Education from The University of Virginia, a master's in Anthropology, and a B.Sc. in Communication Theory.

Valerie A. Larsen is the Educational Technology Consultant for the Alliance for Catholic Education at the University of Notre Dame, where she has instructional design and administrative responsibilities in distance learning and teaches graduate courses in technology integration. She also provides design and training services to the business community. Her research interests include multimedia design, distance learning, and case studies.

Lori Lockyer teaches within the *ICTs in Learning* program in the Faculty of Education, is Director of the Digital Media Centre, and is Head of Educational Development in the School of Medicine at the University of Wollongong, Australia. Over the past nine years she has designed, developed, implemented, and researched technology-supported learning environments within a range of educational settings.

Linda Lohr is Associate Professor at the University of Northern Colorado. She is the author of *Creating Graphics for Learning and Performance: Lessons in Visual Literacy* (Merrill/Prentice Hall, 2003) and teaches courses in distance learning, instructional design, instructional graphics, and human performance technology.

Deborah L. Lowther is Associate Professor of Instructional Design and Technology at the University of Memphis where she also serves as Senior Faculty Researcher for CREP. Deborah has co-authored two books, several book chapters, and journal articles; made numerous presentations; provided leadership and evaluations for multiple technology integration grants; and has provided professional development to educators across the country.

Martha Mann (previously Julian) is an instructional designer and usability analyst for the Office of Safety and Health at the Arizona Department of Transportation. Martha is also assists in the development of the agency's e-learning program policies, design, and development guidelines. She is convinced that state government is a great place to gather scenarios for future instructional design case studies.

Skip Marshall is Senior Instructional Designer and Media Developer for a corporate training group in Tampa, Florida. His primary focus includes developing dynamic instructional environments, interactive simulations, and learning management systems in support of corporate training initiatives.

Gary R. Morrison is a Professor in the Instructional Design and Technology program at Old Dominion University. His research focuses on cognitive load theory, instructional strategies, K–12 technology integration, and distance education. Gary is senior author of *Designing Effective Instruction* and *Integrating Computer Technology into the Classroom* (Merrill/Prentice Hall, 2005). His publications include over 50 articles and over 100 conference presentations.

Julie Muehlhausen, English Department Chair at Crawfordsville High School (IN), has taught English and social studies classes for over 25 years. Her college teaching experience includes English composition and English methods courses. She has designed and instituted an independent reading program, a 4-grade portfolio system, and a 24/7 laptop writing and research program for grades 9–12. Her current interests include pre-service teacher portfolio evaluation and technology for student organization.

Chandra Orrill is a Research Scientist in the Learning and Performance Support Laboratory at the University of Georgia. She also holds adjunct faculty status in the Department of Educational Psychology and Instructional Technology. Chandra's research focuses on teacher professional development and school change with particular emphases in mathematics education and technology integration in mathematics in grades 3–8.

Rose M. Pringle is Assistant Professor in the School of Teaching and Learning at the University of Florida. She teaches science education and has published articles on assessment and the integration of technology in science methods courses. Her research interests include pedagogical issues in teaching inquiry science and the exploration of formative assessments as tools to foster continuous learning in science.

Steven M. Ross received his Doctorate in Educational Psychology from Pennsylvania State University. He joined the University of Memphis in 1974 and is the author of six textbooks and over 120 journal articles in the areas of educational technology and instructional design, at-risk learners, educational reform, computer-based instruction, and individualized instruction. He is the editor of the research section of *Educational Technology Research and Development*.

Shanna M. Salter has worked as a manufacturing supervisor for Intel in Rio Rancho, New Mexico, since May 2000. She focuses her strengths and passions on people and employee relations and recently accepted a position in Fab11X as a Human Resource Specialist. Prior to working at Intel, Shanna was employed for three years by the State of New Mexico as a Juvenile Probation and Parole Officer.

Patti Shank is President of Learning Peaks, an internationally known instructional design and technology consulting group. She is an often-requested speaker at training and instructional technology conferences and co-authored *Making Sense of Online Learning* (Pfeiffer, 2004). Patti was an award-winning contributing editor for *Online Learning Magazine* and writes for Macromedia, Magna Publication's *Online Classroom, Training Media Review*, and other publications.

Krista D. Simons is Assistant Professor of Educational Technology at Purdue University. She is interested in several aspects of technology integration related to K–12 environments. Specifically, she has studied scaffolding in the context of supporting middle school teachers and learners, and effective means of promoting technology integration in classroom instruction.

Rod Sims is a consultant and online professor with Capella University, and since 1980 has specialized in instructional design and computer-based learning. Rod is Executive Vice-President of the International Board of Standards for Training, Performance, and Instruction (IBSTPI) and has published extensively. His current research focuses on alternative instructional design models, transformational learning experiences, and multi-user learning environments.

David L. Solomon has spent most of his vocational life working in the field of learning and performance improvement. Currently, he is Director of Design and Innovation for Big Communications in Ferndale, Michigan, the leading health care communications innovator focused on sales force and physician education and engagement. Prior to this, he held positions in strategic planning and retail performance solutions at BBDO Detroit.

Timothy W. Spannaus is Senior Lecturer in Instructional Technology and Research Fellow with the Institute for Learning and Performance Improvement at Wayne State University in Detroit, Michigan. His current research interests include using technologies to improve teaching and learning in higher education and use of games and simulations for learning. Tim is also Chairman and Chief Learning Architect at The Emdicium Group, Inc., in Southfield, Michigan.

Donald A. Stepich is Associate Professor in the Instructional and Performance Technology Department at Boise State University, where he teaches both online and on-campus courses. He has been working and teaching in the instructional design field for more than 15 years. His interests include using analogies as learning tools and the development of professional expertise.

Toni Stokes-Jones is Associate Professor of Educational Media and Technology in the Department of Teacher Education at Eastern Michigan University. She received her Ph.D. and M.Ed. in Instructional Technology from Wayne State University. In addition to teaching secondary business education and adult/higher education, she has over 20 years of experience as a trainer and instructional designer.

William Sugar is Associate Professor in the Library Science and Instructional Technology Department at East Carolina University. His current research interests are developing effective and alternative technology integration strategies for teachers, as well as examining the interrelationship between human computer interface design principles and instructional design principles.

Brenda Sugrue is Senior Director of Research for the American Society for Training and Development (ASTD), directing all of its research and benchmarking activities. Prior to joining ASTD in 2003, she was a professor of instructional design and technology at the University of Iowa. She has published dozens of articles and book chapters on learning and performance improvement.

Laura L. Summers is Assistant Professor of Educational Technology and School Library Programs Coordinator at the University of Northern Colorado. She has over 16 years of experience as an instructional designer for business, higher education, and K–12 education. She specializes in ethnography, case study, and portraiture research designs.

Sean R. Tangney earned a master's degree in Training and Development from Oakland University in Rochester, Michigan. Sean has developed instructor-led training as well as Web-based training for the automotive industry and a utility company in Detroit, Michigan. Most recently, he has been involved in designing, developing, and implementing electronic performance support solutions in the automotive industry.

I. Andrew Teasdale has a Ph.D. in Instructional Systems Technology from Indiana University and has developed award-winning courseware and content authoring tools while working for General Motors and Eli Lilly. He has taught at Oakland University and Brigham Young University. He has also published in the field of Ancient Near Eastern Studies. He loves mountain/rock climbing, windsurfing, and sailing.

Christine L. Thornam leads the development of a nurse home visitor and supervisor curriculum for distance delivery by the Nurse-Family Partnership (NFP), a national, non-profit organization serving first-time, low-income mothers. Her pediatric nursing experience, combined with more than 20 years of instructional design, multimedia production, and use of educational technologies, inform the blended learning solutions that NFP uses today.

Monica W. Tracey received her Ph. D. in Instructional Technology from Wayne State University, Detroit, Michigan. Dr. Tracey has 19 years of experience in business in designing, developing, and delivering instruction and is an Assistant Professor at Oakland University in Rochester, Michigan, where she continues her research on instructional design which includes model design and validation and instructional strategies.

Naomi Waldron is a Learning Designer at the Queensland University of Technology, where she advises academic staff on the effective use of technologies to support learning and teaching. She previously worked as an instructional designer with a leading Australian e-learning company, designing interactive multimedia for school, vocational education, and corporate training sectors.

Brent G. Wilson is Professor of Information and Learning Technologies at the University of Colorado at Denver and Health Sciences Center, where he teaches courses in instructional design, action research, and emerging trends. For several years he has worked to broaden the conceptual foundations of instructional design to include critiques from value, aesthetic, and user-practitioner perspectives.

Michael L. Wray is the Director of Culinary and Restaurant Administration at the Metropolitan State College of Denver. In addition to collegiate teaching experience, Michael worked as a chef and food and beverage director. At Metro State, Michael has garnered a strong following of students who appreciate his interactive learning environment. He has a BS in Nutrition and Foods from Virginia Tech, an MBA from Salisbury University, and is completing his dissertation in Education Leadership and Innovation.

Contents

Case Studies—Section 2: Post-secondary Audience/Context 75

Case Studies—Section 3: Corporate Audience/Context 145

Case Studies—Section 4: Military Audience/Context   247

Part I

The Case-Learning Process: Strategies and Reflections

by Peggy A. Ertmer and James Quinn

Instructional Design (ID) is a complex, ill-defined skill that is largely, if not entirely, dependent on the context in which it is done (Jonassen, personal communication, March 15, 2005). This means that there isn't a single set of principles and procedures that can be applied in the same way in every situation. While there is no formula for good design (Cates, 2001), there is evidence to suggest that the more we know about ID, and the more we practice solving ID problems, the more "expert" we become (Atherton, 2003; Bransford, Brown, & Cocking, 2000; Ertmer & Stepich, 2005; Hardré, Ge, & Thomas, 2005).

It is our hope that the cases in this book provide you with the kind of opportunities you need to initiate the development of your instructional design expertise. The case studies are purposefully complex and, by design, do not lend themselves to simple, "right" answers. The goal of the case method is not to help you find answers to every possible design issue but rather to increase your understanding of the types of complex problems professional designers encounter in their everyday practice. By analyzing and reflecting on a variety of complex design situations, we expect that you will be better prepared to solve similar problems when they occur in your own practice.

The Case-Learning Experience

Although case methods have been used in business, law, and medicine for over 100 years, it is likely that this will be one of your first experiences with the case approach. This may give rise to a wide range of feelings—excitement, nervousness, curiosity, intimidation. In addition, you'll probably have a lot of questions: How do I analyze a case? How long should a case analysis be? How will I know if I've done it right? Where will I find the information and resources I need to solve the case problems? Although it is our experience that students are typically excited about using case studies in instruction, they often feel a little apprehensive as well, possibly due to their unfamiliarity with this approach. We've written this section, addressed to you specifically, because we have found that initial concerns can be lessened by describing, up front, the types of tasks you will be expected to complete, as well as some of the adjustments you may need to make in your current learning "mindsets." As one of our former students noted:

> In my opinion, if students were told up front that this style of learning (case-based instruction) feels slow and cumbersome at first, and that they should read and re-read the information in the case a couple of times, do what they need to visualize and better understand the scenarios—it might be easier to adjust to. I think case-based learning is a valuable and interactive method that just takes a different mindset than most students are used to.

We think this student makes two excellent suggestions: tell students what this approach *feels* like and tell them how to *do* it (i.e., analyze a case). Although we don't really believe that we can tell you exactly how it feels to learn from cases or how you must go about analyzing a case, we offer a few thoughts and suggestions related to these two elements of the case-learning experience. We begin with suggestions on how to adopt a reflective mind-set and then provide strategies and procedures for analyzing a case.

Developing a Reflective Mindset

One of the primary goals of professional education is to help novices "think like" members of the profession (Shulman, 1992). This entails being able to look back on practice as a way to understand experience (Schön, 1983), as well as engaging in an internal process of reflection and inquiry as a way to improve future practice. According to Hartog (2002), this type of skillful inquiry takes "time, commitment, and practice" (p. 237).

Kitchener and King (1990) described mature, reflective thinkers as being able to view situations from multiple perspectives, search for alternative explanations of events, and use evidence to support or evaluate a decision or position. These qualities form an essential part of the mindset that we believe facilitates learning from case studies. We provide additional guidelines below, gleaned from our own experiences and those of our students, as well as from the results of an exploratory research study conducted by one of the authors (Ertmer, Newby, & MacDougall, 1996).

- There is no one, right answer. If you enter the case-learning experience with this idea firmly planted, you are less likely to be frustrated by the ambiguity inherent in the case-study approach. There are many answers to the issues in each case. The solutions you propose will depend as much on the perspective you take as on the issues you identify. Accept the fact that you will not know how to solve each case. Furthermore, if you have no clue where to begin, give yourself permission not to know. Then begin the analysis process by paying attention to how others analyze the case based on their personal experiences.

  After you have analyzed the case, you may think that it would be helpful to know how the designers in the cases "solved" the problems. However, this is not as helpful as you might think. Being frustrated by a lack of answers can actually be very motivating. If you're left hanging after reading a case, chances are you'll continue to ponder the issues for a long time to come.

- There is more than one way to look at things. One of the advantages to participating in case discussions is that you get the chance to hear how others analyzed the case and to consider multiple points of view, thus gaining a more complete examination and understanding of the issues involved. Not only will listening to others' ideas *allow* you to see the issues from different points of view but it will also *force* you to consider exactly where you stand. By paying close attention to what others have to say, you can evaluate how their views fit with your own. Thus, you learn more about who you are, where you are coming from, and what you stand for. Your views of others, as well as of yourself, may be broadened.

▪ Keep an open mind; suspend judgment until all ideas are considered. This suggestion builds on the previous one. It is important to come to the case discussion with an attitude of, "Let's see what develops." Begin by regarding your initial solutions as tentative. Listen respectfully to your peers; ask questions to clarify and gather additional information, not to pass judgment on ideas different from yours. As one of our students recommended, "Be flexible and open-minded. Remember that problems can be attacked from many different angles." Use the case discussion as a means to gather additional data. In the end, your final recommendation should be informed by the collective wisdom of the whole class, yet reflect your own best judgment.

▪ Be leery of assumptions and generalizations; avoid seeing things in extremes. If data are ambiguous or there is little evidence to support why case players behaved as they did, be cautious of the assumptions you make. Be especially careful to state your assumptions tentatively, suggesting uncertainty. Furthermore, be careful about making assumptions that allow you to propose easy solutions. Before going down any single solution path, ask yourself if the assumptions you are making are realistic based on the facts of the case.

Along these same lines, be careful not to generalize your observations beyond the data provided. Avoid using labels or slogans that lump people together. If you're inclined to see things in black and white, all or nothing, stand back and look at the words you use in your analysis. It is fairly safe to say that you should avoid words such as *always, never, everybody*, or *nobody*. Stick close to the facts when describing the issues, drawing conclusions, and making recommendations.

▪ Expect to get better; focus on the analysis process. At the beginning of a case-based course, you may feel overwhelmed with the challenge of trying to solve case problems. It is important to recognize, first, that this is not uncommon. Many students initially feel overwhelmed and apprehensive. Second, it is equally important to recognize that, as with most skills, design skills and knowledge improve with practice. Furthermore, most students actually start to enjoy the challenge involved in analyzing problematic situations. If you maintain the mindset that you learn as much from the analysis process as you do from identifying a potential solution, then your case-learning experience will be less frustrating. The analytic process is at the heart of the case method. Pay attention to the progress you make in analyzing the cases. Judge your success not by comparing your answer to what the authors of the case did, but by your approach to the analysis process. Did you consider all of the issues? Did you look at issues from the varying perspectives of the key players? Have you based suggestions on available data? If your skills are improving in these areas, you're gaining in precisely the ways promoted by the case approach. And remember that learning is a lifelong process. You'll never know all there is to know about designing. Yet each experience with design situations should move you closer to thinking and acting like a professional designer.

▪ Take time to reflect. According to Campoy (2005), "Good problem solvers review their efforts and the results to incorporate what they have learned for future reference (p. 197). Reflection is a recurring theme in our discussion of how to approach a case study. Quite simply, that's because we believe that reflection enhances everything that happens in the case method. According to Shulman (1996), "We do not learn from experience; we learn by thinking about our experience" (p. 208). Reflection, as a form of metacognition, is a prerequisite for deep learning.

It's true that a case analysis takes more time to complete than traditional course assignments. Yet there is little to be gained by trying to rush the process. Acting or responding impulsively decreases the chances that you will gather all the relevant information, examine all the potential courses of action, and consider the many possible ensuing consequences. Take time to think. Ask questions of yourself, your peers, and your instructor. Hills and Gibson (cited in Grimmett & Erickson, 1988) describe how reflective practitioners might go about their work. The development of this type of reflective mindset can begin with your work on these cases:

> As you go about your work responding to phenomena, identifying problems, diagnosing problems, making normative judgments, developing strategies, etc. think about your responses to situations and about what it is in the situation, and in yourself, that leads you to respond that way; think about the norms and values on which your judgments are based; think about the manner in which you frame problems, and think about "your conception of your role." "Surface" and criticize your implicit understandings. Construct and test your own theories. (p. 151)

- Enjoy yourself. As indicated earlier, the case method may at first feel like a strange and difficult way to learn. Yet, even when students indicate that learning from case studies can be frustrating and "unnerving," they also admit that it is exciting and valuable. Being actively involved, working with stimulating case material, having a chance to express your ideas and hear those of others—these are all enjoyable aspects of case learning. We think one of our students summed it up wonderfully: "I like how cases challenge you and frustrate you. My advice is to relax. Let the ideas flow. Don't say, 'This isn't possible.' And, most of all, be confident that what you are doing now will pay off in the future."

Strategies for Analyzing a Case

There are probably a variety of ways to effectively analyze a case study. We offer the following as one possibility:

1. Understand the context in which the case is being analyzed and discussed. If your instructor is using this text to supplement another, then the cases will probably be used to provide real-world examples of the content or design steps you've discussed. This context can help focus your attention on relevant issues, questions, and concerns related to your readings and other coursework. Also, each case includes a set of focusing questions at the end. You may want to read these questions first, as a way to "prime the pump." Reading case questions before you read the case may help you read more meaningfully and more effectively.

2. Read the case. Your first reading should probably be fairly quick, just to get a general sense of what the case is about—the key players, main issues, context, and so on.

3. Read the case again. Your second (and subsequent) reading(s) should be much slower: taking notes, considering multiple perspectives, thinking about alternative solutions and consequences. The benefits you reap from your case analysis will relate to how much time you spend—not necessarily reading, but reflecting on what you have read.

4. Analyze the case. This is probably the "fuzziest" and thus most overwhelming step of the whole case-analysis process. Assuming that you have already identified the facts of the case, relevant information, key players, context, and resources and constraints, we recommend that you address the following questions/points during your analysis:

   a. Who are the key stakeholders in this case? How would each stakeholder describe the primary issue in the case?

   b. Given the stakeholders' various perspectives, what do *you* see as the primary design issue(s) in the case?

   c. List any assumptions you make about information that is missing from the case. As much as possible, support your assumptions with evidence from the case. Why are your assumptions reasonable?

   d. Generate a list of potential solutions related to each issue.

   e. Specify possible consequences (pros and cons) of each solution.

   f. After weighing the advantages and limitations to each solution, make a recommendation for action.

   g. Describe how your recommendations address the issues listed in the first two points above. Reflect on the extent to which you think that the suggested solution will solve the primary issue(s).

5. Actively participate in class discussion. The case class is a learning community—together you, your instructor, and your peers are working to gain a more complete understanding of the case situation and possible solutions. It is important that you be an active participant as well as an active listener. You must listen carefully to what others are saying so that your questions and contributions can move the discussion along. Coming to class prepared is critical to your ability to participate in, and benefit from, the case-learning experience.

6. Reflect on the case-learning experience. Boud (2001) advocated the use of reflection at three different points during a learning experience: at the *start*, in a preparatory phase when you start to explore what is required of you, as you become aware of the demands of the situation and the resources you bring to bear; *during* the experience, as a way of dealing with the vast array of inputs and coping with the feelings generated; and *after* the experience, as you attempt to make sense of it.

   The case method provides fertile ground for facilitating a reflective approach to learning. Starting with the first step in the analysis process, as you consider the context in which you are studying a case, you are immersed (already engaging) in a reflective process. As you implement your analysis approach, you complete a variety of activities that are inherent to a reflective design approach; that is, you "test the waters" through a process in which you consider previous experiences, connect with your feelings, and draw upon your existing repertoire of images, metaphors, and theories (Smith, 2001).

Finally, at the end of a case analysis, reflection helps you make sense of your experiences and deepen your understanding of the case. By reflecting on both the products and the processes of your learning experiences, you gain insights essential to improving future performance. Reflection can link past and future actions by providing you with information about the strategies you used (learning process) and the outcomes you achieved (learning products). It allows you to take stock of what has happened and to prepare yourself for future action. As noted by one of our former students:

> I have enjoyed the opportunity to reflect upon my performance (on my case analyses) because I think that it encourages me to take stock of where I have been, where I am, and where I need to go on the road to expertise. Self-reflection may, at times, be painful, but the gains stimulate growth and improvement necessary to become the best instructional designer possible.

Becoming an ID Professional: Reflecting on Your Case Experiences

It should be evident by now that one of our primary purposes for using case studies as an instructional approach is to facilitate your growing ability to think like an instructional design professional. As in all professions, learning to "think like a designer" does not happen overnight. Furthermore, reflection has been established as a valuable part of this process. As Weil and Frame (1992) stated, "experience and action do not themselves guarantee learning. We learn by doing and through reflection on doing" (p. 63).

As you analyze the cases in this book, and particularly as you come to the end of using the book, we ask you to consider *how* you learned from the case studies, and then more broadly as a beginning ID professional, how you might use cases in your own design work.

First of all, consider what it was like trying to learn from case studies. Use the following questions to stimulate your thinking about specific aspects of the case-learning experience:

- ✔ How interesting, valuable, and relevant was the case approach?
- ✔ How challenging and/or frustrating was it? What features contributed to the challenge level? Should these features be altered and if so, how?
- ✔ How would you describe your attitude toward using case studies as a learning tool?
- ✔ What strategies did you use to analyze each case? Did you use a systematic approach, or was it more hit-and-miss?
- ✔ Did your approach change over the course of the semester and if so, how?

✔ What did you do when you hit a "snag"? (Did you give up? Did you consult other resources? Did you talk to other students?)

✔ What advice would you give to other ID students who are just beginning a course/book like this?

Second, we ask you to put on a different hat, so to speak, and look at the use of case studies from the point of view of a designer rather than a student of design. Use the following questions to stimulate your thinking regarding the usefulness of the case method as a teaching strategy:

✔ What particular design situations might be amenable to the case approach?

✔ Are there situations where the case method would not be appropriate?

✔ Are there any specific types of learners who would/would not benefit from this approach?

✔ What different purposes might cases serve (e.g., building interest and motivation, contextualizing learning, enhancing problem diagnosis and problem-solving skills) in the education of instructional designers?

✔ How might cases be used with novice learners, "advanced beginners," and so on? How might cases be used in professional development courses for practicing ID professionals?

By reflecting on questions such as these, we hope that when you begin designing and teaching your own courses and workshops, you will feel comfortable using the case approach. We believe that cases offer a powerful means for facilitating the development of instructional design expertise. As you look back on your own experiences using the *ID CaseBook*, we certainly hope that this is true for you, and wish you well in confidently employing the case method in your future instructional design practice.

References

Atherton, J. S. (2003). *Doceo: Competence, proficiency and beyond*. Retrieved August 1, 2005, from http://www.doceo.co.uk/background/expertise.htm.

Boud, D. (2001). Using journal writing to enhance reflective practice. In L. M. English & M. A. Gillen (Eds.), *Promoting journal writing in adult education. New Directions in Adult and Continuing Education* (No. 90, pp. 9–18). San Francisco: Jossey-Bass.

Bransford, J. D., Brown, A. L., & Cocking, R. R. (Eds.) (2000). How experts differ from novices. Chapter 2 in *How people learn: Brain, mind, experience, and school* (pp. 31–50). Washington, DC: National Academy Press.

Campoy, R. (2005). *Case study analysis in the classroom: Becoming a reflective teacher*. Thousand Oaks, CA: Sage.

Cates, W. M. (2001). Introduction to the special issue. *Educational Technology, 41*(1), 5–6.

Ertmer, P. A., Newby, T. J., & MacDougall, M. (1996). Students' approaches to learning from case-based instruction: The role of reflective self-regulation. *American Educational Research Journal, 33*(3), 719–752.

Ertmer, P. A., & Stepich, D. A. (2005). Instructional design expertise: How will we know it when we see it? *Educational Technology, 45*(6), 38–43.

Grimmett, P. P., & Erickson, G. L. (1988). *Reflection in teacher education.* New York: Teachers College Press.

Hardré, P. L., Ge, X., & Thomas, M. K. (2005). Toward a model of development for instructional design expertise. *Educational Technology, 45*(1), 53–57.

Hartog, M. (2002). Becoming a reflective practitioner: A continuing professional development strategy through humanistic action research. *Business Ethics: A European Review, 11*, 233–243.

Kitchener, K. S., & King, P. M. (1990). The reflective judgment model: Ten years of research. In M. L. Commons, C. Arman, L. Kohlberg, F. A. Richards, T. A. Grotzer, & J. Sinnott (Eds.), *Adult development: Models and methods in the study of adolescent and adult thought* (Vol. 2, pp. 63–78). New York: Praeger.

Schön, D. A. (1983). *The reflective practitioner: How professionals think in action.* New York: Basic Books.

Shulman, L. (1992). Toward a pedagogy of cases. In J. H. Shulman (Ed.), *Case methods in teacher education* (pp. 1–30). New York: Teachers College Press.

Shulman, L. S. (1996). Just in case: Reflections on learning from experience. In J. A. Colbert, P. Desberg, & K. Trimble (Eds.), *The case for education: Contemporary approaches for using case methods* (pp. 197–217). Boston: Allyn & Bacon.

Smith, M. K. (2001). Donald Schön: Learning, reflection and change. *The encyclopedia of informal education.* Retrieved November 2, 2005, from www.infed.org/thinkers/et-schon.htm.

Weil, S., & Frame, P. (1992). Capability through business and management education. In J. Stephenson & S. Weil (Eds.), *Quality in learning: A capability approach in higher education* (pp. 45–76). London: Kogan Page.

Part II

Case Studies

Section 1: K–12 Audience/Context

1

Scott Allen

Designing Learning Objects for Primary Learners

by Sue Bennett, Lori Lockyer, and Barry Harper

Scott Allen e-mailed the rest of his design team the good news—they had won a tender for a major project with *SchoolsOnline*, a national initiative to develop online resources for primary and secondary schools.

Scott was happy with the team he'd put together. All members, including himself, Jeff Parker, Penny Johnson, and Tracey Ward, were academics on the education faculty. Each was also an experienced instructional designer and they had all worked together on previous projects. Jeff was well known in the field of multimedia design and, as director of the college's multimedia unit, had developed several innovative educational CD-ROMs that had received a number of international awards. Penny and Tracey worked as professors in educational technology with an emphasis on multimedia design. They both had worked on a wide range of CD-ROM and web-based projects for industry groups, higher education, and primary schools over the past 10 years. In addition to his design experience, Scott brought technical and management skills to the group. All of the group members were also currently involved in a research study investigating the use of learning objects in education. Scott hoped that by conducting this study his team would gain additional insight for the upcoming project.

Scott also believed that this would be an interesting project for two reasons. First, he knew they would work primarily on the design specifications while collaborating with two other small teams: one that would be responsible for proposing and researching the content for design briefs and another that would do the development work. Second, they would be creating educational learning objects, as opposed to a full CD-ROM or web-based project.

Later in the week, Scott attended an initial meeting organized by *SchoolsOnline*. A representative from each of the project teams was there, as well as subject matter and educational experts, the overall project manager, Gordon Anderson, and other representatives of *SchoolsOnline*.

Understanding the Project

After he returned from the initial project meeting, Scott called the design team together. He began by explaining the requirements for the project and how the process would work. As he distributed copies of the project brief for *Our Nation and Society* (see Appendix 1–A on page 21) he said, "To start us off, let's read through the project brief. This is similar to the information we were given to prepare the proposal. As you can see it's still quite general, because it's trying to describe the principles driving the overall project, rather than the specific learning objects that will be developed as part of it."

The team members spent a few minutes reading through the project brief. When they finished, Scott highlighted some of the main points. "Basically, in terms of the learning objects, *SchoolsOnline* wants fairly small-scale resources that are flexible enough for a teacher to use with a whole class or for a student to work with independently. By small, they mean focused on only one or a few objectives and also small in file size. But, because the learning objects need to be substantial enough to use as the focus of a lesson or an activity, these learning objects may be much larger than what most people would normally think of for a learning object."

"And from the brief, it's clear they want a particular pedagogical approach to be taken," Tracey added.

"That's right," said Scott, "there was a lot of discussion about the learning objects not just presenting content but engaging learners in activities. And those activities should be more constructivist than prescriptive. Still, we do have a lot of flexibility in terms of adapting the content that they gave us." Scott went on to describe a learning object that was demonstrated at the meeting, which was designed to involve students in solving a crime. The learning object required students to collect evidence after a robbery by visiting the crime scene to interact with witnesses and collect forensic evidence. The program then required students to select certain pieces of evidence from a list of possibilities, and then compare these with information about suspects to identify who committed the crime. Scott explained that a teacher could extend the task by having students discuss the process in class or asking them to write a report of their findings.

Scott added, "The learning object used simple animation, text, and audio. *SchoolsOnline* wanted to avoid using full-color graphics and video because this would increase the file size. All of the learning objects will need to be developed in Flash™ for a particular set of end-user specifications. That way all of the learning objects will have consistent technical requirements. That's mainly a concern for the development team, but we need to give some thought to keeping the learning objects small while we are developing our design specifications."

"In addition to the file size issue," added Jeff, "my impression is that these ideas are quite different from some of the other conceptions of learning objects that appear in the literature, especially in terms of context. A lot of those sources emphasize the need for learning objects to be context free. However, the learning objects we develop for this project will not be context free."

"Yes, I was also wondering about this issue of context," added Penny.

Jeff replied, "Obviously, these learning objects will be geared toward Australian K–12 students, designed to meet particular national curricular needs, which certainly enhances their reusability in the Australian context. But as a consequence, that will make them less usable in other national contexts."

Scott clarified, Well, I think that the aim of the project is to make something for Australian students. So, I think the main point is that the objects should be reusable within the scope of *this* project, and that we need not be concerned with contexts outside of Australia.

"Let me tell you a little bit about how the project is going to work. I've photocopied a diagram from one of the handouts we got at the meeting and I'll take you through it," Scott said as he passed a sheet of paper to each of the other team members (see Figure 1–1).

Scott continued, "In this diagram they've represented the process and the organizational structure. We're the design team, and there are two other teams with whom we'll work. There are three people on the writing team, who have been busy generating design briefs based on suggestions from subject matter experts on the steering committee. The members of the writing team have experience in technical and creative writing, but don't have backgrounds in education. So, the role of the writers was to capture the ideas produced by the steering committee, document these, and research additional content, as required. The learning outcomes and intended pedagogical approaches originated from the steering committee, as did decisions about what content each learning object should focus on."

Scott went on to explain that the writers had prepared 32 draft briefs, each of which was a couple of pages long and pretty rough. The design team must now choose the best 15 of these ideas to be developed further, and then the writing team will revise the briefs and prepare the content needed.

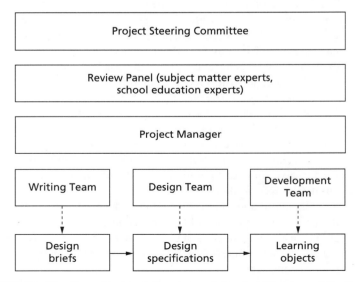

FIGURE 1–1   The Organizational Structure of the *Our Nation and Society* Project.

Scott explained, "The entire process actually involves a fair bit of consultation, so it's not as linear as it looks. And there are reviews and sign-off points between each of the stages." "For example," Scott continued, "after the writing team prepares the content for the briefs we have chosen for further development, the briefs come back to us and we develop the full design specifications, which would then be reviewed by the panel of subject matter and educational experts. Their feedback would be returned to us as the basis for revisions to the designs. The final design specifications would then go to the steering committee to be signed off on prior to any development. Everything will go through Gordon, our project manager, whose job is to keep things on track overall."

After the design specs are approved by the steering committee, they go to the development team from *ScarletMedia*, which is a company we haven't worked with before, although Jeff knows the director. After that point the design team would no longer be involved. By the way, the total time line for the design work is three months. We need to decide how we can do the required work within this time frame. So, what does everyone think?" asked Scott.

"Well, it depends," replied Tracey. "Do we know how many iterations of the review we will have to go through? That part of the process could take ages, especially if the other participants take their time getting feedback to us. I think we need to talk to everyone about setting some time limits."

"I agree," said Jeff. "We need to develop a time line and see if we can get everyone to commit to it. Another thing I'm a little concerned about is how detailed the specifications for the design will need to be. They will need to be detailed enough so that the developers know what we are looking for, and also we need to be sure that we don't recommend something that exceeds the technical limitations involved in developing learning objects. We'll be out of the process by then so we won't have any input into the changes. How does everyone feel about that?"

Scott replied, "I think it's something we need to be aware of and be careful about. I was thinking that we might want to hold some workshop sessions in which we bring in the writers and the developers so that we clarify expectations for each team. I mentioned that to Gordon and he seemed to think it was a good idea."

Penny added, "It would be a good way to bring the developers into the process so that they understand the basis for the design. That way, if they need to make changes due to technical constraints, they are more likely to choose options that align with our original design."

"I'm wondering about the proposed working relationships among the different teams," Jeff said. "Do you know why they've done it like this, Scott?"

"Well, I think they used the whole-team approach in an earlier round of projects. But I got the impression that they weren't convinced that the whole-team approach provided the best combination of people to do the job well. I think they've decided to go this way so they have more say over who is involved," replied Scott.

Tracey added, "Well, whatever the reasons, we're not going to get much of a chance to work directly with the other teams. So if we have the workshops we can try to make sure we are all on the same wavelength."

"Alright, I'll work on a time line and possible dates for meetings, and then get that out to everyone on e-mail," suggested Scott. "I can then negotiate with Gordon and the others.

As a next step for us, I think it would be worth working through one of the briefs. As I mentioned earlier, there are 32 design briefs, each about 2–3 pages long, that provide a short description of a design idea and possible means of implementing it as a learning object. I had the chance to read all of them on my way back from the project meeting last week and took the liberty of choosing one to start with. I think this might help us figure out how to approach our task of choosing the best ideas from among the 32 briefs and then shaping the good ones into workable learning objects."

Everyone nodded in agreement and Jeff said, "Good idea. I think we need to start with something concrete to get a better handle on the project."

"OK," replied Scott. "Let's start with *Mission to Mars*. It seems pretty straightforward. We could each consider it independently first and then put our heads together later." The others agreed. Scott suggested that they make a time to meet later in the week. Everyone checked their diaries and agreed on a meeting time two days later.

Discussing the Brief

The team reconvened as planned to discuss the *Mission to Mars* brief (see Appendix B). Scott began, "Has everyone had a chance to read through the brief?" The others indicated that they had. "Great. Let's start with the basis of the brief then. First of all, it's targeted at kindergarten to Year 2 students and it's trying to get kids to see the difference between the things that they need and the things that they want."

"And it says it's also about how people contribute to the well-being of a community. That comes from a balance of needs and wants, I guess," added Penny.

"Right, so the students are starting a new community on Mars and they need to choose what they are going to take with them in the spaceship to do that. My first question is, do we think this concept is going to work?" asked Scott.

Jeff began by commenting that he saw the brief as focused and simple, but still with opportunity for learners to make decisions. For this reason, Jeff suggested that it would make a good learning object. Tracey added that engaging learners with a challenge could be very motivating, as would the fantasy element.

Penny looked a bit skeptical about this. "Yes, but it isn't that realistic, though, is it? I'm not sure the kids are really going to relate to this. And one of the principles mentioned in the project brief is setting the activities in authentic contexts."

"Traveling to Mars might not be that far off, you know," said Jeff.

"Yeah, right Jeff, but it's not as though it's something they can do now," replied Penny.

"OK, maybe it's not the right context. Can we think of some alternatives?" asked Scott. The team is quiet for a minute while they each read through the brief again and consider the issue.

"I think the essence is that they are in some kind of remote environment. Otherwise all the things a community needs would already be there," suggested Tracey.

Penny added, "And the difficulty with setting it in space is that they're going to need oxygen and water before they get anything else. That's just a bit advanced and might be too distracting. It's just not going to be something they can relate to. And the learning objects have to be pretty small, so we can't make it too involved."

"OK, I see your point. So what if it's something else? I don't know. What about a desert island?" suggested Jeff. "They could have to take things in a boat. We can include some things on the island, like it could have a freshwater lake, vegetation for building materials, and so on."

"And would they be able to come back to the mainland and swap things if they realized they don't have everything they need?" asked Tracey.

"I don't see why not. That would be important for the learning process. They would need to get some feedback on their decisions and have the opportunity to change their minds," replied Jeff.

"So, they would start a settlement or town on this island?" asked Scott.

"Yeah, they'd still need some of the people in the original brief, like a doctor or a police officer. So they could still explore the issues about people's roles and what they add to the community. And we can still show the consequences of their choices," said Jeff.

"Wait a second, this is starting to sound complicated. We're not making *SimCity*. I don't see how we can fit all of this into a learning object. There's going to be too much content. I think we have to think about something a teacher can get through in a lesson. And we're talking about young children who have a fairly limited attention span," argued Tracey.

"That's true," said Scott. "From reading the project brief and from the discussion at the meeting, the learning objects should be pretty flexible. So we need to make sure that an individual student or a small group can use it without direct instruction from the teacher. But also a teacher could integrate the learning object into a lesson, as Tracey said. So we'll have to limit the options anyway to make it contained. One way is to have only so much room on the boat, so they can only take a limited number of items."

"We have to be careful how we limit it though or it won't be as realistic. I think we need to re-think the challenge," said Tracey.

"Maybe we need to think of a more confined setting then," suggested Scott.

"I agree. I still have a problem with the setting. And the desert island doesn't solve it," said Penny.

"Why not?" asked Jeff.

Penny explained, "Well, it's a bit of a cliché isn't it? It's more like something from a storybook than real life. Children of this age relate best to things in their immediate environments, which are basically their households. So if we consider the 'community' to be their families, that might help us."

"Good point, Penny. Perhaps we should ask ourselves how teachers would approach something like this in their classrooms. What kind of context might they use to set the scene for children of this age?" suggested Scott.

"What about a camping trip? Most kids would have some experience with that," offered Tracey.

Jeff agreed, "Yeah, that could work. They'd have to decide what to take with them. They'd only have so much space in their bags or the back of the cars or whatever. We could call it, *'Let's Go Camping.'*"

"That would make it quite personal too, which is important for young children. We would have to lose the policeman and the doctor, but I'm not convinced they add much to the story anyway," said Penny.

"So what feedback will learners get about their choices? As I look at the writers' brief, it seems very behaviorist. For example, learners' choices are very limited and the feedback is not very authentic; if they haven't chosen the things they need, the planet starts to fade, which I think is nicer than people dying, but it's not very realistic. Whatever setting we choose, the learners will still need to get some feedback on the impact of their choices," suggested Tracey. "Maybe we should think of a character, like a guide or narrator, who could do this. Maybe feedback could come from another member of the family. So the scenario could be that they pack things for a camping trip and then when they get to their destination they get the feedback."

Penny begins to draw the flowchart of the learning process on her laptop. She added, "And they only have so much space in their bags so they have to make choices."

Jeff nodded his head and added, "They could be setting up camp and something happens because they haven't got the right equipment. Maybe they forget a warm hat so they get cold during the night."

"And they could get a stomachache if they only have chocolates and chips for dinner," Penny suggested as well. "And then they could change the items and run the whole thing again and see if they have made better choices. Just give me a second to map this out a bit."

The team waited while Penny finished the flowchart and then took a look at it (see Figure 1–2).

"Yeah, that would work. They could interact with the final scene somehow, maybe by clicking on parts of the scene to find out more. The guide could ask them what would have been a better choice," explained Jeff. "Does it still seem a bit behaviorist, though? Focusing on right and wrong answers, and limiting the learners' choices isn't consistent with the constructivist approach for which we're aiming."

"It does raise questions about the nature of the feedback," said Penny thoughtfully. "I mean, how do we distinguish between a need and a want anyway? I might consider something absolutely essential that someone else thinks is completely frivolous. And for balance they'll have to be able to have some things they want but don't need. You could argue that's essential for happiness."

"I agree, but we still have to get across the idea that there is a difference between the things we need for survival and the things that we want," Jeff replied. "So there should be some choices that are better than others."

"What about including some way for learners to express their thinking about how the items they have chosen represent their needs or wants? So, the feedback would query them about their choices, rather than just telling them their choices are right or wrong. For example, there's nothing wrong with choosing to take some chocolate as a treat provided that's not the only food they have," offered Penny.

"It makes the package more complicated because there will be quite a few combinations," commented Scott. "One of the reasons for limiting the choices in the first place is that we need to keep the learning objects small."

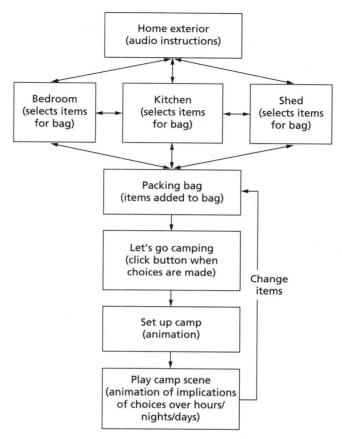

FIGURE 1–2 Initial Flowchart for *Let's Go Camping.*

"I like the idea though," said Jeff. "We could perhaps do it by giving feedback on their choices for categories of items, like Penny's food example. We could ask learners to decide what they would like to take to eat for three meals, for example. Then ask them some questions to get them thinking about their choices. The teacher could extend the ideas quite easily into some class discussion."

Scott added another thing for the team to think about. "*SchoolsOnline* is also quite keen for us to think about how a learning object can be adapted for different age groups. There were some ideas listed at the end of the design brief. It seems to me that this one could work with other age groups, too, if we wanted to extend it."

"I don't see why not. The objectives are still relevant to older learners and we could use the same structure and adapt the content or increase the complexity," suggested Tracey.

Jeff added, "At least for Years 3 to 4 and Years 5 to 6. For secondary students we would need to bring in some more sophisticated concepts."

"You don't look so sure about this, Tracey," said Penny, having noticed that Tracey was still deep in thought.

Tracey responded, "Well, I still like the fantasy element. I think it would be motivating and different. I'm not sure how much the realism really matters. I can see your arguments and also how the camping trip would work, but it doesn't grab me. I'm just not sure which design would be better."

"Well, we're just about out of time, so we won't resolve it today. But it seems that the underlying concept is promising, even though we have moved well away from the original brief," added Jeff. "Can we do that, Scott? Can we recommend such substantial changes?"

"Absolutely," said Scott. "My understanding is that this is definitely part of our role. All parts of the brief are negotiable. In fact, the briefs represent ideas that we, the design team, should use as starting points only. We can accept, change, or discard them, provided that we can convince Gordon and the *SchoolsOnline* steering committee of our reasoning. If we have any reservations about the design briefs at all, now is the time for us to voice them and to offer alternative designs to achieve the objectives."

Preliminary Analysis Questions

1. What criteria (e.g., technical specifications, design requirements) should the design team use to determine the appropriateness and merit of each design brief it has been asked to review?
2. Given the constraints under which the design team is working, suggest specific ways that it can move a draft brief from the form in which it is received (see Appendix B) to what is required by the project brief (see Appendix A).
3. Apply the criteria, developed in response to question 1, to critique the two design ideas presented in this case: *Mission to Mars* and *Let's Go Camping*.
4. Outline the work flow among the three project teams by adding arrows to Figure 1.1. Discuss the potential challenges that arise due to this configuration.

Implications for ID Practice

1. Discuss the skills needed by project managers in order to facilitate effective interaction among different teams (e.g., design, graphics, programming) working on an instructional design project.
2. Describe the core characteristics that define learning objects. What impact does each of these characteristics have on the reusability of a learning object?
3. Discuss the challenges involved in applying constructivist pedagogical strategies (e.g., authentic tasks, social interaction, and negotiation) within computer-based learning object environments.

Appendix 1-A

Project Brief
Our Nation and Society

SchoolsOnline is a national initiative to develop online digital learning resources (i.e., learning objects) in specified curricular areas. This project focuses on *Our Nation and Society* for years K–12.

This Project Brief provides an overview of the scope and major objectives of developing online curricular content for this area.

Online Content

Within this initiative, the features of online content are expected to:

- engage students in meaningful, interactive learning experiences
- relate to intended outcomes and link to national, state, and territory syllabi
- support students' learning in new and effective ways
- exploit the potential of new media and technologies for promoting learning experiences not otherwise available
- cater to individuals or small groups
- adapt easily to a range of learning contexts
- support concept development, transfer of skills and understandings to and from real-world domains, and connections within and across learning areas
- support the development of lifelong learning skills
- encourage students to question and investigate
- provide real-life contexts and scenarios
- support literacy and numeracy development

Project Content Focus

The online digital resources for this project should support the study of history, geography, indigenous studies, environmental studies, values and cultural studies, and study of civic life of particular regional and rural people.

Project Objectives and Scope

This project will provide resources that support students to:

- develop understandings about contemporary society as a springboard for understanding self and others and for examining the contributions needed to bring about preferred futures
- investigate interconnecting social, cultural, ecological and economic systems, political and ethical issues, and alternative worldviews
- develop values, understandings, skills, dispositions, and behavior associated with civic decision making and with principles of the democratic process, sustainable futures, and social justice

The scope of the project is to design and develop high-quality online digital content organized around one or more of the following themes:

- geographical, economic, environmental, ethical, ideological, and political systems, and/or issues
- the way we are now
- what we want for the future

It should be noted that all of the above must be covered in the total body of content developed in the project but that not all elements need to be present in each individual learning object.

Preferred Pedagogies

Constructivist pedagogies should underpin the design of all learning objects. Constructivism recognizes learners as the constructors of their own knowledge, values, and ethical outlook. Constructivist learning is based on tasks that:

- provide multiple representations of reality and the complexity of the real world
- present authentic tasks that encourage conceptualization
- provide real-world, case-based contexts
- support deep thinking
- often involve student collaboration featuring social negotiation and cooperative learning structures
- support students to choose from a variety of possible solutions or approaches to a problem
- enable learners to make connections across disciplines and perspectives

Learning Object Design Brief

Title: Mission to Mars

Target Audience: Kindergarten–Grade 2

Overall Concepts

The learning object will develop students' understanding of:

- values
- sustainability
- dimensions of well-being

Subconcepts

The learning object will develop students' understanding of:

- how people contribute to the needs and well-being of the community
- how we all contribute to the community in productive and fair ways

Learning Outcomes

Students will:

- identify the needs and wants of a community
- distinguish between needs and wants
- recognize healthy and unhealthy choices

Interface Design Considerations

- clean interface
- large drag-and-drop areas
- large-font text
- audio instructions
- colorful, fun graphics

Purpose of Learning Activity

The purpose of the learning activity for K–2 learners is to identify and understand the difference between their own needs and wants and to think about the needs and wants of others.

Description of Learning Activities

Step 1: Students decide what is important to them—what they need to live in terms of people and resources. Students must discriminate between needs and wants.

A brightly colored spaceship appears in the foreground of the screen. Black space, stars, and planets appear in the background. Students are told that they are going to go on a mission to Mars and are asked what they need to take with them to live.

Students consider what they need to live and through appropriate selections, eventually populate the planet with the resources (i.e., people and things) they need.

Students are given a limited set of choices on a menu bar and they are restricted in the number of resources they can choose. The choices may include family members, friends, a farmer, a builder, a police officer, water, healthy food, plants and animals, chocolate, TV, etc. The choices will cover a range of resources appropriate for different cultural groups, specifically including indigenous groups. The choices contain both needs and wants. The choices they make appear as graphical icons on the planet.

If students do not choose appropriate resources to satisfy basic needs such as water or other people, the planet starts to fade. An audio prompt asks them to consider what they really need.

With each appropriate choice, the students receive some form of affirmation (e.g., an audio applause, a smiling Martian). Students can remove resources from the planet and replace them with others until they are satisfied with the results.

Students explain the reasons for their choices either in written form on screen or orally.

Step 2: Students have to consider what the people and things they have previously chosen will need. There is another selection process whereby students must think about the needs of others in terms of resources and make appropriate selections from a set of choices. Students visually witness what happens when certain elements are missing or inserted in the scene. They can manipulate the scene until satisfied. The planet grows until a whole, sustainable community is reproduced.

Step 3: When the community is completed, students can select some 'wants' from options provided. These 'wants' include friends, pets, extra food such as chocolate, etc.

Additional Information

The learning object can be replicated with other information and in other contexts.

It could be also extended in complexity for older learners. This could be done by increasing the size of the "ecological footprint" that the students' decisions leave. Reference could be made to the amount of water consumed, atmospheric pollution generated, and space occupied for farming, industry, and waste disposal.

Denny Clifford

Designing Learning Experiences for Middle School Science Teachers

by Peggy A. Ertmer and Katherine S. Cennamo

Denny Clifford, an independent instructional design (ID) consultant, had never felt so bewildered—Dr. Cynthia Oakes was one of the most complex clients he had ever worked for! Denny wasn't sure if this were due to the difference in their ages, genders, or educational experiences or simply due to the nature of the project, but he found himself completely incapable of carrying on a meaningful conversation with Cynthia. They just didn't seem to speak the same language.

Denny was an experienced design consultant—he had worked for a video production firm for the past five years and was an Air Force technical designer/trainer prior to that. He had created a wide variety of instructional materials, including computer-based lessons, multimedia simulations, and distance education courses. Although Cynthia had personally requested his help with the development of a set of innovative materials for middle school science teachers, this was the most difficult job he had ever accepted. Originally, he had thought that his basic understanding of science and technology would be a distinct advantage, compared with other projects he had worked on; now he wasn't so sure. Maybe if he understood a little bit more about Cynthia's teaching philosophy, he wouldn't be so confused.

Cynthia, a professor of science education at the local university, believed wholeheartedly in a constructivist approach to teaching and learning. Denny learned, early on, that this translated into an aversion to such words as *objectives, criterion-referenced test items, directed instruction,* and *right answers.* Still, Cynthia had requested Denny's assistance in creating some instructional materials to help local middle school teachers teach in a manner consistent with science reform initiatives.

As in most middle schools, students at the local schools change classes for instruction in various content areas; thus, certain teachers are responsible for teaching science to multiple groups of students each day. Although some of these teachers have an interest in science, most are simply assigned to teach science without much training or interest in the subject. Several years ago, Cynthia received a large grant to develop science materials for this group of teachers.

As a national leader in the area of science education, Cynthia developed an innovative curriculum based on a social constructivist view of learning. Quite simply, the curriculum consisted of a set of "problems" for students to solve. Cynthia introduced the curriculum in local workshops, where she explained her constructivist philosophy and provided an overview of the materials. The curriculum was wildly popular, leading to multiple requests from other school districts for Cynthia to present workshops and in-services at their locality.

Now, Cynthia has received a large grant to develop professional development materials for this audience. Money does not seem to be a concern; however, she has introduced a number of constraints to the project.

The Middle School Science Project

First, Cynthia indicated that the purpose of this project was to help middle school science teachers (1) generate multiple ideas from their students about how to solve a scientific problem, (2) listen to and make sense of the students' ideas about science, and (3) know what to do with these ideas (i.e., respond in ways that value the students' ideas and provide opportunities for them to explicate their problem-solving strategies). Cynthia didn't really care what specific content from the science curriculum Denny focused on; instead, she wanted the teachers to learn an alternative way of teaching science to middle school students—that was the content she was most interested in teaching. In fact, she wasn't interested in *teaching* her content at all. She simply wanted to provide opportunities for teachers to "explore issues related to reform-based science teaching" in a "socially supportive" environment.

Second, Cynthia believed deeply in the effectiveness of her approach to developing scientific reasoning. From earlier discussions, Denny learned that science lessons typically began with pairs of students working on a problem from the curriculum and ended with sharing their problem-solving strategies and solutions with the whole class in a large-group discussion. It didn't matter to Oakes if the middle school students gave the right answers to the problems; her interest was in developing the problem-solving *process,* not achieving particular learning outcomes in terms of content. In fact, she mentioned that there *were* no absolute right answers, since "all knowledge is socially constructed." Thus, she wanted teachers to develop their pedagogical knowledge of science teaching in a similar manner.

Third, Cynthia was particularly sensitive to her participants' needs. She was well aware that classroom teachers were extremely busy people. She was hoping to provide instruction in a format that allowed teachers to work on their own time, possibly at school or home. Of course, she expected that teachers would start using innovative approaches to science instruction in their own classrooms.

Fourth, Cynthia didn't have the time, or the desire, to conduct a series of in-services or workshops for the local teachers. She had done this a number of times over the past few years and was no longer interested in continuing in this vein. Her main interest was research. She was deeply interested in the effects of the curriculum on students' scientific thinking. Typically, she provided extensive follow-up for each teacher who participated in her workshops. She observed their classes weekly and followed these with individual meetings in which she discussed her observations. In fact, she had published numerous articles in which she discussed children's learning in her problem-centered science curriculum.

It seemed to Denny that Cynthia was willing to find a way to meet the need for the workshops but wasn't interested in delivering them. In fact, it seemed that she had not really thought much about how to package the instruction. Denny wondered if much of her previous "instruction" on the curriculum had occurred during one-on-one meetings with the teachers. Although she did not want to spend her time conducting workshops, Cynthia indicated that she was willing to meet with teachers for an occasional half-day to "share experiences and stories." But, of course, that would be impossible if the program were eventually distributed nationally, as she envisioned. With the large number of requests for workshops, Cynthia just didn't have time to do it all. That's why she contacted Denny—to design another way to distribute the information.

What to Do?

At Denny's prior meeting with Cynthia, she had made it quite clear that she expected him to provide a list of suggestions regarding his proposed materials and delivery method at their next meeting, scheduled within a week's time. Yet, to date, Denny hadn't completed *any* of his normal ID tasks. For example, he hadn't been able to develop a list of objectives or assessment instruments. He had no specific content to work with; Cynthia seemed to be the only subject matter expert available; in fact, he didn't even have a list of learner characteristics. Despite having had four meetings with Cynthia, Denny hadn't been able to obtain the information that he normally got from clients at the start of a project.

On reflection, however, Denny realized that the following possible resources, mentioned in conversations with Cynthia, may provide him with some direction, or at least a starting point:

- A list of 24 teachers who had completed the workshops in previous years; many of these people were teaching in local schools and, for the most part, were still practicing the techniques they had learned
- A box of videotapes, labeled by observation date, of these teachers in their classrooms as they were gaining experience with this approach
- A copy of the grant proposal that funded the development of the materials for teachers
- A list of local teachers who expressed interest in learning to teach science in a new way
- A couple of articles that had been written by both Cynthia and a former participant who was entering her fifth year of teaching science in the manner Cynthia advocated

Denny had his notes (see Figure 2–1) from these meetings and the resources provided by Cynthia, but the information still seemed only remotely related to his assignment. How was he going to deliver effective instruction when he couldn't seem to begin designing it?

- Group discussions are important to allow opportunities for kids to create shared meaning of scientific ideas.
- Productive discussions allow kids to develop their scientific reasoning, to articulate their ideas, and to reflect on their reasoning and the reasoning of others.
- Teachers need assistance in becoming good discussion faciliators.
- Teachers need continual support while in the process of changing their practice.
- The teacher's role is critical in fostering students' ability to develop skills in scientific reasoning.
- Teaching in a manner consistent with reform initiatives requires a shift away from traditional teaching and change in teacher practice.
- Change in practice is especially important in terms of conducting successful class discussions during science, which are critical to the success of this approach.
- Teachers lack the time and social support necessary to reflect on their practice.
- Materials are targeted for both new and experienced teachers, reinforcing teaching in a manner consistent with reform initiatives in science education.
- Participants enroll voluntarily, so they usually have a positive attitude toward developing their practice. May have some anxiety about trying something new. Important to create trust and a nonjudgmental environment.
- Want participants to reflect on classroom practices of their own and others, and to develop action plans for continual development of practice.

FIGURE 2–1   Denny's Notes from Meetings with Cynthia.

Preliminary Analysis Questions

1. Describe the communication barriers operating in this case. Suggest strategies for circumventing or eliminating those barriers.
2. Describe how the identified resources can be repurposed to address specific ID needs.
3. What type of media, delivery mode, and instructional techniques might be appropriate for this content, audience, and client? Justify your recommendations.

Implications for ID Practice

1. Suggest strategies to facilitate a mutually beneficial relationship between people with different philosophical backgrounds.
2. Draft an instructional strategy for a sample lesson that introduces teachers to a constructivist approach to science teaching.
3. Describe the importance of matching delivery mode, media, and instructional techniques to client and learner needs.

Carla Fox
Implementing Change in a K–12 Environment
by Kara Dawson, Rose M. Pringle, and Skip Marshall

Carla's mind is racing a mile a minute as she sits in the first faculty meeting of the third nine weeks. Now that she is halfway through her first year at Thompson Run Elementary School and is pleased with her fifth-grade students' progress, her thoughts have turned to what the principal, Shannon Ensman, said when she was hired: "Carla, I am delighted to offer you a position at Thompson Run. Obviously, your first and foremost responsibility is to your students and your teaching. However, with your background in instructional design and strong record of innovative teaching, I also expect you to help our school move toward more innovative teaching practices." At the time, Carla saw this as a dream come true—an administrator who recognized her expertise in both teaching and instructional design. Now, as she sits and listens to her colleagues discuss potential schoolwide changes, she wonders if this dual role is possible.

According to Shannon, not only is this possible but it is the reason she hired Carla Fox. Shannon has been principal of Thompson Run Elementary School for one year; she had come with visions of modeling her new school after the school where she had served as an assistant principal for five years. She had visions of promoting and facilitating constructivist teaching and learning strategies and interdisciplinary approaches that could take advantage of the many hands-on materials and technology-based resources the district has invested in so heavily over the past few years. While many faculty members have expressed an interest in exploring and implementing interdisciplinary teaching, technology integration, and alternative assessment measures, there are others who continue to focus on promoting rote memorization and teaching to statewide, standardized tests. As a teacher, Carla is expected to model new teaching approaches and become a model for other teachers. As an instructional designer, Carla is expected to lead efforts to identify, plan for, and implement the necessary changes embodied in Shannon's visions for the school.

Shannon is an administrator who is knowledgeable about how to help teachers change their practices, and she recognizes the costs that the process incurs. Shannon hopes that she will be able to provide funds to facilitate the process and has been working on ways to adjust the school's budget. Her plan is to use monies to provide faculty in-service sessions; to hire substitute teachers, so that her teachers can attend professional conferences and participate in peer observations; and to offer incentive money for teachers interested in curriculum development. Likewise, she is committed to hiring innovative teachers, such as Carla, who embrace constructivist philosophies and who can model for, and work with, current faculty members to promote change.

Carla is a master teacher who has received recognition for her teaching and involvement in schoolwide reform efforts, including "County Teacher of the Year" and "Innovative Instructor for Region 10." She is noted for her creativity, intelligence, and motivational strategies, and her students have consistently topped the state's average in academic achievement. This led to a feature in the local press, documenting her achievements as well as describing how she conducts her classes. Of interest were her ease in interacting with the students, her knowledge in the areas of interdisciplinary teaching and learning, her use of alternative assessment measures, her ability to work with students with special needs, and her passion for technology integration.

Six years ago, Carla graduated from a reputable state teacher education program known for its innovative five-year program that includes two semesters of integrated courses—one in math, science, and technology and the other in social studies, language arts, and English as a second language. Carla also has received a graduate specialization in educational technology. Recently, Carla earned a master's degree in instructional design. When the position at Thompson Run opened, Carla believed that it provided her with a good opportunity to integrate many of these skills into her work.

As the meeting continued, Carla's thoughts are interrupted by the familiar yet unpleasant voice of Mrs. Hodge, a veteran teacher: "I don't see why we're having this discussion. I've been here for 25 years, through six principals, and we've always been comfortable with our achievements. Our students always meet the mean scores on state standardized tests, so what else really matters? All this talk of reform is an unnecessary waste of our valuable time." Mrs. Hodge continues to stress that Thompson Run is not the worst school in the district: "I know that we are not perfect, but much of what I am hearing will not change what happens here." Carla notices that five or six other teachers are nodding as Mrs. Hodge speaks.

Mr. Schlegelmilch responds, "I, for one, agree with Mrs. Hodge. I don't know about the rest of you, but I already give enough time to this school. I would expect compensation for any additional work we are asked to complete, and even then I don't think I'd be happy about the additional demands on my time." Carla definitely agrees with the issue of compensation and often feels anxious about the demands placed on her time as well. But she finds it hard to understand why teachers would not want to work toward continual improvement, particularly in a supportive environment. After all, the goal of schooling is meaningful learning, and there is always room for improvement.

Mr. Puskorious, a relatively new teacher, says with a touch of hesitation, "I really want my students to do well. I am all for reform, but right now I am directing all my energies into classroom-management issues. This is where I really need support."

After an uncomfortable pause, Mr. Zurovachak, a respected veteran teacher says with an air of confidence, "I don't think as educators we can allow ourselves to be comfortable with the status quo or to take solace in the fact that we're not the worst school in the district. If I remember, many of us willingly welcomed our new principal because of her ideas, and now we must welcome and support the changes that she is leading. Yes, we've had successes, but I also think we can take our students so much further. This is an opportunity to do so under supportive leadership and collaboration between veteran and new teachers."

As if on cue, Mr. Fitzgerald, a first-year teacher with an outgoing personality chimes in, "As you know, I have recently graduated, and I am really interested in collaborating with my colleagues to implement many of the strategies and techniques I learned in college. Mrs. Ensman's goals and vision convinced me to take this job because I wanted to grow and develop in a collaborative and innovative school environment."

Mrs. Hodge responds, "One of the hallmarks of Thompson Run has been the collegiality, particularly in the teacher's lounge and at school functions. I don't see how these university innovations, such as alternative assessment measures, technology integration, interdisciplinary teaching, and the like, will improve our students' test scores. We've done some of those things in the past and there was no change in the scores. However, the classrooms were chaotic and the planning took so much more effort and time."

As Mrs. Hodge speaks, Carla notices Mrs. Lynn wince slightly in discomfort. Carla knows from her collaboration with Mrs. Lynn that, although she is a quiet and reserved colleague, she is a dynamic teacher who integrates innovative teaching strategies into her classroom. Carla also knows, through conversations with Mrs. Lynn, that teachers such as Mrs. Hodge were the reason that other reform efforts were dropped in the past. Mrs. Lynn specifically told Carla about teachers' responses to workshops initiated by a past principal related to interdisciplinary teaching, a strategy that integrates subjects in meaningful ways rather than teaching individual subjects in isolated blocks of time. Although the initiative failed on a schoolwide level because of a lack of teacher support, Mrs. Lynn applied the initiatives in her own classroom. Mrs. Lynn also told Carla that she hoped the principal and other new teachers could generate enough interest to bring about schoolwide change. As Carla makes a mental note to talk to Mrs. Lynn about the faculty meeting, Shannon thanks the teachers for their input and suggests that the conversation be continued at the next faculty meeting. The buses are beginning to arrive, signaling the start of a new day. As the meeting adjourns, Shannon asks Carla to stop by her office after school.

As Carla's fifth-grade students file into her room, they immediately begin to work on their insect projects in preparation for their collaboration with Mrs. Lynn's primary students. Whereas some students are creating a presentation based on digital pictures captured during a nature hike, others are using chart paper to plot the variety and number of insects observed. At about 10:00, Carla gives some final reminders to the students about the collaborative work they will be doing with Mrs. Lynn's students, and they depart hurriedly and excitedly to her room. As Carla is walking her students across the school, she notes what is going on in other classrooms. Some classrooms are absolutely silent, with desks in rows and students doing seatwork. In others, students are arranged around large tables but are still involved in individual work while others are communicating and collaborating. As she walks by Mr. Puskorious's class, she notices the chaos, coupled with his loud and directing voice attempting to get control. As he sees Carla, he peeks his head out and says, "Do you see what I am talking about? These kids are impossible to control!" Carla also notices that Mrs. Hodge's room is completely silent. She is seated at her desk at the front of the room, grading papers, while her students are working on the numerous worksheets she has listed on the chalkboard. As her class arrives in Mrs. Lynn's room, Carla feels excitement about the teaching approach she is implementing and the level of collaboration being achieved with Mrs. Lynn. Carla and Mrs. Lynn envision that the collaboration will lead to a jointly sponsored science fair or community action project. As Carla watches her students with satisfaction and pride, she cannot help but think about all the things she wants to do, both in her classroom and for the school.

After the students leave for the day, Carla walks down to Shannon's office. Shannon's first words are, "I just finished talking to the mother of one of your students. Your insect unit was a topic of discussion during many family dinners and she couldn't be more pleased. Nice work." Carla smiles. The principal continues, "I hope you weren't discouraged by the discussions this morning. I saw it as very positive, since last year at this time there were no discussions. I have even received a few e-mails from teachers who didn't speak in the meeting, saying that they are interested and willing to try new things in their classrooms." As the principal speaks, Carla thinks back to her trip to Mrs. Lynn's room this afternoon and the types of learning environments she briefly observed along the hallway. The principal continues, "I received approval for our long-term budget from the central office today. We have discretionary funds to apply toward the types of changes we've been discussing." Carla's posture immediately becomes more alert and she leans forward as she asks, "Do you think such funds will be able to make a difference?"

Shannon responded, "Well, some of the teachers' concerns about time, incentives, and compensation could be addressed. Plus, we'll be able to provide more equipment and resources. But I still think the big issue is having a teacher-led plan for reform. That is why I'd like to compile an ad hoc committee to explore these issues. I'd like you to chair this committee. Are there any teachers you think should be included?"

"Yes, definitely Mrs. Lynn and Mr. Zurovachak." The principal smiles as she jots down these names because both teachers had written e-mails to her, expressing support for reform after the faculty meeting. "Excellent, now that we've got the committee, let's meet as soon as possible."

Preliminary Analysis Questions

1. Identify the characteristics of Thompson Run Elementary that might impact efforts to initiate and sustain change.
2. What is your reaction to Carla's thoughts as she observes her colleagues and their teaching methods? What is your reaction to Carla's teaching methods as described in the case?
3. Evaluate the tentative makeup of the ad hoc committee. Would you recommend changes? Why or why not?

4. Outline a plan for what Carla should do at the first meeting of the committee. Include a rationale for each component of the outline.
5. What factors must Carla and the committee members take into account when outlining a plan of action?
6. What are some indicators of progress that the committee should look for?

Implications for ID Practice

1. Describe how culture and context influence the implementation of instructional design processes.
2. Outline the issues that change agents face when they are members of the system in which change is implemented.
3. How can knowledge of stages of adoption help designers implement plans for change?

Suzanne Garner
Allocating Resources to Meet Multiple Needs
by Teresa Franklin

Suzanne Garner, technology coordinator for Spring Wells High School, had secured a grant for $20,000 from the Teacher Professional Development Grant Fund (TPDG) through the State Education Agency. TPDG funds were to be used to improve teacher skills and knowledge in providing new environments for learning. When she wrote the grant, Suzanne envisioned using the funds for technology training to encourage the integration of technology into the high school classrooms and to meet state professional development requirements for technology funding. Suzanne believed that the use of technology would help promote new and different ways of learning through a technology-enriched and -supported curriculum. She was very excited about the possibility of using electronic portfolios, project-based learning, and problem solving with technology.

After receiving the funds, however, the principal, Terrence Oren, and the curriculum coordinator, Alicia Graham, suggested that the funds might have more impact if they were spent in the content areas to improve the proficiency scores on the state-mandated proficiency tests. Terrence and Alicia suggested providing seminars for teachers that focus on assessment and the implementation of curriculum standards.

The Professional Development Team (PDT), consisting of the principal, curriculum coordinator, technology coordinator, and content area leaders was meeting to decide on the use of funds for professional development. As Suzanne glanced over at Terrence, she reminded herself of the need to impress upon him the success that many schools have had by using technology to enhance teaching and learning in the classroom. Having recently visited several school districts, Suzanne had observed examples of teachers using technology as a way of motivating students to excel in various areas of the required proficiency testing. Suzanne reached into her briefcase and pulled out research she had gathered on the use of technology to improve academic achievement. She passed a copy to all of the members of the team. As the team thumbed through the materials, Suzanne reflected, "How can we work together to meet both the technology and testing needs of this school and keep everyone happy?"

Spring Wells High Today

Spring Wells High is a low socioeconomic, urban high school in the Midwest, serving approximately 1,800 students with 120 teachers and staff. Presently, Spring Wells High has two labs of 30 computers each for Business Education, Introduction to the Internet, and Computer Science courses. The machines in the lab are less than three years old, and all are connected to the Internet. Additionally, each classroom has one computer for the teacher's use and two computers for use by students. The library maintains several new computers, which access the city library and the local university library. The high school building was wired three years ago for Internet access in each classroom, the lab, the library, and school offices. Computers have also been placed in the administrative offices of the high school and in the offices of the coaching staff.

Over the past three years, all of the technology purchases in the school have been the result of SchoolTech Equity funding from the state. The amount of technology equity funds sent to each building was determined by the socioeconomic status of the district and has been under the control of the principal. As part of this funding, schools were required to provide professional development for their teachers in order for them to obtain novice, practitioner, and expert certification. Novice certification signifies that teachers have developed proficiency in the use of the computer as a tool. Practitioner certification signifies proficiency in the application of the tools by students and teachers in the classroom. Expert certification indicates that the teacher has developed proficiency in the use of authoring software and online course development.

Schools are required to have 100% of their teachers with novice certification and 75% of their teachers with practitioner certification by the end of three years after receiving their SchoolTech Equity funds. Spring Wells High School is in its third year of SchoolTech Equity funding. If these standards are not met this year, Spring Wells will lose its funding for technology equipment purchases. Of the 120 teachers in the school, 30 of them still do not meet the novice certification requirements. Forty percent of the teachers have earned the practitioner certification as the result of last year's training.

Furthermore, Spring Wells High has been designated "in emergency" by the State Education Agency due to its low proficiency test scores. This year, the school's principal and curriculum coordinator have been provided with detailed information concerning the student scores in the areas of the state proficiency tests: reading, writing, mathematics, science, and social studies.

The school has two years to increase its proficiency scores from the "in emergency" level to the "continuous improvement" designation. Otherwise, the State Education Agency will take control of the school and implement the budget and educational changes it thinks are necessary to meet the proficiency standards. Everyone involved is well aware of the high stakes issues affecting Spring Wells High.

Worried about the pressure on Terrence and Alicia to meet the testing needs and still maintain the technology funding, Suzanne wonders how this will influence the professional development she plans to offer the teachers. Suzanne has been the technology coordinator at Spring Wells for two years and taught Computer Science 101 for six years prior to that. Suzanne's recent work on her master's degree provided her with many opportunities to examine the instructional design techniques used to improve teaching and learning. Suzanne had planned to use the professional development funds to help teachers gain a better understanding of how instructional design can support not only the improvement of proficiency scores but also the implementation of technology.

Last year, Suzanne provided after-school and summer workshops to help teachers earn their novice and practitioner certifications. Teachers had complained that the training was not provided at a time they could attend, that the training did not meet their needs in the classroom, and that coaching and classroom duties did not require computer use. Suzanne had planned to use the grant to complete the novice certification for the remaining 30 teachers and complete the practitioner certification for 75% of the teachers.

Conflicting Roles and Views

As Terrence called the PDT meeting to order, he passed out copies of the results of the state proficiency tests for each content area to the members of the committee.

"Welcome back from a summer of rest and relaxation," he said with a smile. "I'm sure that everyone is ready for another year of great achievement by our students and teachers. We have good news on the proficiency scores; we increased our scores by 6%!"

Team members looked pleased until Terrence continued. "However, this still fell below the 'continuous improvement' benchmark. I thought that we would meet the benchmarks this time, but apparently not. We will just have to work harder and think of new ways to motivate the students to learn," he added. "Our goal for today is to plan the workshops for the year that will do just that—help us help our students learn."

Peggy Goodwin, the lead teacher for the English department, and Bill Ellis from the social studies department gave each other a pained look. Bill whispered, "Here we go again, more 'innovative' workshops that will not do anyone any good!"

Peggy frowned. Although she was not sure exactly what could be done to improve the proficiency scores, last year's workshops had been a waste. Peggy had hoped to hear that the workshops were already planned and ready to implement. She needed concrete answers as to why the low reading and writing scores were occurring and how they might be improved.

Terrence continued, "We have received $20,000 in additional funds for professional development this year. Suzanne was instrumental in securing those funds for us and has suggested that the funds be used for technology training. She has visited several schools in the state and has seen how using technology in the classroom can be a great motivator for our students. I am somewhat concerned that we have lots of equipment in the classrooms and, except for the science department and courses that use the computers every day, such as business education, very few teachers are using them in their individual classrooms. I have noticed that, as I walk through the halls, most of the computers are turned off and many have never been used."

Terrence paused to see the effect of his statement on the group. After a moment, he continued, "I would like to ask Suzanne to talk for a few moments about the state requirements and the SchoolTech Equity funds."

Suzanne began, "As you all remember, last year we had hoped to meet the state goal of 100% novice certification for our teachers and then to concentrate on the practitioner certification this year. We reached 75% on the novice and 40% on practitioner certification last year. We only have this year to meet the state goal or we will forfeit our technology equipment funds. I am really worried. We can't afford to lose this funding source. But I also know that there is a need to meet the proficiency test requirements."

Sandy Green listened attentively. She had been using technology for more than 15 years. The loss of technology funds would be devastating to her program. Sandy slowly lifted her hand as Suzanne paused. Suzanne nodded to Sandy to speak. "This is very worrisome to hear. The science department uses computers constantly. We need these funds to maintain the equipment we have and to purchase new equipment, so that the students have computers to use with the scientific probes, digital cameras, and software. The science scores are meeting the state requirements. I don't understand why the teachers are not attending the technology training and why they are not using the proficiency template to see how the curriculum aligns with the proficiency standards. It would be crazy for us to neglect this and lose these funds!"

The group around the table began to comment. Phil Nelson, from the math department, spoke up. "I did not get the certification last year. I don't really see any need for it; I will retire in two years and it is too much time spent on technology. I'll admit our math scores are low, but these students need to do computations, not play games on the computers."

Jim Wilkins from physical education asked, "What am I going to do with the technology in my course? I don't mind doing the training, but I coach after school, like a lot of other teachers. If we want to keep the funding, there has to be a better way to work out a training schedule during the day when we are all here, rather than after school."

Peggy Goodwin added, "My new teachers want to use the technology, but we're concerned about having students working on the Internet. I really don't even know where to begin in making technology work in my classroom."

"Where to begin would be to make the computers work more than half of the time," commented Bill Ellis. "The network or computers never work on the days I have something planned that uses the computer. I can't constantly change my lessons depending on whether the equipment is working or not."

Terrence responded after the group commented, "I hear what everyone is saying about the technology, but we must get the proficiency scores in line with state requirements, or we are going to be in more trouble than just losing technology funds."

Alicia added, "I believe that some of the teachers do not know how to align their curriculum with the state proficiency requirements and therefore are not using the proficiency template. This prevents them from determining the instructional needs of their courses as they relate to the proficiencies. Teachers also need new and more innovative ways to assess if the proficiency standards have been met. They need to do these assessments on a daily and weekly basis, not wait until we get the proficiency scores back each year. The use of drill and practice and lecture has replaced some of the active learning that used to occur in our classrooms. This concerns me greatly."

Terrence stated, "Now that we have the state proficiency results in everyone's hands, I would like each of you to meet with your content teachers to discuss possible uses of the professional development funds. We must meet the proficiency standards as well as the novice and practitioner certifications for technology. Each is critical to the success of our students. We will meet again in a week to finalize our decision on the use of the teacher professional development funds."

As the meeting ended, Suzanne leaned over to Alicia and confided in her, "The teachers keep hearing about the need to use technology. However, several have commented that, if Terrence doesn't use the technology, why should they? How do you think we can convince Terrence that he can't just use his computer as a paperweight?"

Alicia chuckled softly, "Yes, it is hard to motivate the teachers to use technology when the principal doesn't. I'm having trouble getting them to use the proficiency template as well."

Suzanne knew she had Alicia's support for using computers in the classroom. Alicia has been an avid computer user and had developed the proficiency template. This template allowed each teacher to match his or her curricular objectives with the state proficiency standards. Once the curricular objectives were entered, the template created a printout of the proficiencies that were not covered. By entering the school proficiency scores from the state into corresponding sections of the proficiency template, the teacher could compare the curriculum to the scores. Each teacher could be provided with a complete assessment of strengths and weaknesses of a course in relationship to the standards. In developing the proficiency template, Alicia had hoped to save the teachers time by using the software to locate the proficiency standards that were not covered in each content area.

"I can't figure it out," Suzanne replied. "You would think that the teachers would use the template to see what is going on in their courses. It tells them exactly the areas where they need to improve their teaching of the material or add more content."

"You would think so, but it isn't happening and, with the few that have put in their numbers, I am seeing more lectures and drill and practice. The fun poster sessions, student-written plays, and social studies field trips are becoming fewer and fewer. The teachers are obsessed with this proficiency testing. I have heard more than just a few teachers say they are not going to lose their jobs to proficiency testing, so they teach what is on the test," Alicia stated with a sigh.

Suzanne added, "It's too bad that this strong testing focus is seeming to cause teachers to eliminate some of the more active learning strategies in their classrooms. We seem to be taking a step backwards. I've got to get the teachers to use the technology to help them do these things, but I am having trouble just getting them to the training."

Preliminary Analysis Questions

1. Describe the range of critical needs facing Spring Wells High School at this time.
2. Identify the available resources and existing constraints that apply in this case.
3. Describe a plan for meeting the needs identified in question 1.
4. Specify the steps required for implementing the plan you developed in question 3, keeping in mind the resources and constraints present in the case.
5. What are the ethical issues related to the use of funding for assessment and curriculum alignment when the grant was originally written for technology professional development?

Implications for ID Practice

1. Develop a set of questions to guide an instructional designer who is attempting to meet multiple needs with limited resources.
2. Recommend appropriate strategies for meeting the technology professional development needs of a variety of teachers, keeping in mind the constraints of a K–12 environment.
3. How does an instructional designer address the ethical issues involved in maintaining grant expenditures in alignment with the stated goals of a grant?

Don Garthon and Susan Harper
Professional Development for K–6 Teachers in Remote Areas
by John G. Hedberg

Don Garthon was on one of his regular visits to the Central Curriculum office for the State Department of Education when Terri Lee happened to spy him. Terri previously had met Don, a faculty member who taught in the instructional design program at the local university, while he was leading a team of curriculum office staff who developed a CD-ROM to introduce a new integrated syllabus in creative arts. She had also seen some of Don's earlier projects, such as problem-based learning packages for the science curriculum. Some of the features she liked about the projects were their practical appeal to teachers and the emphasis that the design team had placed on creating easy-to-use materials. She asked if he had the time to talk about a professional development problem that was worrying her. Terri explained that she had been given the task of developing a professional development program for rural teachers who were working in small schools in remote regions across the state.

"Quite a vast area!" Don noted. "If you like, we can go to your office and talk about this for a while. I have about an hour before my next meeting starts."

After they settled into her small but comfortable office, Terri continued her description of the proposed project. "We are specifically thinking about piloting the professional development program in a few small schools near the Queensland border and possibly some further west in a district like Moree," Terri volunteered.

"The challenge is to help remote teachers learn how to use a new CD-ROM-based performance support tool for teaching and assessing math K–6. It's called *321 Countdown*," she continued. "Teachers in remote schools don't get many chances to attend professional development courses, as they have difficulties finding relief teachers for short periods of time in such out-of-the-way places. So we're starting to explore how we might offer some professional development opportunities for them and provide some up-to-date curricular materials at the same time."

Terri was passionate about supporting the work of rural teachers as she, herself, had spent several years teaching in small towns. It was during that time that she had become aware of the particular challenges that these teachers faced as they tried to obtain new ideas and gain some experience in applying them in the classroom. Terri's expertise in K–6 curriculum and her additional instructional skills resulted in her appointment to the K–6 literacy team at the Central Curriculum office, a posting that later expanded to include other curricular areas after she obtained her master's degree in education.

"Sounds like an interesting challenge, but how do you see me helping?" Don replied.

Terri went on to explain. "We have been given some funding specifically to support teachers who work in schools where there are only one or two teachers, with the expectation that we will be able to expand our scope to support the professional development of teachers across the state. I'm really hoping that we can develop ways to be more responsive to these teachers.

"We have talked with teachers at some of the possible target schools over the past few months and have found that not all the schools we are trying to reach have stable connections to the Internet. In addition, some have limited bandwidth to receive files over the school network." Terri continued, "I have been working with a part-time consultant, Chris Green. I think you know her. She has been trying to sort out the technical issues and also to determine the current interest among potential participants. The two of us have been working with a production team to develop the *321 Countdown* CD-ROM and some additional support materials."

As Don listened to Terri he started to sense that the main focus of this project was on helping teachers effectively use existing materials as opposed to creating lots of new materials. He thought that the challenge might be one he could ask one of his graduates to work on with him to review and possibly generate a working solution within a short time frame. To clarify his thinking, he asked, "Exactly what resources are on the CD-ROM and how do you propose using them with the target group?"

Terri described what the production team had done with the design of the CD-ROM. "Well, we have designed the CD-ROM as a performance support tool so that teachers can type in each student's test scores and then the program will group students at the same developmental level on each subskill included in *321 Countdown*. This means that the teacher can quickly generate a list of those students who are at the same level. As their performance improves and the teacher enters new scores, the program will automatically place students into new groups. Of course, since not all students will progress at the same rate, these groups will change as the students develop new skills. In fact, the composition of the groups could change on a daily basis. The CD-ROM also contains video models of students demonstrating the various subskills as well as video examples of best practices in teaching. What we have found, in talking with teachers, is that even though they are comfortable running small groups, it is the preparation of the activities, the continual assessment of where each child is on numerous subskills, and the ability to manage all this within a doable schedule that presents the biggest challenges for them.

"Also, to answer the second part of your question—how do we propose using them with the target group of teachers—this is where I'm hoping you might be able to help. One of our main challenges has been finding qualified people to work on the project. Unfortunately, no one in our central office has either the time or the skills to design appropriate support materials for these teachers. I'm hoping that you may be able to help us by coming up with some possibilities to help them use the materials in their classrooms. These remote teachers often lack sophisticated technology skills, so we really need help devising some professional development activities that will support them in their initial implementation of the *321 Countdown* performance support tool as well as in *continuing* to use the tool on a regular basis."

Don then tried to summarize the challenge. "Have I got this right? We are looking for ways to provide professional development opportunities for teachers in remote areas. Initially, the goal is to pilot this in a few schools with the ultimate goal of implementing it across the state. You have *321 Countdown* on CD-ROM and additional teacher support tools that can help them as they implement it in their math instruction."

"That's right," said Terri, and added, "And, also, we would ideally like the professional development approach to serve as a model for professional development activities in other subjects. Would you like to look at the materials we have?" Terri offered.

Don agreed and she led him to a large, open office where curricular materials were piled high on a number of different desks. She gathered several copies of the *321 Countdown* CD-ROM, as well as several copies of a teacher's resources kit that included a set of graduated learning activities, organized by topic for each of the math subskills, and an assessment kit that included testing sheets for assessing the students' levels of mathematical thinking.

Don thought about the challenge and suggested, "Why don't I chat with Susan Harper? She is one of my recent Ph.D. graduates who might be able to work on the project. She has a strong background in training. She also has a math background but I admit it's not at the K–6 level. Still, she is a good designer and might be interested in the challenge as she has two young girls in that same age group."

"Great! Why don't you look things over and then get back to me with some ideas and a projected budget? Say, in about two weeks?"

Don agreed and left the central office with several copies of the *321 Countdown* CD-ROM and support materials, as well as a list of the proposed sites for the pilot trial. The more he thought about the project, the more intrigued he became with the possibility of not only developing a pilot professional development program to help a small group of teachers in remote areas, but also having a broader impact across the entire state.

Brainstorming Possibilities

Don met with Susan later that week and asked her if she was interested in being part of a professional development project for rural teachers. Susan had recently graduated from the instructional design program and had considerable experience in math, computer science, and training but was unfamiliar with the preparation of classroom teachers and even less aware of what went on in K–6 classrooms. Susan had developed training courses for sophisticated computer users, but this time the audience would not have the same level of sophistication, nor would its access to technology meet the same standards as those of her previous audiences. Don suggested that they review the materials that Terri had given him and then consider how they might design a set of professional development experiences for these teachers. Susan could make her final commitment after they saw what resources were available.

Two days later, Don and Susan were poring over the materials, which they had spread out over a large meeting room table. Examining the CD-ROM, Don and Susan found that the resources were organized according to three major areas (see Figure 5–1).

1. Teaching math according to the framework
- Overview and introduction to the framework
- Teacher professional development (reporting, planning, programming, and assessing)
- Linked sections:
  - Learning framework
  - Administering the tests
  - Reflective practice

2. Classroom strategies and management
- Class implementation: Strategies, models, and management strategies
- Classroom practice, assessing, and recording
- Linked sections:
  - Organizational models
  - Management strategies
  - Models of group work

3. Activities for student learning
- Devising appropriate math activities
- Resources for students (planning and programming)
- Linked sections:
  - Teachers' own activities
  - Analyzing the tests
  - Database of activities

FIGURE 5–1   Structure of the CD-ROM.

As indicated by Terri in her meeting with Don, the key element was a focus on breaking skills down into various subskills; each learning activity was designed to take students from one subskill to the next. Don noted that the main idea was not that the teacher should sum all the scores across each subskill, but rather view each score separately. That is, it was more important to focus on students' mastery of specific subskills rather than their overall scores. In addition to collating similar levels of performance, Don and Susan noted that the CD-ROM also suggested learning activities to reinforce the subskills at each level and to help move students to the next level. They found two screens that seemed to pull all the different elements together (see Figures 5–2 and 5–3). Even though Susan didn't understand the details of each level in the diagrams, she could see the basic point that Don was making about the importance of focusing on the students' scores on the subskills and not just on an overall score.

Susan suggested, "We can use *321 Countdown* as a way of setting up various challenges for the teachers. Why don't we set up tasks that help the teachers assess their students and determine the next set of learning activities based on the materials provided?"

"Yes, the challenge of this task is definitely to ensure that the teachers are happy working on the various subskills and not just recording overall scores. But if we focus on each subskill, the teachers would be responsible for monitoring over 40 different subskills for each child. That would be a challenge but I think we can use *321 Countdown* as a scaffold to support their instructional planning."

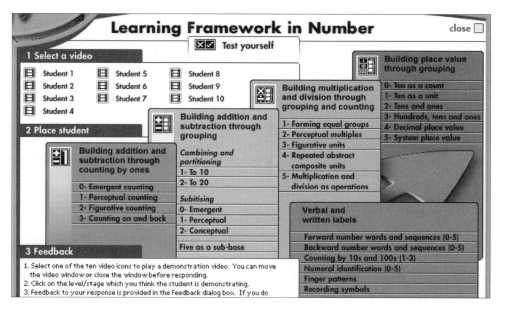

FIGURE 5–2   Math Skills and Subskills on *321 Countdown*.

Source: The *Learning Framework in Number* is a synthesis of research central to the *Count Me In Too* program. The copyright in the *Count Me In Too* program materials and the trade name belongs to, and is vested in the State of New South Wales Department of Education and Training. Reproduced with permission.

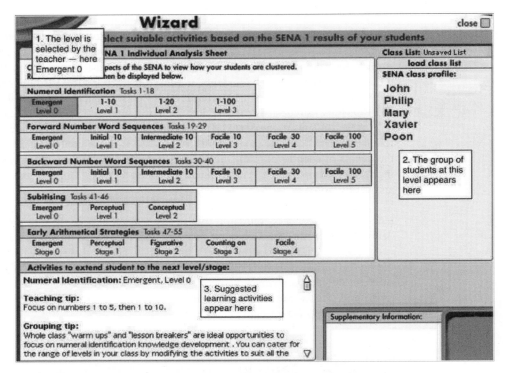

FIGURE 5–3   Screen Shot of Available Support Tools in *321 Countdown*.
Source: The *Learning Framework in Number* is a synthesis of research central to the *Count Me In Too* program. The copyright in the *Count Me In Too* program materials and the trade name belongs to, and is vested in the State of New Wales Department of Education and Training. Reproduced with permission.

Don and Susan also reviewed the support materials that included video models of students demonstrating different levels of performance and models of exemplary teaching, as well as suggestions for how to make reflective notes on student performance. They also noted that the materials included several topics that would support the individual teachers beyond the math curriculum. For example, there were hints and tips for implementing student-centered strategies in other disciplines across the curriculum.

Considering everything they had seen, Don and Susan believed that they would need to devise professional development activities that addressed and integrated each of the different areas:

1. Ideas about teaching math using the *321 Countdown* framework
2. Classroom activities and management strategies to support teacher use
3. Learning activities for each of the small student groups.

Although Susan was a little concerned about her lack of experience in the professional development of teachers, she sensed that this would be an interesting project and indicated her willingness to participate. "Excellent," responded Don, "let's see when we can meet again to refine our ideas. I would really like to have a detailed plan ready to present to Terri at our next meeting. I think we have come up with some good initial ideas, but we also have to consider *how* to deliver the professional development activities to these teachers, not to mention the ultimate goal of implementing whatever professional development activities we propose across the state and in other subjects." "Sounds good to me," said Susan and they agreed on another meeting.

Preliminary Analysis Questions

1. Develop a list of goals, issues, and constraints in this case.
2. What are some of the possible barriers teachers may encounter when using *321 Countdown?*
3. How can Terri determine if teachers are using *321 Countdown* and whether or not they are using it appropriately?
4. How can *321 Countdown* be used as a scaffold for teacher learning and practice? Develop a professional development plan for teachers that introduces and supports continued use of *321 Countdown* in their classes.

Implications for ID Practice

1. Describe a range of possibilities for providing professional development opportunities for teachers in remote areas with poor technology infrastructures.
2. Discuss the challenges that confront designers of professional development programs when they are expanding a pilot program to an entire state.
3. Describe the challenges in getting potential users to begin and continue to use a performance support tool. Devise a possible set of solutions for each of the challenges described.

Jacci Joya
Addressing the Technology Needs of K–12 Teachers
by Julie Muehlhausen and Peggy A. Ertmer

Current Status—May (Year 1)

Jacci Joya walked out of the administration office with a sense of uneasiness. She and one of her co-teachers, Brandon Stohl, had just been asked to serve as technology coaches for the 43 teachers at Cunningham High School (CHS). The high school had recently installed a new grade book program, *QuickGrader,* as well as a new administrative package, *School Manager,* on the school intranet, and the administration was hoping to increase teachers' use (and satisfaction) by providing access to some one-on-one training. Although coaching sounded like a good idea, Jacci's thoughts about what had transpired since February prevented her from getting too excited. On the positive side, she liked the idea of possibly being able to use some of her recently learned instructional design skills, acquired during her master's program at a nearby university. On the negative side, however, recent history indicated little likelihood of even moderate success. She definitely felt skeptical.

Cunningham High School

It wasn't that CHS was hurting for resources. Even though Cunningham was located in a small rural community of just over 16,000 people, a new high school facility had been built just seven years ago, on an 80-acre stretch of land, at a cost of $31 million. Because of the new facility, the administration had made a strong commitment to the use of technology in the school. At the time the building opened, there were approximately 575 computers in various locations, including at least 8 labs, all networked to one of 9 servers throughout the building. In addition, there was a Macintosh™ writing lab operating independently. Every teacher, administrator, and secretary had been given a desktop computer with a printer. Within the past two years, all computers in the building, except for the Macintoshes™ in the writing lab, were upgraded. In addition, labs for math, industrial technology, science, social studies, and foreign language were replaced with 2 laptop carts (28 machines total), which were shared among the classes. The business department retained 3 labs, 2 with laptops and 1 with desk units. Teachers now used laptops instead of desktop computers; one printer was located in each department office. The superintendent, who was hired two years after the new school opened, was committed to converting the middle and high schools into laptop schools.

Thinking Back: February–April (Year 1)

Jacci remembered how upset everyone had been when the information technology (IT) staff sent out a memo last February, announcing that two new programs had been installed on the network and indicating that teachers should begin using them immediately. That is, teachers were asked to take attendance using the *School Manager* program and to record their grades using the *QuickGrader* program. Of course, the teachers were not familiar with either of these programs; they had been using another integrated program for the previous year and a half.

Needless to say, because of the timing of the installation, training had been difficult to accomplish. The IT staff had put together an "each-one-teach-one" method of instruction for teachers, which, unfortunately, resulted in almost no instruction whatsoever. Neither the IT staff nor the one teacher who had been drafted to train teachers knew how to use the program effectively. No one could teach the program to anyone.

To further complicate the situation, the *QuickGrader 4.0* interface was not Windows-based, which made it very difficult for anyone not used to working in a DOS environment to even begin to figure out how the software worked. Moreover, the 144-page user's guide was not well written. Only one copy of the guide had been purchased, and that was kept on file in the technology office. Consequently, only the most adventurous teachers even attempted to use *QuickGrader*.

Within a short time, it became apparent that if teachers were actually going to use *QuickGrader* and *School Manager*, a new training plan had to be developed, yet it looked as though no one was available (or knowledgeable enough) to accomplish this formidable task. The IT staff was overwhelmed with responsibilities related to the proliferation of laptop computers at the middle school, as well as new technology being installed at the four elementary schools. There were not enough individuals who were capable of dealing with the myriad of problems related to computer use at the high school. Furthermore, the communication among the IT staff, administration, clerical staff, and teachers was less than efficient. Vital information could not be relayed clearly to the entire staff. Tension surrounding the use of technology increased.

Meet the Coaches

Still, if anyone could be successful in this situation, Jacci and Brandon certainly could. They were both long-time members of the technology committee and were well respected by the administrators, teachers, and IT staff. In addition, they were flexible in their approaches to problem solving and eager to help their colleagues. An officer in the Army Reserve and a high school science teacher, Brandon was particularly adept at performing "techie" duties and could troubleshoot minor hardware, software, and network problems. Brandon had taught C++ and liked to tinker with computers. Unfortunately, he had a tendency to take over when solving problems, thus keeping others in the dark about the magic he performed.

A veteran teacher of 25 years, Jacci taught English and language arts in grades 9–12, as well as composition and English education methods courses at the college level. Her specific skills were related to language and instruction. Jacci had a strong knack for being able to interpret technology language, either written or oral, for the specific needs of the high school staff. Furthermore, her coursework at the university had resulted in a number of exceptional instructional products. She had a good understanding of how to reach an audience with diverse technology needs and was eager to work as a liaison.

Both Jacci and Bill had previously worked one-on-one with teachers and other staff members to solve problems and provide training, as well as to facilitate group instruction and communication. Brandon was prepared to put out fires, whereas Jacci looked for ways to prevent problems and, through good communication and instruction, help others learn to use the programs.

Developing Training: June–August (Year 1)

In order to prepare herself to coach others, Jacci needed to learn as much as possible about the *QuickGrader* software package. The expectation was that the staff would be able to use *QuickGrader* for both attendance and exporting grades to *School Manager*. To date (from February through the end of the school year), teachers had been taking attendance with *School Manager* (although they complained that it was incredibly slow) and had been using *QuickGrader* for their own recordkeeping, but without exporting grades to *School Manager*. Jacci studied the user's guide but could not make much sense of it. Moreover, she could not access the program because it had not been set up properly for the network. The customer representative who had sold the two software packages to the school had not been on-site to help the staff during the school year. When she finally arrived on-site in June, after school had been dismissed for summer vacation, she was not very familiar with the *QuickGrader* program herself. Thus, Jacci's training amounted to one day in June, at the convenience of the sales representative, looking over the shoulder of a technology staff member, whose main interest was the *School Manager* administrative package. Brandon was also present to observe the training but would not be available for the upcoming teacher training because of army responsibilities scheduled for that time.

The administration expected all the teachers to begin using both software programs on the first day of school (Year 2). Thus, they had to be trained during the one-day in-service scheduled for the day before school started in August. To facilitate staff training, Jacci asked six teachers to come to the high school one day in late July to learn at least as much as Jacci herself had learned about *QuickGrader*. This had to be done on the day when the sales representative was going to be in the building to work with the administrative and IT staff, so that she *might* be available to help with any problems with instruction. On that day, the six teachers (without compensation) learned the basics about setting up the grade book and taking attendance, as well as using the grade scale and grade symbols. The plan was that they would assist Jacci while she conducted both morning and afternoon training sessions for the teaching staff during the August in-service. The participating teachers brainstormed potential problems their colleagues might have learning the program, as well as the kinds of handouts that would be helpful.

In-Service Training: August–December (Year 2)

Although Jacci felt reasonably well prepared when she began the first training session on the morning of August 28, things still began somewhat rocky because the IT staff had not attached some network cables in the lab that the teachers were using. As a result, some teachers were unable to connect until an IT person solved the problem, about 45 minutes into the instruction. Some of the teachers commented to Jacci that this was just one more example of an ongoing lack of communication between the IT staff and teaching personnel. One frustrated teacher, Vera Moreno, expressed her anger, noting, "IT staff always seem to be doing *something* with the network yet never seem to remember to tell those of us who may be affected by their actions. Then, when we try to work with a program that the school has mandated, we can't; the IT person is completely unavailable or deeply involved in another job and cannot or will not respond. I don't know about the rest of you, but this certainly doesn't increase my confidence for trying to use these new programs on an ongoing basis."

Nevertheless, Jacci was pleased with the turnout. All but two CHS teachers attended the training sessions. Once the network cable problem was solved, the morning teachers breezed through the training. All six teachers, who had been trained in late July, were on hand to help their colleagues. The afternoon session, however, which included many teachers who were less adept with technology, proceeded more slowly. Only two of the teacher helpers participated because the others had their own class preparations to complete. Still, at the end of the day, all but two teachers had been trained, the participants had a set of handouts to get them started, and they all knew that Jacci would be available to help them. In addition, even though Brandon had not been able to make this initial training session, he would also be available to help them during the school year.

In order to support the high school faculty as they began to use the programs in the fall, Brandon and Jacci frequently talked with administrative staff about the types of data they were expecting to receive. The principals, guidance counselors, and secretaries outlined the specific data they needed and described the specific reports, such as grade sheets and midterm reports, that they expected the teachers to generate. Throughout the first grading period, Jacci created instructions for the teachers, based on the administrators' and secretaries' specific needs, as well as the teachers' specific requests for help. These directions were sent by e-mail to the teachers just prior to their need to implement the instructions. Jacci used the *QuickGrader* user's guide, the help portion of the software, and her own exploration of the various options within the program to develop these instructions.

Brandon and Jacci continually tried to assess their own performance and to anticipate future problems and needs. For example, reactions to the e-mailed directions were mixed. One teacher complained that she thought that Jacci was treating the staff like "village idiots;" one said that she loved the directions because she could follow everything step by step; others requested that Brandon and Jacci meet with them one-on-one because they "just couldn't figure out the directions"; most of the teachers, however, thanked Jacci for the instructions. A few teachers explained that they were able to do their own exploration of additional features of *QuickGrader* because the basics were explained through e-mail.

Probably the most revealing reaction Jacci received was quite unintentional. A teacher came to her with two grade sheets for the end of the first six weeks. She asked why they did not look identical, since she "had done the same thing with both classes." Jacci replied that she did not know why they looked different but that they did not look like the grade sheet that would have been created using the directions that she had e-mailed them the week before. The teacher replied that she had not looked at the e-mail (which actually contained several sets of instructions vital to the end of the six weeks) because she did not like to follow numbered directions but preferred to "figure things out herself." The next morning, when Jacci went to the main office, a secretary showed her the grade sheets that 12 other teachers had submitted; only 3 had followed the directions. No one, other than the teacher who had wanted to know why her sheets did not look the same, had asked for help.

Unanticipated Problems: August–December (Year 2)

It was at about the same time that it became apparent that the *QuickGrader* software was inadequate in one key area. The high school had an attendance policy that reduced students' grades for unexcused absences. Students' grades were dropped 3% for every unexcused absence; this roughly translated into one-third of a letter grade per unexcused absence. The teachers received notification of how much to reduce the students' grades at the end of a grading period. In the past, the teachers merely changed the students' letter grades without considering the mathematics involved; for example, if a student had two unexcused absences, an earned $B+$ would become a $B-$. When the teacher averaged the students' grade at the end of the semester, the teacher used the value of the $B-$, not the numerical score earned with the $B+$ grade.

Realizing that *QuickGrader* kept the numerical score and would not allow the teachers to use the overwritten grade for averaging purposes, Brandon and Jacci tried to figure out the best way for teachers to determine semester grades when all grading periods would have to be averaged. Brandon wanted to put in a constant that could be used for each unexcused absence, so that the numerical score could be altered, thus resulting in the reduced grade. Such a system would have been fine if all the high school teachers had used the same grading scale, such as 90–100: *A,* 80–89: *B,* 70–79: *C,* 60–69: *D,* and 0–59: *F.* However, the teachers had the flexibility to use their own grading scales. Any change to a uniform grading scale for the school would have led to a dramatic confrontation with the faculty. The software just wouldn't allow the kind of freedom the teachers had enjoyed throughout the history of the school.

In response, the IT staff developed an elaborate disk system for transferring grades from the grade book program to the administrative program. A member of the IT staff created a spreadsheet using the *School Manager* program and then copied it to individual disks for each teacher. The teachers then were responsible for transferring students' letter grades to the spreadsheet on the disk and returning them to the department secretary. The secretaries then copied each spreadsheet to the administrative software to record the grades and generate report cards.

Looking for Alternatives: January–March (Year 2)

By January, calls for help had become much less frequent. Minor problems occurred related to faulty disks and disk drives, as well as to teachers' putting the wrong grades into the spreadsheet on the disks, but, in general, the disk solution to importing grades seemed to be fairly successful; at least it would carry them through to the end of the year.

Jacci began looking for other grade book software that might meet the needs of the school better but was limited to software that would interface with *School Manager,* even though the only feature that *School Manager* was using directly was attendance. At one point, Jacci thought she found a potential solution when she discovered that there was a newer version of *QuickGrader.* After further investigation, however, Jacci realized that, even though version 5.0 looked better on the surface (the interface looked more like a page from a grade book, and there were a few icons and buttons for frequent commands), behind the scenes, where the real work was done, it was almost identical to version 4.0. Apparently, upgrading to 5.0 would not solve the current computer grading and attendance problem at the high school. Logic indicated that *any* grade book software that was more user-friendly would be better than *QuickGrader,* at least on the grading side. However, Jacci couldn't help but think that logic and local needs just did not seem to carry much weight in this case.

Teacher Feedback: April–June (Year 2)

As the school year was drawing to an end, Jacci decided to gather some data from teachers about the grading program. She created and e-mailed a questionnaire to all of the teachers. About a dozen replied. Nine respondents checked "Although I have little difficulty with

QuickGrader, I check myself according to e-mailed simplified directions to make sure I can handle required operations." Eight teachers noted that the "double bookkeeping" in order to send data to the administrative package was a serious flaw in the grading system; they wanted to be able to send grades through the network rather than by disk and spreadsheet. Other comments related to the choice of grade book software in general, saying, "The grade book seems to be the last thing considered when selecting school software. Let's not use it if it is not quicker and easier *for all involved.* The company support staff for this program is awful. She knew how to do little more than read the manual. I would think that a worthwhile company would provide training for all (a day would be enough)." Another was "We have gone backwards here." And "Thanks for asking our opinion." Respondents appreciated the work that Jacci and Brandon had done.

Jacci and Brandon did not want this problem to continue during the upcoming school year. The high school teaching staff needed a simple grade package that they could use easily, with minimal training and assistance, yet the administration was committed to using the *School Manager* program. How could Jacci and Brandon help their colleagues work with these two programs?

Preliminary Analysis Questions

1. Given the resources and constraints available, evaluate Jacci's and Brandon's technology training efforts.
2. How might the administrators and the IT staff have increased teacher buy-in for the new software products?
3. What are some of the ways that the administrators or IT staff might have prepared the school personnel for effective implementation of these new programs?
4. What can Jacci and Brandon do now to assist the teachers? Be specific.

Implications for ID Practice

1. Describe the roles and responsibilities of technical support personnel in a K–12 environment.
2. Discuss the advantages and limitations of having K–12 technical support staff make decisions about software purchases for teacher use. Describe the ideal composition of a software evaluation and purchasing committee in the K–12 environment.
3. Outline an evaluation strategy related to the selection and purchase of new software.
4. Discuss the importance of timing as it relates to the introduction of new software in a work environment. How can users be brought up to speed when implementation is expected immediately?
5. Outline strategies for training a large number of people, with a wide range of skills, in a short amount of time.

Tina Sears
Evaluating the Impact of a K–12 Laptop Program
by Michael M. Grant, Deborah L. Lowther, and Steven M. Ross

Andersen was a rural, southern community tucked in at the base of the Blue Ridge Mountains in upstate South Carolina. Like other small, close-knit towns in the state, over half the students in the four-school district qualified for free or reduced lunch. Furthermore, a number of students were minorities due, at least in part, to the large number of Hispanic families that had recently moved into the area.

Hillendale Textiles was an anchor of the community. Not only did many of the parents work one of the three shifts, but CEO and owner Bradley Cook had often stepped in to provide the school district with funds for special projects, such as the high school's football stadium and new band uniforms. It was easy to see why the rotund Mr. Cook had the ear of the school administrators and the school board. It was just as easy to see why they listened to him.

The Pilot Laptop Program

Another special project was now in the works: During late October, Mr. Cook received a call from Darren Chaude, a business associate at Toh, Inc., an aggressive computer systems firm headquartered in Southeast Asia but well established in the United States. (Hillendale Textiles used Toh, Inc. hardware for its fabric manufacturing lines.) Darren rang because he knew that Mr. Cook was an active supporter of his local school district and might be interested in Toh, Inc.'s laptop program for K–12 schools. Toh, Inc. had just become highly visible in portable technologies and was vying for market share with extreme competitive pricing. Darren shared his opinion that the program had been shown to not only improve students' learning, but also to prepare them for the high-tech job market. He further explained that the program included 60 hours of teacher training from a national expert, free teacher laptops, full technical support, and discounted prices on volume purchases of laptops. Mr. Cook was very impressed with Darren's description of a recent visit he had made to a fifth-grade laptop classroom. Darren said he had never seen students with such a high level of computer skills or who appeared so motivated to learn.

The conversation piqued Mr. Cook's interest, so he decided to investigate the possibility of funding laptops in Andersen County School District. After some initial investigation, and following further discussion with Darren, he decided on a pilot program with the eight fifth-grade classrooms. He did not want to buy laptops for all grades, particularly if the program proved to be unsuccessful. His two primary reasons for funding the program were to improve student learning and to increase employee loyalty by supporting a program that benefited their children. Of course, it wouldn't hurt that he'd get a great tax write-off as well!

Capriciously, Mr. Cook skipped consulting the district before signing the contract with Toh, Inc. He wanted to present the news at the Winter Teacher Meeting, which was attended by all teachers and administrators—and the newspaper. With a certain amount of shock (which was to be expected) and an equal amount of gratitude (which was also to be expected), Andersen County School District set about to make Mr. Cook's vision a reality.

As District Technology coordinator, Tina Sears was appointed project director. Plucky and adventurous, Tina, and a small committee of committed parents, fifth-grade teachers, and the school principals ordered the equipment from Toh, Inc., scheduled the teacher professional development sessions, and prepared to document the changes in teaching and learning. The committee penned some program goals and distributed them in a flyer to the parents and school board (see Figure 7–1).

Teacher Professional Development

With the equipment on the way and the summer holiday steadily marching by, Tina spoke with Toh Inc.'s teacher trainer, Mark Waters, a nationally recognized expert in the field of K–12 technology integration, about running the professional development workshops for her teachers. His full-time job was as a professor at a large mid-Atlantic university; he also consulted for Toh, Inc. with schools that were beginning new laptop programs. Mark's approach centered on encouraging teachers to engage students in using the computer as a tool during problem-based activities. In essence, the teachers wouldn't just learn how to use computers, they would learn *how to teach* while using computers to meet their objectives. Mark emphasized that computers wouldn't just be an add-on to the curriculum; they would be integral to achieving the objectives outlined in the curriculum. Computers would not be a reward for the "smart kids" or for finishing work early; *every* student would use computers to support and enhance classroom activities.

Essential to the two weeks of professional development in the summer was a series of simulation activities in which Mark modeled the role of a fifth-grade teacher while the teachers assumed the roles of fifth-grade students. For example, while learning about plate tectonics, the teachers/fifth graders would use concept-mapping software, or while learning about similes, the teachers/fifth graders would use presentation software. Mark began

---

Andersen County School District
Pilot Laptop Program

PROGRAM GOALS

The purpose of the pilot laptop program is to:

1. Equip each 5th-grade classroom with high-performance laptop computers
2. Ensure students and teachers are computer literate
3. Increase student achievement through the use of laptop computers

PROFESSIONAL DEVELOPMENT PLAN

In order to achieve the program goals, the 5th-grade teachers will participate in a comprehensive two-week professional development (PD) summer seminar and monthly three-hour sessions during the school year. The training activities will engage teachers in three types of activities: *experiencing* classroom simulations, *creating* materials and resources to support technology integration efforts, and practice *modeling* scenarios to build implementation and management skills. The specific PD objectives are below.

The teachers will be able to:

- Create lesson plans that engage students in effective use of laptop computers as a tool to improve achievement on the district's standardized assessments
- Integrate effective student use of laptop computers into everyday teaching and learning
- Manage classrooms that have students using laptop computers

---

FIGURE 7–1   Pilot Laptop Program Goals and Professional Development Plan.

each lesson, "Today, we're going to learn about . . . " and filled in with "science, social studies, math, or language arts." Then he would say, "The point of this lesson is not to learn everything there is to know about . . . " and filled in with "Word™, PowerPoint™, Excel™" or some other popular software package. Throughout the two weeks, Mark illustrated how the software applications had specific uses, and how teachers should match each application's use to their curricular objectives.

Implementing the Laptop Program

As school began in early August, the heat didn't give in and neither did Tina and her newly trained fifth-grade teachers. During the school year, monthly three-hour, follow-up workshops were conducted to maintain the momentum generated during the summer workshops.

The teachers planned lessons collaboratively, and Tina guided them through making the best uses of technology for learning.

Documenting progress continued to nag at Tina. She couldn't let the evaluation slip her mind. To move this task along, Tina called on a friend from a neighboring district who had received computers for her library from the local literacy club. Her friend told her that she had used student, teacher, and parent surveys, but had really wanted to tell the "true" story of how the computers were being used. To do this, she regularly videotaped the students as they were accomplishing different activities, then created an edited version to show at the annual literacy club fund-raising dinner. The videotape was an incredible hit and resulted in the library receiving 10 more computers.

Tina decided she would definitely include videos, but wanted to go even further, so decided to hold focus groups with the teachers and students to learn things that wouldn't show up on a survey. She also added technology to the district's annual teacher evaluation form, which was a huge improvement since the evaluation hadn't been changed in years. And, of course, she needed to include the Iowa Test of Basic Skills (ITBS) scores as part of the data collection as well. She dashed off these descriptions in a fax to Andersen County's school superintendent, Dr. Tammy Burns (see Figure 7–2).

It was unseasonably warm for January, and Dryer Elementary was alive with activity for fifth-grade parent night. Tina beamed throughout the whole evening. The shiny laptops were on display and videos of students using the laptops were cycling through the closed-circuit TVs near the classroom ceilings. As the images on the screens changed, Tina recalled seeing students retrieve census data from the web and then place it in Excel™ to make predictions on future population trends. She also saw students team-writing a paper by wirelessly passing the story from computer to computer. The video revealed that students used technology tools seamlessly to support their learning, including the thesaurus, online dictionaries and encyclopedias, concept mapping software, and graphing calculators. The students also instantaneously searched the web when questions arose during discussions or problem-solving exercises.

It was obvious to Tina the changes were not just with the students; video clips affirmed that the teachers were changing, too. They were not glued to the front of their classrooms. They moved about, talking with individual students and small groups.

The next day it seemed cooler—closer to normal for January—as Tina met with the fifth-grade teachers and recorded their pride from parents' night. As expected, a photo of Mr. Cook surrounded by laptops and excited fifth-grade students made the newspaper front page.

Spring announced its arrival early in March, and now, everyone was sweating again. Tina was pleased that the time in her muggy, yellow office was abbreviated today. She had scheduled videotaping two of the fifth-grade laptop classrooms. This was always a highlight in her day because of the amount of progress that had been made in many of the laptop classrooms. In the most innovative classrooms, students were so engaged in their assignments that they hardly noticed the video camera (an enthusiasm she wished would transfer to all the classrooms). Teachers were busily moving from group to group answering and asking questions. Students and teachers frequently used the digital projector to share and discuss their work.

FAX Transmittal Form

To:	Dr. Tammy Burns
	Andersen County School District
FAX:	864-555-5234
Phone:	864-555-5235
From:	Tina Sears
	District Technology Director
FAX:	864-555-5123
Phone:	864-555-5124
Subject:	Pilot Laptop Program Evaluation
No. of Pages:	1 page

Dr. Burns,
See the evaluation plan below for the pilot laptop program for the eight fifth-grade classrooms.
Thanks, Tina

Pilot Laptop Program Evaluation

Purpose
Mr. Bradley Cook, CEO of Hillendale Textiles, generously donated laptop computers to our eight fifth-grade classrooms. He has agreed to provide laptops for all elementary classrooms, if evidence can be provided to show that use of the laptops improved student learning. Therefore, the purpose of this evaluation is to demonstrate how providing laptops for each fifth-grade classroom improves student learning.

Evaluation Plan
Our district has planned the following activities to demonstrate the positive impacts of having laptop computers:

1. Add "Technology Use" to the district annual teacher observation form.
2. Throughout the year: Collect videotapes of successful laptop use.
3. At the end of the year: Conduct teacher focus groups to see how the teachers feel about using laptops.
4. At the end of the year: Give teachers, students, and parents a survey to see how they feel about the use of laptops.
5. Compare last year's ITBS scores with this year's scores.

FIGURE 7–2   Tina Sears' Evaluation Plan.

With a subtle smile across her face, Tina reminisced. All the classrooms' activities and excitement reminded her of when she was selected as the only teacher in the district to have computers placed in her classroom. Back then, students were limited to basic programming and using simple software like Logo™. Many students were motivated with turtles and geometry.

Yet, even with her limited resources she used the computers to create a learning environment where more students wanted to learn. *Her* class was even on the front page of the newspaper, which probably contributed to her appointment as District Technology Director. Her pluckiness surely helped, too.

Tina collected the last of the parent, teacher, and student surveys, which had straggled in. It was a 70% response rate; the phone calls to homes had eeked out enough returned surveys. She felt quite pleased that almost everyone marked "Yes" to her two key questions: (1) Do you think students are learning more? and (2) Have the laptops made students more interested in learning?

Initial Evaluation Results

School had been out for a couple of weeks now and so had Tina's air conditioning. She carefully transferred the data—the bulk of which were positive survey results and teacher focus group responses—to the final report that she had written. For example, one teacher said, "I've never seen so many of my students so excited to learn." Another commented, "I've been teaching for 15 years and have rarely seen so many student products that were written so clearly and demonstrated such deep levels of learning." Tina also created an edited version of the videos that showed multiple examples of classroom environments that were improved due to the use of laptops. She was confident that the report and video would please Mr. Cook and would be a great springboard to expand to the other grades. She printed out the report and dropped it in the mail, along with the videotape. A smile on her face telegraphed her elation over the report; the sweat on her brow divulged her prayer for the HVAC repairman.

. . . . .

Torrents of rain pounded outside. The almost 100-degree weather was a constant for summer in South Carolina, and Tina's small air conditioner strained to keep up. Adding insult to injury, it was only hotter *after* it rained.

BOING! You've got mail.

E-mail would be a welcomed distraction. Tina quickly opened the e-mail and followed the lines of text across the bright screen (see Figure 7–3).

The message was from Dr. Burns and included an original message from Mr. Cook, sponsor of the laptop program. It was obvious that Mr. Cook was unhappy with the evaluation results.

As she read Mr. Cook's message, Tina's usual effervescence quickly diminished. How wrong could she be? It had been a whirlwind year, but how could Mr. Cook think that the program was not a success? While he had focused on the lack of change in the test scores, he had discounted positive survey results. He had also dismissed her reports from the teacher focus groups and the video. The fifth-grade teachers had accomplished so much; she had witnessed it first-hand. Luckily Mr. Cook conceded funding for a formal evaluation the following school year, postponing his decision about discontinuing the laptop program.

Subject:	FW: Laptop Evaluation Report
To:	Tina Sears <tsears@andersen.k12.sc.us>
From:	Dr. Tammy Burns <tburns@andersen.k12.sc.us>
Date:	July 25

Tina,

Below is an e-mail from Mr. Cook regarding your laptop report.

Begin to schedule the stakeholders' meeting so that we can have an evaluation plan in place for Mr. Cook by October 1.

Thank you,
Dr. Burns

Subject:	Laptop Evaluation Report
To:	Dr. Tammy Burns <tburns@andersen.k12.sc.us>
From:	Bradley Cook <bcook@hillendaletextiles.com>
Date:	July 25

Tammy,

I am disappointed in the lackluster results documented in the Pilot Laptop Evaluation Report submitted by Ms. Tina Sears, Andersen County School District Technology Coordinator. The report documents the positive attitudes by teachers, student, parents, and administrators, and the video clips were moving. But most important to me, this report documents no improvements in student scores on the ITBS. I am considering pulling the funding and dropping the expansion to the other grade levels.

However, if the district can produce a solid evaluation plan that better demonstrates the impact of laptop computers on student learning, I will fund a full evaluation to occur during the next school year. If this report yields positive results, I will extend the laptop program to the remaining elementary grades. For me to consider this new evaluation to be thorough, the school district will need to host a meeting to discuss points of view from teachers, principals, parents, and parent-teacher associations. In addition, the Hillendale Textiles foundation board and myself will need to be present as the sponsors of this program.

Let's talk soon,

Bradley

FIGURE 7–3 E-mail from Superintendent, Dr. Tammy Burns, to Tina Sears, District Technology Director.

Maybe the information in the report had not been definitive enough. Maybe the data she had collected were not convincing enough to warrant another significant expenditure from the textile manufacturing company's foundation. Cook's threat to kill the funding flooded her mind. "I've got to do something about this evaluation," she ruminated. "I can't let the other teachers and students down. I've seen so much progress with the laptops." She began to question herself, and now she needed to host a meeting with all the stakeholders.

Without a doubt, she needed help with the requested evaluation. Fortunately, Mr. Cook was willing to pay for it, so she should get some outside help. That would relieve some of her pressure and help mitigate her bias. She decided to contact the Toh, Inc. consultant, Mark Waters, who helped with the teachers' professional development. He had been a breath of fresh air with the teachers and the professional development. Somewhere in the back of her mind she recalled him mentioning something about program evaluation.

Planning the Future Evaluation

School started back. Mark had been a gold mine. Tina couldn't believe her luck. Mark worked within a center on campus that helped local and nationwide schools with documenting changes from instructional interventions, just like her laptop pilot program. The unassuming director of the center, Dr. Lisa Colm, was a nationally recognized and well-respected leader in the field of school evaluation. With backgrounds in educational psychology, statistics, and psychometrics, Dr. Colm's personality tempered audience's reactions to these sometimes challenging topics. While discussing program results to legislators, school boards, and other bigwigs, she often asked, "Is this in the best interest of children?" She made the results and numbers real—because they represented real teachers and real children.

After some discussion, the center agreed to handle the laptop pilot's external evaluation. Together with a team from the center, Dr. Colm agreed to facilitate a meeting, a week later, among Andersen County School District's stakeholders: teachers, principals, parents, the PTA president, community members, Mr. Cook, and the Hillendale Textiles foundation board, as well as the school board members. "A tough crowd for sure," Tina sighed. She was just relieved she didn't have to lead the meeting.

In the small, cramped boardroom at the school district office, all of the chairs were filled. Tina sat quietly in the back and fanned herself. While Dr. Colm expertly maneuvered the discussion around the laptop pilot program's purpose and goals to the various attendees, three members of the evaluation team scrawled copious notes. The purpose of the project, how the teachers and students had used the laptops, anecdotes from teachers and parents, and emphases on student test scores were all covered.

As purses and yellow notepads were picked up, sweat-soaked tissues were tossed, and the various stakeholders filed out, Tina approached Dr. Colm and the evaluation team. She was apprehensive; she knew these folks were her best help, or the project was sunk. Dr. Colm smiled and reassured Tina: "I'm confident we can help."

Stakeholder Questions

Do teachers teach differently when lessons include student use of computers?

In what ways do parents support the laptop program?

How do students' scores change, if at all, on the ITBS?

In which subject areas do student ITBS scores increase the most?

How often do students use the laptops?

In which subjects do students use the laptops the most?

Do students behave differently when they use the laptops?

How confident do teachers feel to integrate students' use of laptop computers into their instruction?

FIGURE 7–4　Whiteboard Notes from Dr. Colm's Evaluation Team Meeting.

The Next Day

Back at the university, Dr. Colm and the evaluation team met in their cool, blue conference room to debrief the stakeholder meeting from the day before. The relaxed team compiled all their notes onto a large whiteboard wallpapering one side of the room (see Figure 7–4).

Reviewing the whiteboard, Dr. Colm sighed. She was confident that her team could readily craft a proposal within the time line. However, addressing all the stakeholders' questions, particularly those focused on the ITBS test scores, would be more difficult to achieve and even harder to make others understand why it was difficult. Yet, with a confidence that came from having addressed these issues many times before, she turned to her team and smiled, "Well, team. Let's get to work!"

Preliminary Analysis Questions

1. You are a member of Dr. Colm's evaluation team. Consider questions raised by stakeholders in the meeting (see Figure 7–4). What other questions might have been raised at the meeting? Be sure all viewpoints are represented.
2. Why do you think Mr. Cook decided to fund one more year of the laptop program even though student achievement gains were not realized?
3. In what ways should the "formal" evaluation be different from the evaluation conducted by Tina Sears?

4. In addition to student achievement, what other factors could be examined to determine whether or not student use of laptops impacts student learning?
5. Describe the evaluation method (instruments, data collection, and analysis) needed to measure the achievement of program goals and to address the stakeholders' questions.

Implications for ID Practice

1. What influence should testimonials have on making technology purchasing decisions?
2. How can evaluators convince stakeholders that alternative evaluation measures, other than standardized tests, are needed to answer complex questions related to measuring student achievement?
3. What techniques can evaluators use to ensure that results are unbiased?
4. What are some of the challenges evaluators face when scaling up from a small program to a larger program with the same goals? How would data collection and analysis methods differ depending on the size of the program?

Case Study
8

Maya Thomas
Implementing New Instructional Approaches in a K–12 Setting
by Chandra Orrill and Janette R. Hill

Subject: Math ideas
Date: Wed., April 21 08:10 GMT
From: r.ponten@middlecity.k12.ga.us
To: m.thomas@middlecity.k12.ga.us

Maya,

Next year, I will be teaching pre-algebra to at-risk, low-level 7th-grade math students. For self-survival, I have got to find an innovative way to reach and teach these kids. I am open to trying ANYTHING! I envision making this like a laboratory class, where we "do math" by doing activities and lots of different things. Obviously these kids are not pencil-and-paper learners. They have got to learn by doing. In my classroom I have 7 student computers and 1 teacher station with an Internet connection, so the possibilities are not limitless but are promising.

What do you think?

Ruth Ann Ponten

Maya Thomas, the staff development and instructional consultant for the Middle City School District, looked up from her e-mail and remembered her most recent science class with similar kids and knew that there had to be some way to help Ruth Ann succeed with her students. She picked up the phone to call Ruth Ann and set up a time to talk.

The next afternoon, Maya drove out to Middle City Middle School. As she drove through the rural area, she reflected on the changes that had occurred in the past decade. The community was in a major state of transition. This once quiet community of farmers and working-class folks was changing. College-educated professionals were moving in because they were attracted to the community's tight-knit feeling and immaculate old houses. This physical change was also bringing other modifications, such as different expectations about education and a willingness to try new ideas for teaching and learning. These changes made Maya's job exciting as well as challenging.

Maya arrived at the school at the beginning of Ruth Ann's planning period. Maya entered the room, dodging a couple of students who were rushing off to their next classes. She quickly got inside and sat down at a desk. Ruth Ann, who was writing something on the board, turned and greeted Maya, then resumed what she was doing. After she finished writing, she came over to talk. She explained to Maya that she was so frustrated the last time she taught the pre-algebra class that she just couldn't bear to do it the same way again. Maya listened patiently, knowing that often teachers need time to vent before being able to get to work. Maya found herself thinking about the last class that she taught before becoming a staff development specialist after seven years of teaching. They were a bright group but simply were not motivated to succeed in school. She remembered the helpless feeling of knowing there must be better ways to help her students learn and the frustration of not knowing what those ways were. She empathized with Ruth Ann's stress and feeling of helplessness—this was a tough case.

They talked for about an hour, and, as they talked, Maya took notes identifying some of the assumptions and beliefs that Ruth Ann seemed to hold. Maya began asking Ruth Ann questions about her previous class and about the students she expected next year. Ruth Ann explained that the previous class had been very difficult because the students were out of control. A few of the kids just did not care about what was going on in the class and distracted the rest of the students. Ruth Ann continued to say that, even when the students were on task, they were so deficient in their basic mathematical abilities that she just was not sure where to begin with them. She also mentioned that some of the kids seemed really interested in the technology, which is why she had mentioned that in her e-mail. But Ruth Ann also pointed out that other students seemed to not like the computers at all. She finished by noting her extreme frustration that the students simply would not do their homework.

During the conversation with Ruth Ann, Maya asked about the kinds of students that tended to be enrolled in the class. Ruth Ann commented that it was almost never the farmers' kids or the kids of the college-educated professionals who were tracked into these classes. In fact, these were the kids of the unemployed or blue-collar parents; they tended to move between parents and between schools, and they tended to be latchkey kids. Ruth Ann added that these were kids who probably did not have parental support when they got home in the afternoon. Maya pondered how these factors might influence students' reactions to being immersed in a laboratory setting such as Ruth Ann envisioned.

As Ruth Ann talked, Maya realized how often she mentioned getting the kids to work more math problems. Even though Ruth Ann had originally said that she would be open to doing anything to help her kids, Maya realized it might not be as easy as just *saying* it. It was apparent to Maya that Ruth Ann typically taught from the front of the room, giving assignments with many problems, so that students had a lot of opportunities for practice. Learning in this environment meant memorizing formulas and calculating accurately.

Ruth Ann had mentioned a laboratory-style class in her e-mail; now she also added that she thought the math needed to tie more to the "real world." Ruth Ann also mentioned that she knew that having students work problems at the board was not enough—that there had to be a better way to teach math. But, she added, she did not know any other way to teach math.

Maya realized that helping Ruth Ann develop a more hands-on, real-world learning environment would be difficult, given the differences in Ruth Ann's desired outcomes and her current practices. Maya knew from personal experience that changing teaching styles was a lot of hard work. She wondered how best to support Ruth Ann in helping the kids succeed.

Maya went home that evening, thinking about Ruth Ann's situation. On her power walk that night, she formulated a plan to help support Ruth Ann: She would talk to some students and teachers to explore the current state of the pre-algebra curriculum, as well as the kinds of things that might improve it. She was determined to begin the next day.

First thing the next morning, Maya started her detective work. She began at the curriculum office to find out which students had taken seventh-grade pre-algebra the previous year and which ones were in the current sixth-grade class. She deliberately selected a few students from each group, dividing them into three subcategories: those who had done very well, those who had struggled, and those who were likely to be in the seventh-grade at-risk pre-algebra class the following year. One-by-one, she talked to about 10 kids over the next week and a half. To round out the analysis, Maya also interviewed each of the teachers about the curriculum and their perceptions regarding students' performances. She also talked with the assistant principal for curriculum about her thoughts on the pre-algebra course (see Tables 8.1 and 8.2 for a summary of student, teacher, and administrator information).

In addition to talking to various people during data gathering, Maya spent time combing through the state and national math standards and the pre-algebra textbook (see Table 8.3 for a summary of curricular information).

Once she had completed the interviews and reviewed the current curricular materials, Maya analyzed the data she had collected. She wanted to be well prepared for her meeting with Ruth Ann the next week. She was surprised to see that the factors working against success in math went beyond those she expected. Maya had anticipated that students of non-college graduates would be lower performers and would demonstrate lower achievement than other students. However, she also found, among a segment of the population, what looked like a cultural tendency to be resistant to education in general. There was an attitude of "My mom and dad didn't get a high school education and they're doing fine" or "My friends aren't doing well in school" or "My community doesn't care if I succeed here because school isn't an important part of my life" or a combination of these. Maya was saddened by this. She wondered, "How do you help students with these kinds of attitudes see the value of pre-algebra in everyday situations?"

About three weeks later, Maya and Ruth Ann finally got to spend half a day working on ideas for the class. Maya presented a short synopsis of her findings. Ruth Ann was surprised, and like Maya, she was saddened by the poor attitudes of the lower-achieving students. Ruth Ann was also surprised at the discrepancies between what the national standards called for and what her book was providing. She told Maya that she knew the book had problems but did not realize that it neglected so many important skills. Then, Ruth Ann and Maya looked over a variety of new curricular materials and discussed what issues there would be in integrating them into the math curriculum.

TABLE 8.1 *Summary of Field Notes from Student Interviews*

Source	Notes
High 7th-grade math achievers at Middle City	– "6th- and 7th-grade math was boring. They've already covered all this stuff and I want to do something new." – "I just don't see how this math will help me when I grow up." – Many like some group work but don't like being graded in groups because students don't always do their part in a group. – The overwhelming student definition for math is that it means working a lot of problems. – Many students claim to like using the calculator because it makes things easier. – Several commented that their favorite part of math is the puzzles (number and shape) that they get to work on when they have extra time in class. – Most students don't really like the computers because they do only drill and practice.
Poor 7th-grade math achievers at Middle City	– "6th- and 7th-grade math was boring." – "6th- and 7th-grade math didn't make any sense to me." – "All the teacher did was work problems on the board and expect us to do them at our desks." – "There was too much homework." – "My mom works and can't help me with my homework." – "I hate math." – "Man, my dad says that this math is useless. I don't know why I have to do it." – Students reported liking classes that involve hands-on activities, such as science. – Most of the students said they like working in groups. – Most said that they like solving problems. – A few commented that they used to like math but that it is not fun anymore. – They don't really like the computers because they do only drill and practice.
Poor 6th-grade achievers (next year's 7th-grade at-risk pre-algebra class)	– None like math—it's boring and hard. – None see connection to real life. – Most like hands-on work in science. – None want a teacher who makes them do a lot of homework. – "I can't get any help with my homework at home." – "This math won't matter when I grow up—just as long as I can add and stuff. I can just use a calculator." – They all hope that the teacher will help them more than just talking at the board because that is boring and because they don't always understand what the teacher is doing. – Most haven't really used the computers a lot. – They all seemed to think that there are too many problems to work in the book. Their homework takes too long, and they don't know how to do it.

TABLE 8.2 *Summary of Field Notes from Interviews with Ruth Ann and Assistant Principal*

Source	Notes
Ruth Ann	– Feels that regular curriculum doesn't work for this kind of learner
	– Hates to teach at the board and let students practice yet does this all the time in all of her classes
	– Believes that low-achieving kids can benefit from doing hands-on activities in authentic situations
	– Worries about class conduct—the pre-algebra kids tend to be rowdy and off-task and often skip class
	– Wants to look at innovative ways to grade, but is bound to the *A, B, C, D, F* policy of the school
	– Doesn't like the current book used for these kids because it is too choppy—ideas are covered in strange orders and for the wrong amount of time
Assistant principal for curriculum	– Supports Ruth Ann in whatever efforts she takes; these kids aren't succeeding. So any success is a giant step
	– Would like to see a more progressive approach to math but stressed that the state standards *must* be met
	– Wants to have a written pre-test, midterm, and post-test
	– Knows that there is little money to support the purchase of materials for the students
	– Wants synergy with other in-school programs, if possible

Ruth Ann: My first reaction to these materials is that I have no idea where to start. I mean, I can see that these problems are really good—they are open-ended and would get the kids engaged. But how would I help them solve these problems when they don't even have the basics? I'm a person who believes that you need the foundations, first. Develop the skills—then you can move on to these problems.

Maya: OK. I can understand your point. The students you're targeting do come in with really low skills. But don't you think that we need to explore some different ways to help them? I mean, after all, if the traditional drill and practice worked for these kids, you wouldn't have them in this class, would you?

Ruth Ann: That's true, and I can see how these materials could really make the kids think. But how do I know I'm meeting the state standards? I don't see how this is going to help them do better on the test.

Maya: I'm glad you see some potential here. Maybe you and I can work together to see how they meet the standards.

Ruth Ann: Won't the kids panic when they see these? I mean, these kids don't like school—they don't do their homework and they certainly aren't going to like all the writing.

TABLE 8.3 *Summary of Curriculum Information from State Standards,*
National Standards, and Textbook

Source	Notes
State standards	– Include a lot of computational skills.
	– Many do not correlate to national tests (NAEP, PSAT) in their focus.
	– Include some explicit practical links (e.g., calculate sales tax).
	– Require considerable mastery of concepts involving variable use and graphing.
	– Include fractions, decimals, and percents.
	– Include lots of discrete skills—no discussion of integrating or applying many.
National standards	– NCTM breaks into 10 key areas: number and operation, algebra, geometry, measurement, data analysis and probability, problem solving, reasoning and proof, communication, connections, and representations.
	– Concerned mostly with understanding, with less attention to computational skill.
	– NAEP calls for students' ability to connect knowledge across mathematical areas.
	– NAEP is centered on five major strands (algebra, number sense, geometry, statistics, and measurement) and three major kinds of abilities (computational understanding, procedural knowledge, and problem solving).
	– NAEP supports use of manipulatives and assessment using constructed responses.
Textbook	– Includes a lot of practice in computation.
	– Focuses on the topics listed in the state standards.
	– Does not focus on communication, connections, or representations.
	– Is visually appealing and interesting.
	– Includes a link to everyday life in each chapter, but problems do not come from that.
	– Includes regular multiple-choice test-practice activities to prepare students for national standardized tests.
	– Review problems are offered regularly throughout each chapter to review computation.
	– Includes a technology integration idea in every unit.
	– Chapter problems include one or two higher-order thinking problems.
	– There is no explicit call for manipulatives or alternative materials; everything can be done with paper and pencil.

Maya:	You might be right about the writing. Do you think that the kids will see these materials as more relevant to their everyday lives?
Ruth Ann:	Well, yeah. Still, what if the students refuse to do the work? And what if *I* can't work the problems?
Maya:	Maybe we can come up with some incentives to help get the kids interested. As for you not being able to work the problems, we'll make

	sure that you have some practice ahead of time, so you'll be fine. It may actually be a great way to get the students interested: Have them help you!
Ruth Ann:	Well, I can see that the students would at least have answers to some of their questions about how they'll use it in the real world. I worry, though, about the grading. How will I grade this work?
Maya:	Yeah, grading will be different in this kind of class. This is something I think we can work on together.
Ruth Ann:	I mean, all this writing—how will I know what they're thinking? I'm afraid that I won't see where they are having problems in this. They just don't have to do enough problems to indicate where the gaps are in their skills.
Maya:	I think you'll be surprised. I talked to a teacher at a workshop a couple weeks ago who is using this kind of approach. She said she actually knows *more* about her students' thinking now than she did when they were just working problems. She says it's been wonderful.
Ruth Ann:	And what about the parents? I know that they'll be screaming at me—this isn't what they know as math!
Maya:	I can see your point here.
Ruth Ann:	Hmm, I just don't know, Maya. I mean, we just went through textbook adoption a couple years ago, and we were so sure that we chose the best stuff out there. How can I go and change what I do now? I know the kids need something more than the textbooks, but this is a big change. Well, let me keep these materials and look at them more closely. [Ruth Ann is flipping through the notebooks.] Hey, here's an activity for graphing. We'll be doing that in one of my classes later in the week—maybe I can try it there.
Maya:	Great. How about if we sit down again next week and talk about this some more?
Ruth Ann:	Sounds good!

Maya left feeling hopeful, but there was still no firm commitment to a new approach. Ruth Ann raised a number of issues that Maya thought indicated that Ruth Ann might not be comfortable with adopting a new approach. It appeared that, although Ruth Ann wanted to implement a new approach in her classroom, she was reluctant to jump in. Maya believed that Ruth Ann wanted to change and was working in a system that valued change. However, there was still a strong core in the community that might hold tight to tradition, and Maya thought that Ruth Ann might be a little uncomfortable actually implementing the approach that she had initially said she wanted.

How could she and Ruth Ann work together to create a better math experience, given all these constraints? What kinds of support could she offer Ruth Ann that might help her use these innovative curricula to get the kids interested in math? How could they meet the assessment requirements set forth by the assistant principal and still keep the instruction focused on the learning and development of mathematical knowledge? These were the questions that were going through Maya's head as she reflected on the conversation with Ruth Ann. Although she knew that it would be a lot of work, she felt confident that she could help Ruth Ann. This is what she enjoyed about her work.

Preliminary Analysis Questions

1. Critique the steps Maya took to identify the needs in the case, including the collection and analysis of data.
2. What are some of the options Maya can explore to support the learning environment Ruth Ann requested?
3. What are some of the critical factors Maya needs to attend to if this effort is to be successful?
4. Consider how the work with Ruth Ann could be used as a starting place for schoolwide mathematics reform. Does that change the way Maya should work with Ruth Ann and the other math teachers? Does it change the options they should consider?
5. How might the community and parents influence the success of this effort?

Implications for ID Practice

1. Discuss how characteristics of an organization affect the outcomes of a needs assessment.
2. Discuss how factors such as culture and resource availability impact change management.
3. To what extent should a change manager determine the direction a change should go? Who owns the change process?
4. What are some ways to move people from one stage of adoption to the next?

Case Studies

Section 2: Post-secondary Audience/Context

Case Study
9

Jackie Adams
Evaluating a Federally Funded Faculty Training Program
by Melissa J. Dark

Part One: Creating an Evaluation Plan

Upon graduating with a master's degree in instructional design, Jackie Adams accepted an instructional design position with a federally funded project at a large university. As the instructional designer on the job, Jackie's main responsibilities were to work with technical subject matter experts in the development, delivery, and evaluation of in-service faculty education. The Advanced Manufacturing Technology Education (AMTE) project was a new venture, which meant that Jackie would be clarifying her job at the same time she was developing the in-service faculty education program. The first thing Jackie did was read the grant proposal and talk with her new boss, Ray DeMilo.

Jackie learned that the AMTE project was one of many projects funded by the Advanced Technology Education (ATE) program. The goal of the ATE program was to improve science and engineering technician education at the undergraduate and secondary school levels. The ATE projects focused on curriculum development, instructional materials development, teacher/faculty enhancement, and/or student recruitment. The AMTE project focused specifically on teacher enhancement as a means of advancing technology education. The rationale behind AMTE was to provide educators with state-of-the-art knowledge in their technical disciplines, so that their students, in turn, would benefit from the most current advances in technology. Over the life of the three-year grant, the AMTE project was to provide faculty development to 100 science, math, and engineering technology educators each year.

Over the course of the next several months, Jackie worked with several subject matter experts to plan in-service workshops in high-tech areas, such as computer numerical control, programmable logic controllers, robotics, electromechanical controls, lasers, solid modeling, and rapid prototyping.

Jackie had been on the job about four months when Ray asked to discuss her progress to date. Ray told Jackie that he was pleased with the progress of the project and that her skills in instructional design had significantly contributed to this progress. Jackie felt great. He went on to explain that he had just received a bulletin announcing new legislation that was going to have an impact on all federally funded projects, including AMTE. The new legislation required greater and more stringent performance assessment of all federally funded projects. Jackie asked Ray what that meant for AMTE. According to Ray, they needed a more detailed evaluation plan to assess the performance of their project. Ray delegated the evaluation to Jackie and asked her to submit a detailed plan for evaluating the project in a month. He also told her that the evaluation plan would need to be submitted to the funding agency and filed in the grants office at the university.

After Ray left her office, Jackie worried about how to approach this task. She had never written an evaluation plan before. Jackie thought that she and the subject matter experts she was working with had been making good decisions in designing the instruction for the target audience and establishing the goals and objectives of the in-service workshops. However, because they were just getting started, Jackie did not feel ready to think about measuring outcomes of the teacher in-service workshops.

Concerned, she remembered reading a little bit about evaluation in the grant proposal. She pulled out the proposal and reread the section on project evaluation that Ray had written for the grant (see Figure 9–1).

Jackie read the section several times, trying to make sense of it. However, she did not have a background in quality. The most that she understood was that the "quality system" was supposed to provide a standard for evaluating and continuously improving AMTE's operations. There was no information in the section about how this was to occur. She pondered this for a few days and finally wrote down some thoughts (see Figure 9–2).

As she looked at what she had written, Jackie reflected on what she needed to do with the evaluation plan: (1) give it to her boss, Ray DeMilo; (2) send it to the funding agency; (3) file it with the university grants office; and (4) use it to conduct the evaluation.

Preliminary Analysis Questions

1. Use Jackie's questions (in Figure 9–2) to decide what she needs to do to complete this evaluation.
2. How can Jackie determine whether the short- and long-term outcomes are being achieved? What evaluation data does she need to collect?
3. How should Jackie design the instruments for this evaluation?

The focus for the AMTE evaluation plan will be the development of a quality system that will provide a well-defined and agreed-upon standard for evaluating and continuously improving AMTE's operations. The use of standards to establish quality systems in industrial and education settings is growing rapidly and provides an excellent framework for the development of AMTE's evaluation plan.

Quality systems based on such standards typically include the development of both a program for assuring an organization's quality and all the activities and operations required to implement it effectively. AMTE is proposing to establish a comprehensive quality system, which will cover elements such as documentation, implementation, review and correction for all activities having a bearing on the quality of the information, and services and activities supplied by AMTE.

A key factor in the management of AMTE's quality system will be the development of a quality audit, which will be used to provide the data for evaluating and improving the effectiveness of its quality system. The objectives of AMTE's quality system audits will be to a) maintain or improve efficiency of its operations and image, b) determine how disciplined and effective the organization's operations are, and c) meet an appropriate level of quality assurance as specified by an agreed-upon standard or contractual agreement. The standard for the AMTE quality system audits will define its policies, lines of responsibility and accountability, and procedures, in addition to work instructions, and recordkeeping requirements as appropriate. Audits will be conducted periodically by internal AMTE auditors in order to maintain and improve the quality system, as well as external reviewers who may provide a more objective assessment of the project.

FIGURE 9–1 AMTE Evaluation Plan.

Evaluation Planning Notes

According to the grant proposal, the mission of the center is to

"improve significantly the educational experiences and opportunities of students preparing for careers in manufacturing and distribution by keeping teacher enhancement as a major focus."

Tie evaluation to mission.

Answer the following questions:

Why evaluate?

Evaluate what?

How should the evaluation be conducted?

Who should be involved?

When should it be done?

FIGURE 9–2 Jackie's Evaluation Planning Notes.

Implications for ID Practice

1. How is evaluation important to the theory of instructional design?
2. How is evaluation important to the practice of instructional design? At what point(s) in the ID process should it be considered?
3. Evaluation is sometimes compared to quality management. How does this comparison apply in instructional design?

Part Two: Conducting a Meta-Evaluation

The AMTE project had been operating for a year and a half. Ray DeMilo, the project director, came in to see Jackie Adams, the project instructional designer. Ray shared with Jackie a letter that he had received from the funding agency regarding an upcoming meeting. The funding agency would be sending out a six-member team to review the project's progress and impact. This was a routine practice on large grants to ensure that the money was spent as intended and that the project was meeting its goals, as well as having the intended impact.

According to Ray, this meeting was very important. Upon conclusion of the review, the six-member team would report the success of the project to key administrators at the university and the funding agency. The review team had asked to meet with Ray's boss, Ron Bentley, the dean of the school, and Ron's boss, Bruce Stingel, the vice president for academic affairs.

Since the beginning of the grant, Ray and Jackie had talked about the importance of a good plan for project evaluation. Ray and Jackie knew that if they had a good evaluation plan they could accurately measure the impact of the project and identify areas where the project could be improved to increase impact. The upcoming review session would examine how well AMTE had achieved its goals and how goal attainment had been measured and reported. Ray told Jackie, "Well, kid, that evaluation plan is going to be important now. We will get to show the agency, my boss, and my boss's boss what we are all about. I know you did a good job." Jackie appreciated Ray's vote of confidence but didn't feel quite so confident herself. She did not feel comfortable having a lot of people review her work. Furthermore, the stakes seemed high. If she did a good job, it would reflect well on everyone, and they would have a better chance of securing additional funded projects in the future. If she did a poor job, it would not bode well for the institution and future projects.

As the meeting kicked off, Ray and Jackie became acquainted with the review team. The team included four post-secondary educators with a background in science, engineering, and technology and two engineering practitioners from industry. Each person on the review team was responsible for reviewing and documenting a different aspect of the project. Hank Lundstrom, an engineering technology professor, was the lead team member. Hank's job was to assess Jackie's evaluation plan. Hank had served on accreditation teams in the past, thus giving him more experience in evaluation than his fellow team members.

During the two-day meeting, Hank spent the entire first day with Jackie. At the beginning of the meeting, Hank explained to Jackie that the team would be reviewing the project's progress and impact. He went on to explain that the impact of the project would be assessed using data gathered from the project evaluation plan. According to Hank, the value of data gathered would be directly related to the evaluation plan methodology, and his job was to document this. The team would then get back together, report their findings, evaluate the project, write a report, and present it to the dean, the vice president, and the program officers at the funding agency.

Jackie shared the AMTE evaluation plan in detail over the course of the first day. During the time they spent together, Hank asked a lot of questions and listened intently as Jackie explained the evaluation plan. Hank had a very factual and impersonal manner throughout the meeting. He did not comment much on the information that Jackie shared, making it hard for Jackie to determine whether or not he thought it was a good plan. By the end of their meeting, Hank had detailed what he had learned from Jackie about the AMTE evaluation plan in a summary report. He thanked Jackie for her time and let her know that he would be sharing his summary with the rest of the team in order for them to write an evaluation report. (Note to Instructor: See the instructor's guide for a copy of Jackie's evaluation plan.) As Hank walked away, he felt confident that he had enough information to start on his review.

Preliminary Analysis Questions

Part A: Questions Related to the Evaluation Plan

1. What are the main evaluation questions Jackie appears to be addressing?
2. What are the strengths and weaknesses of the evaluation design for answering the questions?
3. Given the goals stated in the ATME proposal, are these questions sufficient?

Part B: Questions Related to Instrumentation

1. How appropriate are the instruments for the goals of the evaluation?
2. Are the evaluation questions answered in enough detail, or are other instruments needed?
3. What, if anything, would you change about the instruments and why?

Implications for ID Practice

1. What is meta-evaluation? How is it important to instructional design?
2. In what kinds of situations is it appropriate to conduct a meta-evaluation? What are the challenges and advantages to conducting one?
3. How do issues related to measurement instruments impact the practice of instructional design?

Ross Caslon
Supporting Faculty Use
of a Course-Management System
by Ann Kovalchick

The Summer Intersession

Ross Caslon was baffled. As soon as possible, he needed to initiate a series of training sessions for 750 faculty members at Lane State West (LSW) on how to use WebPath, a course-management tool, to support web-based instruction. LSW was planning to roll out WebPath, university-wide, within the next year. WebPath allowed faculty members with limited technology skills, or faculty members who had limited interest in learning technology skills, to gain familiarity with the Web as an instructional resource. Yet the System Administration (Sys Admin) group of the Office of Technology and Communications (OTC) seemed reluctant to set up and support a test environment and to provide demo course accounts to use in faculty training sessions. They preferred to build their own course-management tool and didn't appreciate the high degree of customization WebPath offered, since it complicated their efforts to automate LSW's information and data integration systems.

The director of OTC had formed a WebPath implementation project team consisting of Zinny Welch, OTC's UNIX® Group manager, and Sam Gilbert, its database administrator. Jamie Witkowski, a lead member of the Help Desk staff, had also been asked to participate. After working for five years in the local school district as a technology lab manager, Jamie had taken a position at LSW, so that she could complete her graduate degree. Due to her previous experience working in an educational environment, she had established herself as a leader among the Help Desk staff as she sought to better coordinate LSW's technical support services. As the only instructional designer on the project team, Ross worried that the others were unlikely to imagine the challenges most faculty members faced when using technology as a teaching resource. Zinny and Sam were entirely focused on engineering the production server environment and developing the data-processing models that would support WebPath's portal and course features. Zinny had made it clear that the UNIX® Group didn't want to deal with the "end user needs," though to Ross it seemed that the group of programmers and server administrators had some very clear ideas about how the faculty should be allowed to *use* the technology tools.

As with most IT (instructional technology) technical staff charged with network and system administration, the UNIX® Group was primarily concerned with data security, redundancy, integrity, and backup and preservation. Given the complexities of maintaining a university network, the UNIX® Group also sought to automate where possible, and this meant that a standardized set of user practices was desirable. OTC's director hadn't designated a project sponsor, and it was unclear exactly who was supposed to manage the project team, leaving the four of them to work out their conflicting priorities without clear leadership. Ross wasn't sure how successful he would be ensuring that the faculty did more than use WebPath simply to post their course syllabi.

At the moment, Ross felt bogged down by Zinny's concern about not setting too many precedents for providing services that couldn't be automated. Until they figured out how to completely automate the process of creating course and user accounts in WebPath, he wanted to limit access to the system. The university had yet to tackle the challenge of upgrading and synchronizing a number of information systems. LSW's student data system (SDS)—the source of the faculty, student, and course data that populated WebPath course accounts—and LSW's directory service—the source of user-authenticated data—weren't linked in a logical fashion. Furthermore, no one from the SDS group was on the project team. As a result, the UNIX® Group faced some thorny data-management issues. Zinny had also disabled the chat tool, claiming it presented a security risk, since it did not run under SSL (Secure Socket Layer) and, until the vendor could resolve that, he considered it a network and data security risk.

Ross had persistently stated at every meeting over the past six months that the features the faculty needed in order to use WebPath meaningfully ought to drive the management of the WebPath implementation. How could he reasonably expect the faculty to use WebPath when he couldn't provide an authentic learning environment for them to see how WebPath might be used? It was hard enough to assist the faculty in using new technologies on campus when critical support services were not developed or coordinated. While most classrooms were supposedly wired with Ethernet connections, the faculty constantly pointed out that they were unable to use computer technologies at the point of instruction. Consequently, Ross assumed that most students would be expected to use WebPath outside of their classroom experiences.

Across the university, interest in using online technologies to support distance and non-formal education was increasing. The staff in LSW's hugely successful print-based correspondence study program in the Office of Continuing Education (OCE) was anxious to use WebPath to jump-start LSW's entrance into the distance education market. Ross knew that the OCE staff planned to use WebPath to deliver the same content that the faculty had previously given them to edit into print-based modules. In addition, the faculty's skepticism regarding the level of support available worried Ross. If the faculty didn't feel that the IT unit was responsive, it wouldn't be possible to help them see the added value that instructional technologies could offer. He had to speak up: "Look, I can develop a series of faculty training sessions and include the technical support staff in the academic departments. They're our first line of support—they'll help relieve the load of calls directed to the Help Desk." Ross looked over at Jamie Witkowski. Jamie's Help Desk was chronically understaffed, and, with only one full-time staff member on hand who was familiar with WebPath's features, Ross was also worried that the faculty wouldn't be able to rely on the Help Desk for user support. "We've got to provide training for the technical staff in the academic departments as well as for the faculty. We need some demo course accounts for people to use and to play with as part of a training and orientation process." Ross hoped that, by including the technical support staff, the Sys Admin group would see the value of moving ahead with account creation before all the kinks were worked out. Getting a training environment up and running as soon as possible was his first priority.

"It *would* help if the technical support staff had a few trial course accounts," Jamie added. That way we could start learning the product, too. None of the Help Desk staff are familiar with the product." Jamie passed around a sheet of paper with a Venn diagram. "Here's a model of how I think we should approach this roll-out" (see Figure 10–1).

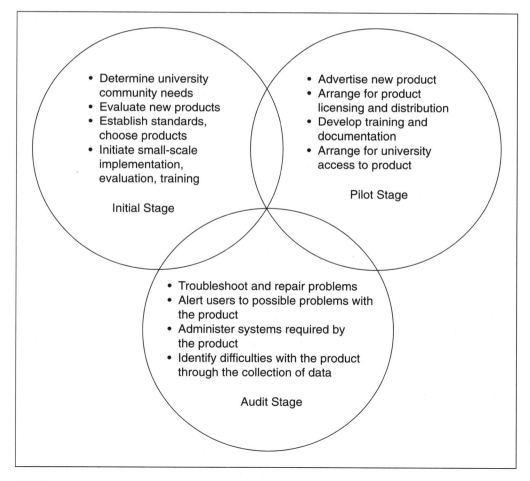

FIGURE 10–1   Conceptual Model of New Product Roll-Out.

With a quick glance at Jamie's model, Zinny waved away the paper and reluctantly agreed to set up a dozen test courses for training the faculty and technical support staff. "That ought to be enough. We really can't burn the calories to support a training environment, too, not if we're going to have this roll-out ready by the end of the summer." Zinny was worried that his group had too much to do and not enough staff. He had initially thought that the WebPath implementation would be a simple process, but the complications were piling up fast, and he was annoyed that the product had some bugs that required constant tinkering by Sam. He wanted Sam working on other projects; adding test courses would mean that Sam would end up running a lot of manual processes until they could get the information systems functioning properly.

Ross winced. Twelve temporary accounts could hardly provide an optimal training environment for the faculty or for the departmental technical support staff. Ross consistently heard from the faculty that "OTC wasn't any help." Although Jamie had worked hard over the past year to staff a functioning support desk, the OTC had to undo years of negative perceptions among the faculty regarding its technical services in support of instruction. Ross had two years worth of survey results of the faculty's perceptions of the use of information technologies for instruction. Unfortunately, not much attention had been paid to these data. Although it was true that the response rate had been low, Ross wondered if little attention was paid because the results had reflected a degree of dissatisfaction with OTC's academic support, yet LSW was not an exception. Didn't everyone know by now that the major barriers to faculty use of information technologies were the lack of support and the lack of time to learn technology and redesign course materials? Maybe WebPath made it a little easier, but it alone would hardly make a dent in addressing these two problems.

"I like this model, Jamie," Ross said, studying it carefully. "I think we're in the initial stage right now." Reluctantly, he added, "With the 12 demo accounts, I guess we can do a small-scale implementation and training pilot project." He was the junior member of the team and doubted that his recently completed MA degree in education from LSW carried much weight. Even most of the faculty thought he was still a student, since he had been working on the degree for years. He had to take what he could get.

Zinny spoke slowly as if having to, again, point out the obvious. "This model also includes the evaluation of new products. WebPath is basically a lousy product. The company isn't mature enough. The technology isn't mature. Its software design model is faulty. Even its business model is bad—the company basically wants to build us a customized system that will make us wholly dependent on it for upgrades, and we'll pay out the nose on consulting fees. So we've got to simplify our level of technical support and aim for bare bones functionality." Zinny folded his arms across his chest. He had made his point.

The Fall Semester

"Very nice! What a high-end facility! It's perfectly designed for using any technology imaginable!" Professor Ruth Newton was clearly impressed. An enthusiastic and early adopter of technology, Ruth was one of LSW's champions. When the Web was in its infancy, she had painstakingly mastered HTML in order to build an interactive chemistry lab and, since then, had received a number of external and internal grants to develop materials for delivery in a web- and CD-ROM format. Ross knew she considered WebPath with some disdain. She thought the interface was too bland and had wanted to give it her own look and feel. Ross was secretly relieved that she couldn't. Her handcrafted interface for her own web materials was filled with things that blinked, dashed across the screen, and usually froze up any machine that didn't have sufficient memory or the very latest browser. In addition, her page took forever to download over a dial-up modem connection. Ross was fairly certain that students could reliably access her materials only from an on-campus location.

Ross handed her the list of participants (see Figure 10–2). "Seven faculty confirmed by late yesterday that they would attend the session today. And then there will also be three technical support staff from different departments."

Ross had followed up on Jamie's suggestion that Ruth lead the WebPath training session. Jamie and Ruth had worked together on a project, and she admired Ruth's technical skill. Though plenty worried that Ruth's "high-tech" experience might eclipse the instructional emphasis he had wanted to incorporate into the training session, Ross had to admit that she had effectively used animation to create a series of 3-D analyses of molecular change for use in her interactive chemistry lab. She had crafted a visual model of a DNA helix that students could rotate in order to see proteins linked to the helix under various conditions. She had been motivated to do this to address a recurring problem: Students were unable to visualize dynamic molecular change using the two-dimensional images typical of

---

Introduction to WebPath: Using the Web-Based Instruction

Confirmed for attendance on 8/31/01

1. Joe Cabrini, Asst. Professor, Biology, College of Arts & Sciences: jsc7u@lswest.edu
2. Prasad Mehta, Professor, Aviation: pmf4r@lswest.edu
3. June Schoney, Asst. Professor, Marketing, College of Business: jjs8r@lswest.edu
4. Pat McGuffey, Instructor, Art Education, College of Fine Arts: pam2w@lswest.edu
5. Debbie Anderson, Asst. Professor, School of Nursing: dja6y@lswest.edu
6. Chen Yin-Zdong, Assoc. Professor, Political Science, College of Arts & Sciences: yzc5t@lswest.edu
7. Rini Frankel, Manager, Sports Recreation, School of Health: rrf5t@lswest.edu
8. Dave Barnouw, Tech Manager, Math, College of Arts & Sciences: djb6e@lswest.edu
9. Cherie Six, Webmaster, College of Fine Arts: cms4r@lswest.edu
10. Frank Huey, Lab Manager, Physics, College of Arts & Sciences: fwh8z@lswest.edu

FIGURE 10–2   Participants in WebPath Pilot Training.

a textbook. She also claimed that her students' test scores had improved since she began using her materials as required homework exercises. The information Ross had gathered seven months ago indicated that both the faculty and technical support staff had limited knowledge of how WebPath might be used to support effective instructional strategies. Ross thought that Ruth might be able to share her experiences and that, along with the $300 stipend provided to the faculty attending the training, he would be able to build a group of willing WebPath users.

Ross pulled out the training session materials. "Maybe we could take a few minutes and review the training session agenda? I never heard back from you whether there were changes and how. . . ."

"Jamie! This is a fabulous room! I see you're equipped for wireless too!" Ruth fondly greeted Jamie.

"It's probably the smartest classroom on campus," Jamie answered. "Though, of course, it's not a classroom. Mostly we use it for our staff meetings and conferences."

"Ross! I have an idea." Ruth turned toward him. "Let's use the question-and-answer period to demonstrate some of the advanced technologies available here. Jamie, you're set up for Internet video conferencing aren't you? You wanted to show collaboration, right, Ross? I could go down the hall to Jamie's office and take questions and answers online. . . ."

The Spring Semester

Ross had spent all of Friday afternoon looking at the WebPath courses offered in the fall by the seven faculty members who had attended the training session at the start of the semester. He could identify only three courses that appeared to have been in use over the whole semester. The other four courses had some content in them but mostly contained syllabi, bibliographies of course readings and recommended readings, lectures posted using SlideShow, lecture notes, and study guides. The three courses that seemed most active had used the discussion threads and two of those courses had extensive lists of URLs in the Cybrary. He looked carefully at all the course syllabi and then quickly added up the total number of different types of assignments and assessments listed within the syllabi of the seven courses:

1. Six courses required a final paper.
2. Four courses required a final individual project.
3. Two courses required a final group project.
4. One course required a final individual presentation.
5. Three courses listed multiple-choice midterm exams.
6. One course required students to keep a biweekly lab journal.
7. Three courses used weekly in-class quizzes to review reading assignments.
8. Two courses required students to submit a bibliography.

All courses except one listed weekly lecture topics and readings. The exception was Pat McGuffey's course, which she had organized around students' weekly presentations.

Ross looked again at the syllabi of the three courses that used the discussion threads. Two had used the discussion tool to encourage weekly postings, though the student postings struck Ross as weak and perfunctory. The other course had used the discussions to manage post-lecture topic reviews and looked to be the most heavily used, although he knew the particular course, June Schoney's *Introduction to Marketing* course, was a large class of nearly 175 students.

It seemed to Ross that there was nothing more than information delivery going on here, yet the pilot faculty had all reported positive reviews of their experiences using WebPath (see Figure 10–3). They thought it was easy to use, especially the e-mail feature, since it allowed them to send e-mail quickly to all class participants. They also liked the fact they could easily post lecture notes, as well as direct students to a list of online resources using the Cybrary. In spite of the positive reviews, however, no one was interested in redesigning his or her course to obtain the $500 stipend he could offer as an incentive. Debbie Anderson had expressed some interest, but, after talking with Ross, she decided it would take too much time, and she needed to spend the summer working on research that would count more toward tenure.

The report back from the technical support staff suggested that WebPath was a lot of trouble for them. After the training session, Ross had offered course accounts to the faculty in the departments where the technical staff worked, based on their recommendations. Although it looked to Ross that these faculty members had used their WebPath courses in

---

"I enjoyed the ability to post announcements in cyberspace."

"I use it to enhance my traditional course but not to replace traditional features, like books."

"The discussion board is neat."

"Probably the two features that WebPath has that my existing on-line syllabus does not are the announcements and the e-mail."

"It was great! I could access it from the airport in Houston once when I needed to add an assignment."

"Good one-stop model for moving around documents!"

"I like that I didn't need to know how to make a web page to make a list of web links for my students to visit."

"The students really appreciated the online grade book."

"It was wonderful to be able to upload handouts rather than have to spend time in class passing them out."

"I was better able to organize my course."

"The students loved it. They really learned a lot!"

FIGURE 10–3 Faculty Comments Regarding Use of WebPath.

much the same manner as the seven faculty members who had attended the training session, the technical staff had described numerous problems to him. One faculty member had to abandon the WebPath course altogether after trying to upload his 30-page syllabus and the account had inexplicably froze. "I couldn't fix it and there didn't seem to be any point in telling you," Cherie Six had said to Ross. "I just designed a separate website for him."

All three of the technical staff had reported that none of the faculty in their departments had asked how to use the asynchronous discussion or e-mail tools. They had been excited to find a chat tool option in WebPath, but, when they attempted to use it and found it disabled, it really dampened enthusiasm. Frank Huey had gone ahead and found a chat tool, which he set up on their NT server, and it had been wildly popular.

Dave Barnouw concluded that the math faculty members weren't interested in using WebPath because there was no easy way to produce specialized math characters. Frank had also said that the physics faculty members weren't too impressed with Web-Path, since it "didn't do anything." Cherie reported that the fine arts faculty liked the fact that they could scan artwork and easily post image files for students to review after class, although she had heard some students complain that now they had even more work to do.

Ross knew that the director of OTC would want the project team to offer suggestions for WebPath training and implementation when they met with him next week. He also knew that Zinny was recommending against its implementation. Jamie could go either way. Her analysis had shown that there had been a lot of user login problems, but that was a relatively simple training problem. Ross didn't have much to go on. There wasn't even one course he could point to that had used WebPath for more than information delivery. All he really had was a list of positive comments.

What WebPath training and implementation suggestions should he make?

Preliminary Analysis Questions

1. What are the primary factors in this case that might have implications for training?
2. Given the factors identified in question #1, how would you design training to meet various stakeholders' needs?
3. Suggest strategies to increase the probability that faculty members will apply what they've learned during training to their own online teaching.
4. Describe the impact of unclear project leadership on Ross's effort to encourage the effective use of WebPath.

Implications for ID Practice

1. What information-gathering and analysis methods can instructional designers use to determine the effect of context on ID decisions?
2. How can an instructional designer meet the needs of learners who go to training with vastly different backgrounds and ways of thinking and who have widely different goals?
3. What are the ways that an instructional designer can affect an organizational context to ensure transfer of learning?

Case Study
11

Jennie Davenport and Pedro Lopez
Converting a Powerful Workshop to an Online Format
by Simon Hooper and Aaron Doering

Jennie Davenport was beginning to wonder if she were making any progress in resolving the instructional design challenges in the project she had been assigned to coordinate. Both Jennie, a project manager with eduLearning Systems (eLS), and Pedro Lopez, a professor of learning sciences at Midwestern State University, had been recruited by Professor Clark Essex, a renowned sexual health expert at the university, to design an online version of his very successful "Man-to-Man" (M2M) HIV/AIDS prevention workshop. This workshop had been designed to improve sexual health for gay and bisexual men and had been delivered face-to-face at cities around the United States on a monthly basis for the past five years. This particular target audience had been shown to be at high risk: Specifically, target audience members were in danger of becoming infected with HIV/AIDS though sexual contact with infected partners.

This danger had increased even more in recent years with the widespread emergence of the Internet as an anonymous communication medium and the meeting place of choice for many gay and bisexual men. Specifically, HIV/AIDS infection rates were higher for men who used the Internet to find partners than for men who met their partners using more traditional approaches such as gay bars and traditional print media.

Several hypotheses had been proposed for the elevated risk of using the Internet as a meeting medium. Some who used the Internet to find partners were unaware of the health issues involved in engaging in unsafe sex. Others may have chosen to ignore potential dangers because of a wide range of intervening variables such as the effects of alcohol or drug use, pressure from partners to engage in high-risk sexual behavior, or internalized homonegativity (i.e., negative attitudes toward homosexuality that obstruct many gay men in the coming-out process). A third explanation is that the Internet simply improved "dating efficiency." It was faster to meet partners by using the Internet, resulting in an increase in the frequency of sexual contact.

Professor Essex had recently received substantial funding from the National Health Foundation (NHF), a government agency, to design and develop a highly interactive multimedia version of the M2M workshop that would be available via the Internet (IM2M). Although Essex was an expert on contemporary HIV/AIDS education initiatives, he candidly acknowledged that he did not understand what should (or could) be done to deliver his workshop successfully via the Internet. However, he was eager for the project to be "state-of-the art" and make full use of the capabilities of the Internet, and was delighted that Pedro had agreed to participate in the project.

The time line written into the NHF grant called for the project to be designed, developed, and evaluated over a two-year period. The first nine months were to be used for brainstorming and developing three levels of prototype. Product development would be conducted during the following six months, and during the last nine months the project would be evaluated using a randomized control study to compare the effectiveness of the face-to-face and online versions of the workshop. The project proposal called for the online version to follow the 10 components of the sexual health model including talking about sex, culture and sexual identity, sexual anatomy and functioning, sexual health care and safer sex, challenges to sexual health, body image, masturbation and fantasy, positive sexuality, intimacy and relationships, and spirituality.

The NHF project proposal was written primarily by Professor Essex, but with significant input on the instructional design approach from Pedro. Prior to joining the faculty, Pedro worked for eight years as a project manager at an educational software development company that relied heavily on a "learning by doing" approach to instructional design. He was currently writing a book with the working title of "Authentic Pedagogy and the Use of Participatory Design in Instructional Design" and his numerous research articles were considered to be "cutting edge" and had received enthusiastic critical review. He was delighted to have the opportunity to work on the design of the online version of the workshop as he relished opportunities to put his theories into practice.

Following notification of funding from NHF, Professor Essex contracted with eduLearning Systems (eLS) to develop the online environment after hearing positive reports about the company from a senior colleague working in human resources at the university. The colleague recommended eLS after working with the company on the development of an online version of a training program to help the university meet the requirements of the Health Insurance Portability and Accountability Act (HIPAA). eLS was an e-learning software company that prided itself, as its advertising said, on "designing and developing instructionally sound, cost-effective education and training solutions to improve performance," and to deliver these solutions on time and within budget. Indeed, eLS had won several prestigious awards in recent years for developing training applications. Some of the company's successes included the design and development of a multimedia application used to improve the performance of human resource managers at a large computer corporation, and a cultural diversity training product used by a Fortune 500 company. According to eLS, the cultural diversity training was credited with raising awareness among 92%, and changing behavior by 84%, of participants.

Jennie, one of the most successful project managers at eLS, had previously coordinated two projects and had developed several learning objects that were integrated routinely into other e-learning products. Her charge was to work with Pedro to translate the face-to-face workshop into an online environment. Moreover, as project manager, it was Jennie who was ultimately responsible for the success or failure of the project. Given this level of account-ability, she was highly motivated to identify clear project goals, to use these goals to estab-lish criteria for project evaluation, to verify changes in behavior, and to determine the success of the project.

Man-to-Man Workshop

The face-to-face version of the Man-to-Man workshop was presented to approximately 50 to 60 participants who traveled to a single location and met for approximately 16 hours over a two-day period. The workshops were facilitated by faculty from the departments of coun-seling psychology, human sexuality, and the university's medical school. All workshop pre-senters had received extensive sexual health workshop training and held advanced degrees in their fields.

The workshop curriculum included the 10 components of the sexual health model, and used diverse instructional strategies such as lectures, games, opportunities for individual reflection, and discussions in both small- and large-group settings. The instructional strate-gies made use of a broad range of instructional media such as video clips, still images, and slideshow presentations. Workshop participants were recruited through local print and elec-tronic media. For example, advertisements had appeared in *Leather and Lace,* a publication focusing on the local gay, lesbian, bisexual, and transgender community; *City Guide,* a local entertainment newspaper; and on local community electronic bulletin boards. Workshops were open to all participants who identified themselves as being gay or bisexual.

The face-to-face workshop had been shown to be highly effective in reducing the inci-dence of high-risk behavior. In fact, in an evaluation comparing workshop participants with a control group who viewed print and video sexual-health materials, data showed that inci-dents of risk behavior among the experimental group decreased by 32% after six months, and 27% one year later. In contrast, risk behavior among the control group decreased by 12% after six months and 8% a year later. Evaluation data pointed to a range of reasons to account for the success of the workshop, but many participants mentioned that the small-group experiences were particularly powerful: Within supportive small groups, participants were challenged to grapple with various issues that promoted heightened self-analysis and this process seemed to have had a transformative effect on the attitudes and behaviors of the participants.

In addition, Professor Essex stressed the importance of using "hot cognitions" (i.e., use of sensual and/or erotic stimuli such as photos and movies) in certain phases of the face-to-face workshops. Cognitive behavioral therapists use the term hot cognitions to indicate that emotional stimulation is often crucial to the therapy process. Using hot cognitions may affect decision making and behavior change more so than learning in nonaroused educational contexts. Moreover, Professor Essex maintained that research had demonstrated that the use of sexually explicit media in such settings gradually reduced participants' discomfort and shame while simultaneously facilitating positive behavior change. Counseling services were offered on-site for participants whose reactions to the workshop experiences made them feel especially uncomfortable.

From M2M to IM2M: How Do We Get There?

Although Jennie and Pedro had only a few brief conversations about the Man-to-Man project, both were already beginning to see that they had quite different ideas about how to translate M2M to IM2M. Both were focused on achieving the same goal, but they were having difficulty agreeing how the face-to-face workshop could be translated to an online environment.

"I think that our design approach for this project is important because it addresses an issue that is likely to become increasingly common in the next few years," said Pedro. "As access to the Internet continues to expand, more and more people will want to learn how to develop an online format for a face-to-face workshop or class."

"Absolutely," agreed Jennie, "and I've already been involved in leading a couple of such projects. As you know, I was the project manager for the HIPAA training modules. My team members and I were asked to convert a classroom-based training module about patients' privacy into an online experience. The modules were completed by employees at the university and the project was very successful: We documented a 100% completion rate! I really think that I can apply what I've learned in that project to the Man-to-Man project."

"So, how did you approach designing the online version?" asked Pedro.

"Well," began Jennie, "it was clear that the original classroom-based HIPAA workshop was quite effective, so we assumed that customizing the content to specific cultural groups and including learning checks would further increase the effectiveness of the intervention while allowing us to reach a larger online audience. The online setting was the perfect environment for customizing content and guaranteeing that learning was taking place. Since much of the content was already in place from the live training, we were able to focus on the customization and learning checks to further improve the training and make it more appealing."

"Well, I haven't seen that workshop but from how you describe it, it seems to be primarily about delivering information," said Pedro. "But in the Man-to-Man workshop, we're looking at very different learning outcomes. This project is not just about the delivery of information—it's much more about behavior change, and that has more to do with modifying people's opinions and values than it does with learning content. I mean, look at what people know about smoking—everyone recognizes that smoking is bad for their health, but such knowledge doesn't cause people to quit. The same is true here; we're not just trying to inform people about safe sex techniques. Our job is to change people's beliefs about themselves. By doing so, people will begin to make effective choices. I'm not so sure that we can take the existing content and reproduce it online with only minor changes in delivery."

"I see what you mean," noted Jennie. "I certainly agree that the Man-to-Man workshop is more than just about delivering information, but so was the HIPAA workshop—not only were the employees required to learn information about HIPAA, the training was also designed for them to perform a range of tasks related to the correct application of HIPAA requirements. In the classroom-based version of the workshop, the trainers had incorporated a lot of question-and-answer sessions and group discussions, and we managed to translate these to the online environment.

"In fact," said Jennie, trying to sound as upbeat as possible although she was pretty sure she wasn't convincing Pedro, "we required participants to post comments for each discussion thread, and the result was that we obtained 100% participation in the online discussion forums, which was much higher than was ever the case in the classroom version of the training!"

"While there might be some similarities in terms of the usefulness of online discussion forums," responded Pedro, "I don't think an online discussion forum is realistic for the Man-to-Man project. An online workshop isn't like an online class—workshop participants attend voluntarily so we can't require them to submit responses to a forum."

Just as Jennie feared, Pedro's comments confirmed her suspicions that she and Pedro were not getting any closer to agreement on the overall design plan for the IM2M, let alone getting to the point of planning a detailed design.

"Also," Pedro continued, "I don't believe we can recreate the small-group experience online because we can't reproduce the empathy of a face-to-face discussion in an online discussion forum. The media associated with each environment differ greatly and the experiences made possible by the face-to-face environment cannot be replicated. Physical proximity makes a huge difference when it comes to discussing important personal matters. Being physically close to another person produces a powerful affective response that may be impossible to recreate on the Internet."

"Do you really think so?" asked Jennie. "More and more people are routinely using the web to meet and date. People frequently discuss their most personal problems in online settings. Look at the emergence of blogs—you can find a threaded discussion or a blog on just about any topic. If these men use the Internet regularly to meet with other men, surely they will also be willing to engage in discussions about their personal lives. Of course, we may have to tweak the format somewhat from the face-to-face version, but I have no doubt at all that this is not only possible, but highly practical."

"Well, it *is* true that people seem to discuss almost any topic on the Internet these days," mused Pedro, "but I'm still not clear on how we can translate the face-to-face interactions to the Internet environment so that we can achieve the same outcomes that Professor Essex has been achieving. For example, you know how Professor Essex uses what he calls 'hot cognitions' in the face-to-face workshop—how are we going to handle these in an online environment? Shouldn't we be concerned about the possible ethical and legal implications of hot cognitions? I mean, could the university or eLS be found liable if it can be proven that an individual who committed a sex crime did so after being aroused as a result of completing the Internet materials?"

Jennie appreciated that Pedro had raised some important points that had also been nagging at her. However, she wasn't about to mention this to Pedro at this point: She thought it better to wait until they had more time to come up with some potential ways to move forward. Besides, hearing Pedro mention Professor Essex reminded Jennie that she had a meeting with him in about 30 minutes and that she needed to finish her meeting with Pedro.

"You've brought up some really important issues," responded Jennie. "However, I have a meeting with Professor Essex shortly, so we'll have to finish for now. What about this as a way to move forward? Why don't both of us give some thought to how we might structure the online version of M2M over the next week and come back with some more detailed ideas for a proposed design? I'm sure that we can work out something that will meet the challenges that we have discussed."

"Sounds good to me," responded Pedro, "but I certainly think we have our work cut out for us."

Jennie had met with Professor Essex only once before to clarify some details about the time line, the budget, and to agree on how they would work together over the course of the project. Based on her experience on other projects, Jennie knew that some clients did not realize that their involvement would be necessary as design and development proceeded, and she believed strongly in having a clear agreement on mutual responsibilities from the very beginning of a project. However, while much of their first meeting went well, she was surprised to find that Professor Essex seemed unwilling to work with her on the development of detailed measures of effectiveness for the online version of Man-to-Man. She had come prepared, having read the NHF proposal that he had developed and which included project goals written according to NHF requirements. Although they were written clearly (see Figure 11–1), she thought Professor Essex needed to identify more detailed measures that she could use to establish evaluation criteria that would be applied during the online workshop to assess changes in participants' behaviors.

Project Goal

Our project goal, which will guide all design and development activities, is to broaden the impact of an HIV/AIDS prevention face-to-face workshop by adapting it to an online environment. The result will be an Internet-delivered sexual-health intervention for gay and bisexual men who use the Internet to date other men.

Project Objectives

The objectives of the project are as follows:

- To develop an HIV/AIDS prevention workshop for gay and bisexual men for delivery over the Internet.
- To use the 10 components of the sexual health model as the basis for the Internet-delivered workshop.
- To incorporate contemporary principles of e-learning and distance education into the online workshop

---

FIGURE 11–1 Project Goal and Objectives Submitted to the National Health Foundation.

"If the goals were good enough for NHF, surely they should be good enough for eLS to work with," Jennie recalled him saying. Unfortunately, or fortunately, Jennie wasn't sure which, their meeting time was up before they could get into more detail about the need for more measurable goals. She hadn't really expected such resistance and had been somewhat taken aback by Professor Essex's reaction at their initial meeting. In any event, she persuaded Professor Essex to meet again today. Since their first meeting, she had thought through how she would present her arguments for the need for more detailed measures and was hopeful, if not exactly confident, that she could convince him of the need for what she was requesting.

As she walked toward her car after her meeting with Professor Essex, Jennie reflected on her day. It was very important to her that the project be completed to a high standard, on time, and within budget, but Jennie already knew that this project would not be like any of the previous projects she had coordinated. Would she and Pedro be able to come to agreement on the design issues they had discussed? Could they translate the face-to-face workshop to an online format while maintaining its power and effectiveness? Given Professor Essex's attitude, would she even be able to measure its effectiveness? And what about the legal and ethical issues that Pedro had raised? "I think Pedro was right," she thought to herself as she drove off campus, "we do have our work cut out for us."

Preliminary Analysis Questions

1. Pedro presents a number of challenges to Jennie regarding the translation of a face-to-face workshop to an online environment. Evaluate the validity of the challenges in the context of this project.
2. Given the differences between Pedro and Jennie's approaches to designing interactive online experiences, propose how they might proceed in their discussions and continued work.
3. Professor Essex depended strongly on hot cognitions for the success of his face-to-face workshops. To what extent can these be incorporated into the online version of the workshop?
4. Consider the project goal and objectives from the perspectives of Professor Essex and Jennie Davenport. Develop a list of criteria that can be used to measure project success.

Implications for ID Practice

1. Consider the potential and limitations of designing Internet versus face-to-face workshops on sensitive content.
2. Discuss the risks and benefits associated with encouraging Internet communication (synchronous or asynchronous) when the topic is emotionally laden.
3. How does instructional design for behavior change differ from instructional design for knowledge acquisition? Describe differences in terms of goals, strategies, and evaluation.

Malcolm Gibson

Designing Authentic Online Experiences for Adult Learners

by Joanna C. Dunlap

Dean's Conference Room, Bentley Hall, Craiger University—9:05 A.M.

"OK, let's go ahead and get started," directed Dr. Teresa Tsagas. "Does everyone have an agenda? As you know, the purpose of our work session today is to pull together all of the sections of the PTTP proposal, including the work that Malcolm has done. In fact, assuming all of you have already had a chance to look at the attachments Malcolm sent a couple of days ago, I'd like to go ahead and start with Malcolm, since his work is the core of the proposal. Malcolm, would you mind getting us started by walking us through your proposed certificate program structure, and then the online module?"

Background

Craiger University is located in one of the top five technology states, ranking number three in terms of the number of high-technology companies. However, the information technology industry in the state is in crisis because there are not enough resident skilled employees to meet demand. Instead of continuing the practice of hiring people from out of state, a number of the state's information technology (IT) organizations have formed the Information Technology Consortium (ITC) with support from the state government. The mission of the consortium is to increase substantially the number of IT graduates over the next five years by funding programs that will increase the availability of highly qualified IT professionals. The ITC has released a *Preparing Tomorrow's Technology Professionals (PTTP)* Request for Proposals (RFP; see Appendix 12–A) that offers financial support to educational institutions that propose innovative methods for preparing an increased number of technology professionals for the workplace. The ITC will award up to $2 million to educational institutions during a first round of funding.

The School of Engineering at Craiger University has a computer science (CS) undergraduate program that the department chair, Dr. Teresa Tsagas, and the faculty believe could be easily repurposed for the PTTP initiative. According to the RFP, one of the possible program formats deemed appropriate for preparing IT professionals was online certificate and degree programs. The CS faculty had been thinking about making the computer science major available online for the past year and a half but hadn't moved forward because of a perceived lack of resources. The PTTP money could be the shot in the arm that the department needed to leap into online delivery.

Initial Plan of Action

Dr. Tsagas and the CS faculty decided to propose a program that would make use of the existing face-to-face courses required for the CS major to offer four online certificate programs. Given this structure, people could take all four online certificates and apply them to the bachelor of science degree in computer science, or people not interested in a degree and just needing to update their knowledge and skills could take one certificate or a subset of certificates.

To create the certificates, the faculty divided the existing courses into the four categories depicted in Figure 12–1. In general, the faculty proposed that the CS curriculum be evenly distributed across the four certificates. Since each certificate would build on information gained in the previous certificate, they would be taken in sequence, from beginning to advanced. Each certificate program would be completed in 40 weeks (each course would be 8 weeks long). If a student applied the certificates to the BS in computer science, the major could be completed in two years.

One requirement of the RFP was to provide an example of the proposed approach to an online instructional module or course. To help the CS faculty address this requirement, Dr. Tsagas contacted Malcolm Gibson, a local instructional technologist with expertise in web-based course development. Because he is also an information technology professional, Dr. Tsagas asked Malcolm to review and provide feedback on their proposed certificate program structure in light of the RFP.

After reviewing the RFP and Dr. Tsagas' proposal, Malcolm accepted the contract, hoping it would lead to more instructional design and online course development work, not only with the CS department but with Craiger University overall.

Certificate I: Fundamentals of Information Technology

CS 145   Calculus
CS 115   Computing Fundamentals
CS 160   Data Structures
CS 165   Discrete Structures
CS 180   Assembly Language

Certificate II: Algorithms and Basic Languages

CS 150   Advanced Calculus
CS 210   Applied Linear Algebra
CS 225   Algorithms
CS 215   Differential Equations
CS 250   Fundamentals of Programming Languages

Certificate III: Operating Systems and Software Engineering

CS 245   Operating Systems
CS 315   Principle of Software Engineering
CS 260   Theoretical Foundations of Computer Science
CS 265   Numerical Analysis
CS 280   Graph Theory

Certificate IV: Advanced Computer Science

CS 390   Applied Probability
CS 410   Computer Architecture
CS 360   Advanced Software Engineering
CS 482   Ethical Decision Making in Computer Science
CS 475   Software Development Project

FIGURE 12–1   Preliminary Certificate Structure.

Project Challenges

During Malcolm's first information-gathering meeting with Dr. Tsagas and the CS faculty, he realized that it was going to be a challenge for him to work on this project. For one thing, he didn't become involved in the project until late in the process. The CS faculty had already been putting together information for various sections of the proposal, and the structure and content of the proposed program and curriculum were already determined. In addition, the proposal was due in six weeks. That didn't leave him a lot of time to develop the sample online module.

Malcolm was also very concerned about the faculty's proposed certificate structure because he didn't believe it would meet the goals of the PTTP initiative. Unlike other certificate programs, Craiger's proposed certificates were unable to stand on their own. The certificates relied on repurposing the same courses, in the same sequence, currently being delivered in the face-to-face program. The existing program appeared to Malcolm to be a sequence of isolated, decontextualized concepts and problems leading to a simplified capstone project completed in the final semester. If the current program were already "preparing tomorrow's technology professionals," there would be no need for the PTTP initiative.

Finally, Malcolm's expertise related to designing instruction that incorporates authentic learning activities. A lot of the content for this project (e.g., computer programming) was procedural. Malcolm hadn't really designed instruction for rule-based content before and wasn't quite sure how to do it in a meaningful and relevant way for students, which was a core requirement of the RFP. He was also concerned about his ability to develop a course that would be delivered in an accelerated, eight-week format. With as much diplomacy as he could muster, Malcolm expressed his concerns to Dr. Tsagas.

"Malcolm, I understand your concerns, and the fact that you have them reinforces my decision to hire you. If I'm hearing you correctly, your primary concerns are the structure of the certificate programs and the time line?"

"Yes," responded Malcolm, "I guess that's accurate." "But," Malcolm thought, "I really am worried about everything!"

"Well, I can't do anything about the time line, but I would like to give you some leeway to explore—and present back to us—different ways to structure the curriculum into certificate programs. We need all the help we can get if we want to present a competitive proposal to the ITC, so if you want to take a stab at it. . . .Would you like to propose a different structure to the faculty at the next work-session meeting?"

Malcolm agreed to develop a web-based module (one week of a proposed eight-week course) for inclusion in the proposal (and for stimulating further faculty buy-in for converting the CS courses to an online delivery format) and to propose a different structure for the certificate programs. Unfortunately, Malcolm had even less time to accomplish both tasks than he thought. Since the proposal was due in six weeks, he really had only four weeks to complete his task in order to be prepared to work with the CS faculty during their final session.

Malcolm's Work

Based on Dr. Tsagas's request, the first thing Malcolm did was to reexamine the certificate plans of study that the faculty had constructed (review Figure 12–1). Based on his understanding of the marketplace and the requirements of the RFP, Malcolm generated an alternative certificate structure for the faculty to review (see Figure 12–2). Using the new structure, Malcolm decided to develop a module for the Programming with PHP and JavaScript course (a course he added to the Web Engineer Certificate). As a web developer, he was very familiar with the content and skills that students needed to learn in that course and, with only four weeks to develop an example good enough to help win the funding and future work at Craiger, he knew he wouldn't have time to work on any unfamiliar content.

TO: Dr. Teresa Tsagas

FR: Malcolm Gibson

RE: DRAFT—CS Certificates

Per your request, below is an alternative mapping of computer science curriculum to four certificate programs, organized by in-demand information technology positions. Each certificate stands alone—it's a vertical orientation as opposed to the original horizontal orientation. For example, in the Systems Engineer Certificate, the courses are sequenced from beginning to advanced—as opposed to the original structure of the certificates where the certificates themselves are structured from beginning to advanced. This structure, based on positions in the information technology field, better addresses the PTTP initiative because it is focused on preparing students for specific jobs in the workplace.

The challenge is that the current courses will not directly map to this alternative structure. As you see, the Data Structures course is now split out across all four certificates, but the content of each Data Structures course will be specific to the position students are being prepared for—i.e., network engineer or web engineer. Sorry, I didn't include course numbers because I am not that familiar with what is covered in each of your existing courses. But I am assuming that content from existing courses can be repurposed for use in these courses. I look forward to discussing this at our next meeting.

Systems Engineer Certificate
Fundamentals of Systems
Systems Algorithms and Data Structures
Programming Language: C/C++
Systems Architecture
Applied Systems Engineering

Network Engineer Certificate
Fundamentals of Networking
Network Algorithms and Data Structures
Programming Language: C/C++
Network Architecture
Applied Network Engineering

Database Engineer Certificate
Fundamentals of Databases
Database Algorithms and Data Structures
Programming Language: SQL
Database Architecture
Applied Database Engineering

Web Engineer Certificate
Fundamentals of the Web
Web Algorithms and Data Structures
Programming with PHP and JavaScript
Web Architecture
Applied Web Engineering

FIGURE 12–2 Malcolm's Proposed Certificate Program.

For the next four weeks, Malcolm worked continuously in order to meet the deadline. Three days prior to the scheduled work session at Craiger, Malcolm sent his version of the certificate program curricular structure and the web-based module as attachments to Dr. Tsagas and the CS faculty for their review prior to the work session (review Figure 12–2 and see Appendix 12–B).

Back in the Dean's Conference Room—9:06 A.M.

Malcolm stood up, walked over to the table in the front of the conference room, and projected a slide of his curriculum-restructuring memo for everyone to see.

"Hello again, everyone. Since you've already had a chance to review this, I don't want to spend too much time on it, if we don't need to. Maybe we could start with your comments and concerns."

It was obvious that the faculty had read the materials and had looked at the online lesson. Over the next 15–20 minutes, Malcolm fielded a quick succession of questions. The faculty began by expressing their concerns about facilitating online instruction.

Dr. Will Jacobs started the discussion. "When I'm explaining programming concepts, I like to look at my students' faces to see if they're getting it. I can tell by looking at them if they don't understand what I'm presenting, and then I can try to say it in a different way. How will I know if the students get it in an online environment?"

"Can I jump in?" asked Dr. Judy Ruzic. "You know, some of the content in our courses is really challenging. I often see students before and after class, working together on different problems. Sometimes they form study groups. I just don't see how they can do this on the Web."

"That reminds me. I don't know about the rest of you, but I am mostly worried about controlling and managing student activities in an online course. If I don't see them, how will I know they are doing their *own* work? Or doing any work at all?" asked Dr. Eli Anton.

"I'm less worried about that, Eli," considered Dr. Angela Wang. "I'm worried mostly about keeping students engaged in the learning. I've seen some online courses that are just the syllabus and calendar online, with assigned readings and questions to answer in an online discussion area. Or the course is just an online textbook—either way, boring. There has got to be a better way of doing online courses, or I'm not particularly interested in participating."

Dr. Chris Newman took up where Dr. Wang left off. "Angela's right. Besides being concerned about keeping students engaged, I really like 16-week-long courses because they give students time to reflect. If a course is condensed to 8 weeks *and* is online, how will students have time to reflect on what they are doing in class and on what they are learning?"

After Malcolm addressed the faculty's questions about online facilitation, Dr. Tsagas called for a 10-minute break before discussing Malcolm's proposed certificate structure. As the faculty filed out of the conference room, Malcolm reviewed his notes about the new structure. He knew from the quality of the faculty's questions about the online module that he would need to be sharp during the rest of the work session.

Preliminary Analysis Questions

1. Why did Malcolm structure the certificates the way he did?
2. How do you think the faculty reacted to Malcolm's curricular restructuring for the proposed certificate programs?
3. Why did Malcolm design the module the way he did? How well do you think he did with his instructional strategy selection, given

   - The goals of the PTTP initiative?
   - The nature of the content?
   - The accelerated delivery format?
   - The web-based delivery medium?

4. How do you think the CS faculty reacted to Malcolm's web-based module?
5. How would you conduct a formative evaluation on Malcolm's web-based module?

Implications for ID Practice

1. Discuss the differences in design when incorporating authentic learning activities, time for reflection, and collaborative activities into online instruction versus face-to-face instruction.
2. Discuss the challenges and constraints involved when using the strategies outlined in question 1 in a course that will be delivered in an accelerated format.
3. Discuss the advantages and disadvantages of repurposing existing courses, as opposed to developing new courses for online delivery.

Appendix 12-A

Preparing Tomorrow's Technology Professionals Request for Proposals (RFP)

Preparing Tomorrow's Technology Professionals

Request for Proposals

In June of this year, the Association of Information Technology Professionals (AITP) released a study—*Building Our Information Technology Infrastructure.* This study stated that, although the number of information technology (IT) professionals in the United States has stayed the same over the past two years (at approximately 10 million), industry is attempting to fill about 1 million new positions. To address the shortage of IT professionals in our state, the Information Technology Consortium (ITC) is working to ensure the availability of qualified IT professionals by providing financial support for educational institutions that will work with us to increase the number of IT graduates that enter the workplace.

Program Description

During this initial round of funding ($2 million is available), the ITC will consider awarding funds to educational institutions that propose projects that address one of the following needs:

- Programs that increase the number of students graduating from existing two and four-year undergraduate programs

- Online certificate or degree programs
- Certification programs for professionals who need to update their technology knowledge and skills

To be competitive, the project must provide clear evidence that the new curriculum responds to changes in industry standards. New curriculum must prepare students for the IT industry, and learning activities must be relevant to the IT workplace.

Proposal Contents

All proposals must include

- Cover sheet—title and type of project, contact information, date submitted
- Project summary (one page)
- Description of the program, curriculum, objectives, outcomes, audience, and delivery format
- Timeline showing when students involved in the proposed program will be ready to enter the workplace
- Data supporting the proposed curriculum's ability to address the needs of the information technology industry in the state
- Letters of support from the educational institution, the faculty, and industry partners
- Budget and project timeline
- Example of curriculum (e.g., if proposing an online program, provide an example of an online module or course)

Appendix 12-B

Module for Programming with PHP and JavaScript Course

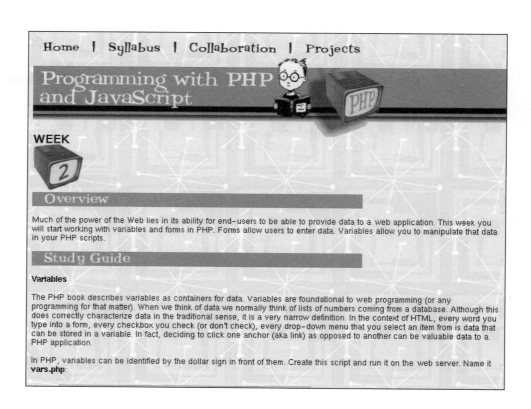

Home | Syllabus | Collaboration | Projects

Programming with PHP and JavaScript

WEEK 2

Overview

Much of the power of the Web lies in its ability for end-users to be able to provide data to a web application. This week you will start working with variables and forms in PHP. Forms allow users to enter data. Variables allow you to manipulate that data in your PHP scripts.

Study Guide

Variables

The PHP book describes variables as containers for data. Variables are foundational to web programming (or any programming for that matter). When we think of data we normally think of lists of numbers coming from a database. Although this does correctly characterize data in the traditional sense, it is a very narrow definition. In the context of HTML, every word you type into a form, every checkbox you check (or don't check), every drop-down menu that you select an item from is data that can be stored in a variable. In fact, deciding to click one anchor (aka link) as opposed to another can be valuable data to a PHP application.

In PHP, variables can be identified by the dollar sign in front of them. Create this script and run it on the web server. Name it **vars.php**:

106

```
<html>
<head><title>Vars</title></head>
<body>
<?php
// Assign values to variables
$pi=3.14;
$pie="Apple";
$py="Pythagoras loves to eat $pie";
$two="The countdown finished...\"two\", \"one\", \"liftoff!\"";

// Print out the variables
print("1. PI is $pi<br>");
print("2. $pie is a fruit<br>");
print("3. $py<br>");
print("4. {$py}s<br>");
print("5. $two<br>");
print("6. \$two<br>");
?>
</body>
</html>
```

HTML Forms and PHP

There are two things to keep in mind when using HTML forms with PHP:

1. The form tag must have an action attribute whose value is a PHP script that will process the form data:

   ```
   <form action="process_form.php">
   ```
   ("process_form.php" would be replaced with the name of your own PHP script)

2. Each field on the form should have a name. This name becomes a variable in the script that processes the form data:

   ```
   <input type="text" name="age">
   ```
   The name *age* can be accessed as the variable *$age* in the script that processes the data.

PHP `print()` made easier

HTML forms (and HTML in general) has a lot of quotes. Since quotes in print statements must be preceded by a backslash, it can make for a pretty miserable time. Take this print statement:

```
<?php
print("<table border=\"1\"
cellpadding=\"10\"
bgcolor=\"#ffffff\">");
?>
```

To print out this simple table tag, there are a total of six quotes that have to be preceded by a backslash (As an aside, one nice thing about print statements is that they can span multiple lines as shown above. This can make your PHP much more readable). Here is a variant on the print statement that eliminates the quoting problem:

```
<?php
print <<<WOODCHUCK
<table border="1"
cellpadding="10"
bgcolor="#ffffff">
WOODCHUCK;
?>
```

In short, after the word **print** type in three less-than symbols and a word. I chose a goofy word to emphasize that you can use any word you like. On the following lines you put in all of the text, variables, quotes, etc. that you want to print out. To end the print statement you repeat the word and end it with a semi-colon. If you have a lot of HTML to print out and you want to avoid placing a backslash before each quote, this is a good alternative.

There are some guidelines to follow if you use this type of print statement:

1. The first **print** line and the last line with the word should appear on their own lines.
2. The last line with the word must not be indented.
3. No spaces should follow either the first or last line.
4. Although it is not required by the language, convention says that the word that you choose should be entirely in upper-case.

Readings/Surfings

1. Add to the PHP script you created in Week 1. Tell the user what kind of browser they are using (hint, see the last page of Chapter 2).
2. Create a quiz form. The quiz should have at least one of each of the following:
   ○ Multiple choice question (using radio buttons)
   ○ Short answer question (using an input field of type *text*).
   ○ An essay question (using a *textarea*).
   Even though this quiz can be built entirely as HTML, name the file **quiz.php**. We will be adding PHP code to it later in the course.
3. Add a link to **index.html** that goes to your quiz.
4. When users press the submit button on the quiz, it should go to a php script that prints the answers that the user selected on the form.
5. A simple red "bar" can be done this way in HTML:

> **<table bgcolor="red" width="100"><tr><td> </td></tr></table>**

    A. Create a script **bar.php** that simply prints a red bar exactly as shown above.
    B. Create a file **barform.html** that has a form that takes two values: A number for the width of the bar, and a name for the color of the bar. The action of the form should call **bar.php**. Change **bar.php** so that it uses the form fields (variables) for the color and width.
6. Add a link to **index.html** that goes to **barform.html**.

Hacker's Challenge (aka, Optional Question)

1. Combine the contents of **barform.html** and **bar.php** into **bar.php**. That is, **bar.php** should contain the form followed by the code that prints the bar. Try entering several values for colors and widths to confirm that you can do it repetedly.

Super Hacker's Challenge (aka, Boy, this is really optional)

1. Add another type of question to your quiz: a multiple choice question with more than one correct answer (e.g. Which of the following numbers are prime numbers: 1, 2, 3, 4, 5, 6, 7, 8). You will need to use an input field of type "select" with the *multiple* attribute. Creating the quiestion is not the hard part. The hard part is printing the user's answers.

1. Now that you've completed two weeks' worth of PHP, how confident are you feeling? Does PHP feel like an "in-town" horse and buggy or does it feel like a barely controlled stagecoach flung along by galloping clydesdales?
2. What would you like to do with forms in *your* work that isn't obvious based on what you've done this week?
3. **Macro View:** Talk a little about your problem-solving process. How are you getting your questions answered? What resources do you use? Have you tried using any Web resources?
4. **Micro View:** What about debugging? What is your routine when you seem to have most (or all) of the code in place and you are trying to get rid of a "parse" error?

In PHP's early days, large shipping containers were used for variables. These two programmers are preparing to assign a number to the variable they've pulled out of the rack in the background.
The archives don't explain why there is a lawnmower behind their chairs.

Case Study
13

Pat Kelsoe and Jean Fallon
Implementing Innovation within an Established Curriculum
by Carol S. Kamin and Brent G. Wilson

Background

State Medical University trains physicians, nurses, and health professionals in a variety of specialties. The training of physicians is fairly traditional, with two years of basic science instruction followed by third- and fourth-year clinical experiences. The primary teaching strategy for clinical experiences has been apprenticeships in hospital settings. However, due to a changing health care environment, fewer than 5% of all pediatric interactions result in hospitalization, and hospital stays have been greatly shortened. Therefore, increasing numbers of medical students do their required rotations in pediatrics offices around the state.

The pediatrics department is considered to be among the top 10 in the country, with a strong history of pediatric research. There are many older faculty members known to be excellent teachers and mentors. The chair of the department noted, "The faculty on this campus wrote the textbook on pediatrics." All medical students are required to take the pediatric clerkship in their third year. Thus, year-round the pediatrics department gets between 15 and 18 new third-year students every six weeks.

Dr. Jean Fallon is eager to begin a new project that will use technology to change how the pediatric clerkship is taught. She has called a planning meeting to brainstorm ideas, so that she can apply for a pilot grant through a recently released request for proposals (RFP) from the Office of the President.

Meet the Characters

Jean Fallon—clerkship director and primary subject matter expert (SME): A physician in academic medicine, Dr. Jean Fallon recently switched her focus from laboratory research to educational research when she became the director of medical student education in pediatrics. After working for a year on a National Institutes of Health grant, she returned the award, at some risk to her tenure prospects, in order to assume these new responsibilities. The promotion and tenure guidelines recently changed to allow faculty to be promoted based on educational scholarship, and Jean wanted to take advantage of this opportunity. Colleagues have told her that she has given up a "sure thing" and has switched to an unproven track for promotion. Her mentors and section head have advised her to work on her interest in educational research after she is tenured. Nevertheless, she is enthusiastic and interested in initiating and evaluating innovative teaching methods. She is also ambitious and wants to make a difference in pediatric medical education nationally, as well as locally.

The pediatrics course in the third year of medical school is the only direct experience all medical students are sure to have caring for children. Physical examination courses and other generic skills are taught with an adult emphasis. As clerkship director, Jean is interested in adopting the recently created national pediatrics curriculum that stresses field experience, but she wants some standardization of this learning experience. She believes that, as practicing physicians, students will need the lifelong skills inherent in independent learning, problem-based learning, and electronic information retrieval. She is open to innovative instructional solutions.

When asked to name the one thing she wants medical students to know when they complete the clerkship, Jean's reply was, "To look at an infant or a child and know if his or her condition is urgent."

Pat Kelsoe—medical educator: A doctoral-level instructional designer, Dr. Pat Kelsoe is a brand new assistant professor in pediatrics accustomed to collaborating on development teams. She has been an instructional designer for the past six years, with all of her experience in academic medicine. She helped two other medical schools transition to problem-based learning. She worked full-time while she completed her doctoral degree in instructional technology a year ago. "I dragged my family across the country to accept this position; there's no way I'm going to take this job lightly," emphasized Pat.

There was no job description for Pat's position when she interviewed, so she asked the chair what success would look like in five years. His response was, "I want the department to have a national reputation as a center for scholarly work (educational research) in pediatric medical education." After she accepted the position, the chair confided, "The medical educator position is a new one for our department; some of the old guard were opposed to it."

To prepare for the planning meeting, Pat asked for past course materials and evaluations for the pediatric clerkship. She received 45 pages of qualitative comments from an open-ended student survey. After conducting a content analysis, she found that the strengths of the course appeared to be the teaching that was conducted primarily by pediatric residents. The primary weakness appeared to be the lack of course organization. The students who were dispersed to clinical sites seemed to enjoy the experience but felt somewhat isolated from their peers and unsure of the intended learning outcomes. They were not sure they were getting what they needed from the course or how it compared with what their peers at other sites were getting.

Sam McConnell—senior colleague: Dr. Sam McConnell, a senior faculty leader, was also asked to attend the planning meeting to discuss potential changes to the pediatric clerkship. Sam thought the new clerkship director had the potential to be a star, given the research she was doing, and was upset that she did not wait until after she was tenured to take this educational position. He has heard some of the grumbling from other faculty members about the medical educator position, and he, too, wonders why she was hired and what she will do to help the department's already excellent teachers.

Sam gets outstanding evaluations of his teaching, but he thinks one is either born a good teacher or not. He gives lectures on Wednesday afternoons and has students and residents in his clinics. As far as Sam is concerned, seeing patients is the only way to learn medicine. After all, that's the way he learned pediatrics. Most pediatrics faculty members prefer to teach residents who are going to be pediatricians. He's one of the few senior faculty members who teaches medical students, but he does it because he is committed to recruiting the best students possible for pediatrics. Sam is always disappointed when he gets a student who shows absolutely no interest in specializing in pediatrics.

Sam wonders why this group is meeting, anyway. He is convinced that students just need to work harder and see as many patients as possible. The clerkship gets good reviews, and the department has highly qualified applicants for its residency program. He believes that "if it's not broken, don't fix it." There is constant pressure to produce revenue by getting large grants and seeing more patients. Sam believes that this is the only way to keep a medical school department afloat in a volatile health care environment. Even though pediatricians love to teach, as far as Sam is concerned, everyone knows that teaching does not generate revenue for the department.

Harry Lipsitz—department chair: Though he has received a lot of heat from some senior faculty members for creating a medical educator position and appointing a junior faculty member as clerkship director, Harry is excited about the potential of these young professors. He sees that there are many research questions to be asked in pediatric education and is anxious for his department to be a leader in this area. He believes that he has two very talented and hard-working faculty members who share his vision for the clerkship. Harry is concerned, however, about their overriding interest in technology. He recalls a colleague who took a sabbatical to create an educational software program. This colleague worked very hard on the project, but nothing ever came of it. Harry is afraid that ventures into educational technology could take a lot of time and money and end up being unproductive.

Harry considers that his most important job is to get these two junior faculty members promoted under the new evaluation system. They will be two of the first faculty members to attempt to secure tenure under these new guidelines. Although it's true that educational innovations are a risky venture for untenured professors, he believes that these two could perform some interesting studies and obtain some interesting research findings.

The Planning Meeting

Faculty members begin arriving in the department conference room. After several minutes of friendly banter, Jean begins the discussion:

Jean: Thank you all for making the meeting. I know it's a busy time of year, but I want to get this project off the ground. There are a lot of great things already in place with the clerkship, but there seems to be some room for trying out new ideas. The President's Office just came out with a grants program, and I thought we could compete for some of that money.

Sam: Always happy to take someone else's money!

Jean: That's right, and I think this project could be worth the investment. I've been thinking—our clerkship students often have great experiences out in the field, but they sometimes don't see any critical cases. It's a bit risky out there. Our students can get a great education, but we leave a lot to chance. So, I've been playing around with a possible solution. What if we developed a set of cases, such as computer-based case studies, covering some cases we think everyone should see—say, an urgent case of abuse? Then we'd be giving students something that's very close to real life, and we'd be able to guarantee they will actually encounter it during their clerkships.

Harry: You mean, show some video on the computer?

Jean: Yeah, show some video, either actors or real patients, depending on what we're thinking of. Give students a look at some symptoms and a situation, and let them ask questions, order tests, somehow leading to a diagnosis. Then we could give some feedback.

Harry: Wouldn't that be kind of expensive—putting all that into the computer?

Pat: Yes, a project like this could easily run up a budget. But I see the grant from the President's Office as a way to get it started. It could lead to some new ways to think about the clerkship.

Sam: [shifting in his seat]: Hold on a second. After having directed the clerkship for 12 years prior to your arrival here, Jean, I have to say that it's one of the most respected in the country. Our students come out very well versed in pediatrics. We get a good number of them deciding to specialize in pediatrics after their rotations.

Jean: That's important; we want students to be attracted to our department. I'm just thinking—maybe some video cases could even increase the attraction.

Harry: I'm still worried about the scope and cost of this kind of project.

Pat: Video production is getting cheaper and easier, but it's still a lot of work. We don't have a production facility here within the university; we would

	have to hire some of this work out. And we'd need to develop some expertise among ourselves.
Sam:	That's just what I need, some fancy new technology to learn. I remember taking a *HyperCard* class once—never again!
Pat:	I don't think faculty members should have to do all the authoring. We could get a couple of interns or part-time help to do most of the production. Your expertise, though, would be very helpful in determining how to approach a case, Sam.
Sam:	I don't want to do *any* of the authoring. It will take far too much of my time and time is money.
Pat:	Maybe I should clarify. We would have a team working on the case. The design and technical aspects would be handled by me and the interns. But we need experts to review the cases to ensure that they are realistic. This is what I mean when I say authoring.
Sam:	Oh, well I could do that. Of course, you'd need some expert advice, since you're not a physician or pediatrician.
Harry:	Tell me more about your ideas for the video case. Would it be like a tape that you watch?
Jean:	Pat, why don't you share the ideas you were telling me about PBL, or problem-based learning?
Pat:	As you know, PBL is heavily used in medical schools, but I'm not aware of very many problems or cases being presented electronically. Here is what Jean and I were talking about. We present a video case, with some footage and some background information—make it interactive, so that students can explore some information, order tests, and ask questions. That part is kind of standard, like an interactive case or a problem online. The part that I'm excited about is somehow connecting the students online—getting students and a faculty member on the Internet, talking to each other about the case. Students won't be so isolated in their different field sites; they will be able to learn from each other. Research suggests that case discussion is what makes this type of learning so powerful.
Harry:	Wow, that sounds exciting. You're trying to get the best of both worlds— video on the computer, but then having people connect and talk about it from different locations.
Jean:	That's right. You get the benefit of field experience but also some assurances that key learning experiences will be encountered and shared. That increases our confidence that they're all learning similar content. Not only would students have the lectures on-campus but they would stay connected throughout their field experiences.
Harry:	It can get kind of isolated out there. Having some way to work together would be good.

Preliminary Analysis Questions

1. In small groups, complete a role-play exercise and finish the meeting. Delineate specific design ideas that would address the concerns of all parties, and satisfy the needs of the clerkship and the department.
2. Identify Sam's biases regarding this proposed new approach to pediatric education. Suggest strategies for dealing with these biases.
3. How should Jean deal with the chair's concerns as expressed in the meeting?
4. Develop a two-page outline responding to the grant proposal. Include in your proposed design five or more of the following concerns and how you will address them:

   - Dealing with file size, download time, video format, and integration of media
   - Getting access to the web and technology throughout the state
   - Managing development cost, time, and resources
   - Encouraging high-quality reasoning, reflection, and defense of decisions
   - Encouraging collaboration, modeling, and exchange of ideas
   - Getting high-resolution and realistic presentation of symptoms and problems
   - Enculturating students to fieldlike situations
   - Overcoming resistance from faculty members and students
   - Using the project as a springboard or basis for research

Implications for ID Practice

1. Organizations, like people, have habits. These are the comfortable, established ways of doing things. Innovators and change agents often create tension within their working units by pushing for new goals, new methods, or both. What mistakes could innovators make if they were unaware of the political tensions arising from these different purposes and habits within the organization? What steps can innovators take to ease these tensions?
2. Innovations typically happen within the normal constraints of an organization—limited time, money, and expertise. Add to that list desire or will. In the face of these serious constraints, what "magic" has to happen for innovations to succeed? Draw on your own experience in addressing this question.
3. Think about cases in your experience of technology introduction, whether for learning or other objectives. Based on your experience and your reading, respond to the following questions:
   a. Organizations regularly go through significant changes—using new practices, adjusting to new requirements or competitive conditions, adopting new technologies. What can a work unit do to prepare itself for these inevitable changes? What can individuals do to help their unit successfully undergo a major change process?

b. In many work groups, at least one or two members are critical of change and tend to resist a proposed innovation. Is there a positive role critics can play within the organization? What kind of decision-making processes can best include the critic's input in a positive, productive way?

c. Many innovations live or die depending on the energy and leadership of a few innovators. How can we come to depend less on the radical innovator and more on collective processes? Put another way, how can an organization get full value from its innovators by encouraging them, tapping their energy, while at the same time minimizing the trauma and chaos involved in many change efforts?

d. Some models of organizational change suggest that innovators and early adopters are motivated by different things than are resistors or reluctant users. If this were true, then how would you motivate and support each of these groups of individuals in a change process?

Ricardo Martinez

Meeting Challenges in the Delivery of Online Instruction

by Patti Shank

Georgina Bates, a respected professor of human resource development at Western College, sat at her desk, checking student e-mails, and sighed. She was becoming increasingly concerned and anxious about the frustrated tone of these and previous student e-mails. Students in her graduate-level online course, *HRD 512: Organizational Psychology,* did not seem to be getting the hang of learning online, and they had just completed week 6 of the 12-week course. She expected a little confusion at first, as many of the students had never taken an online course before. Her close colleague, Dr. Ben Wu, who had taught in the school's online MBA program for two years, promised her that the students would soon get the hang of it, even though there was often some confusion at first. She grabbed her phone and put in a call to Ben. "I'm upset and it's all your fault!" she yelled into the phone. "Good day to you, too, Georgina," answered Ben. "What's up?" Georgina sighed. "Ben, you said my students would be getting the hang of learning online after a few weeks, but it's been 6 weeks and that's clearly not happening." "What exactly is the problem?" Ben asked. "Geesh, Ben, if I knew, I wouldn't be calling you!" she exclaimed. Ben offered, "How about I come over around 2:00 and we look at it together?" "Yes, please," she answered.

Background

Previously, all human resource development (HRD) courses had been in-person, on-campus. In the past year, some department faculty members discussed using Internet technologies in their courses in response to directives from Western's president. He had publicly declared his desire to provide more technology-based and technology-enhanced courses in order to keep up with other higher education institutions. Additionally, many graduate students complained about having to come to campus two or three nights a week, and student travel could easily be reduced through online or hybrid courses.

Georgina saw the value of using technology in the HRD program. She believed that using technology was a necessary skill for students and faculty and was frustrated with faculty resistance to the idea, so she offered to teach HRD 512 online. She expected that her successes would help the more reluctant faculty members in her department consider online or at least hybrid courses. The pressure to succeed was high.

Georgina had dabbled in website development using *FrontPage*™ and she found the development of her course website only slightly more complicated than the development of the small personal site she had developed a few months earlier. The biggest difference, to her, was that the course website had far more pages. The authoring, though, seemed much the same.

Students in the graduate HRD program usually got to know each other pretty well, as they often attended classes together in somewhat of a lockstep fashion. For most of them, HRD 512 was their first experience with an online course. Despite some anxiety, many felt positively about giving the new format a try.

Georgina's courses had always been popular. She typically received extremely high student evaluations and was known by students to be a tough but excellent teacher. Even though some students were nervous about the new course format and expectations, they were excited about the course and the benefit of not having to drive to class. Georgina explained in an introductory e-mail to the class that she had very high expectations for online participation, the use and evaluation of online learning materials, and online discussion.

2:15 P.M.

Ben read through a few student e-mails that Georgina had displayed on her computer screen. "These *are* troublesome," he admitted (see Figures 14–1, 14–2, and 14–3).

"These folks sound confused," Ben declared. "I know I had some difficulties with students feeling confused the first few times I taught online. Maybe that's your problem here. Didn't you just have mid-semester evaluations? Are other students confused?" Georgina showed him the list of comments from the recent mid-semester evaluations (see Figure 14–4).

"Look, I'm an expert in finance but I'm certainly no expert in developing online courses, so I got help when I started to see problems," said Ben. "I guess I figured I could do this myself, since I know how to use *FrontPage*™," she answered. Ben put his hand on Georgina's shoulder and said, "I think this is a pretty specialized skill, and even a reasonably tech-savvy person like you might not know all the ins and outs. It can't hurt to get some advice from someone who designs and develops online courses for a living, right?" He recommended that she meet with the instructional designer he worked with at the business school.

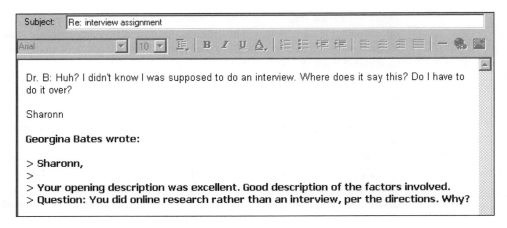

FIGURE 14–1   E-mail from Sharonn Concerning an Assignment.

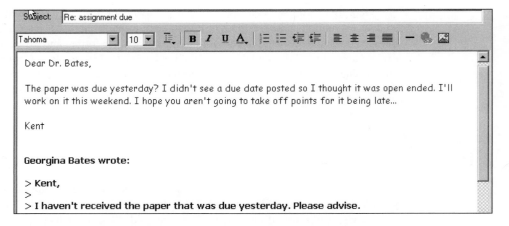

FIGURE 14–2   E-mail from Kent about the Assignment Due Date.

Georgina wondered aloud if she should just forget teaching online to avoid these kinds of problems and potential embarrassment. Ben assured her that she just needed some help tweaking the course in order to make it great. Georgina wasn't so sure but agreed to meet with Ricardo Martinez, an instructional designer and web developer for the business school, if Ben could arrange it. She was feeling somewhat frantic and hoped that Ricardo could meet with her soon.

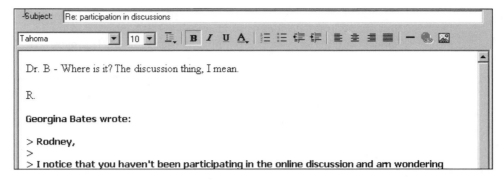

FIGURE 14–3   E-mail from Rodney about the Discussion Forum.

Comments from Mid-semester Student Course Evaluations, HRD 512

- I had heard great things about Dr. Bates, so I was looking forward to the course. It's an OK course, but I feel kinda lost a lot of the time. I'm not sure if I'm doing the right thing.

- Once you figure out what to do and how to do it, it's a good course. Some really good questions and links. . . my bookmarks are growing rapidly!

- I was told I missed answering some discussion questions and am aggravated because it'll affect my grade. I didn't know I was supposed to do this and am feeling like a dope. She needs to be way more clear about what she wants.

- Where's the discussion? What are we supposed to discuss? Are all online courses this frustrating?

- Dr. Bates needs to tell us what she wants for the assignments. I thought I was doing the right thing but I wasn't. Discouraging.

- When is the final project due? Do you want assignments e-mailed to you or brought to your office?

- Once I found everything I was fine, but it wasn't clear where to find instructions for the assignments.

- Help! Too hard to take this course online! Can we meet in person?

- Great topics. A little hard to follow at times.

FIGURE 14–4   Student Comments from Mid-semester Course Evaluation.

4:40 P.M. Ricardo's Office

Ricardo was in his office, troubleshooting a *JavaScript*™ quiz he had developed for one of the school's marketing courses. He wanted to make sure it worked right before he left for the day. Ricardo had been working for Western's business school for almost 2½ years.

After graduating from the online master's program in instructional technology, he was hired just after Western decided to build an online MBA program. Although he could make more money working in corporate training, he found that his laid-back style fit better in an academic setting. He especially enjoyed working with the faculty.

Ben peeked around the corner and saw Ricardo hard at work in his office. "Hey, Ricardo! I'll buy you two boxes of your favorite milano cookies if you'll share some of your amazing insight about online course development with my friend, Georgina Bates. She really needs your help." Ricardo agreed, "And I will *definitely* take you up on the cookies!"

Next Day, 11 A.M.

"Ricardo, I really appreciate your willingness to help me," said Georgina. "Dr. Wu has sung your praises, and I'm hoping you can help me figure out how to fix my problem." "Glad to help. Dr. Wu told me a little about what's going on," replied Ricardo. "Sounds as if both you and the students in your course are pretty frustrated. Tell me more about the problem." Georgina showed Ricardo the e-mails from students and a list of problems she had compiled (see Figure 14–5).

"Yep, looks like frustration alright," commented Ricardo. "Let's take a look at your course, OK?" he asked. Georgina brought up the course homepage on Ricardo's computer (see Figure 14–6).

"Let me get a feel for how students actually take the course, OK?" Ricardo asked. Georgina nodded her head in agreement. Ricardo clicked on the link for Week 2 and pulled up the Week 2 page (see Figure 14–7).

Problems with HRD 512

1. Some students aren't regularly participating in online discussions. When I e-mail them to find out why not, the most common reply is "What discussions?"

2. I'm chasing after too many students who haven't handed in assignments on time. Some students complain that they didn't know when they were due. Due dates are listed on the site!!!

3. Some of the assignments that are completed on time do not match the criteria specified for the assignment. Some students have complained that they don't know what I want them to do.

4. Students continually e-mail me with questions that are answered in the online course materials.

5. I need to look for a new job.:-(

FIGURE 14–5   List of Course Problems Compiled by Georgina.

HRD 512: Organizational Psychology

Welcome to HRD 512! This course provides a survey of organizational psychology and will help you gain knowledge and skills in a variety of important areas, including motivation, group dynamics, organizational communications, and organizational culture.

Click on these links to get more information about the course:

- Introduction to the course
- Readings
- Week 1
- Week 2
- Weeks 3–4
- Weeks 5–6
- Weeks 7–8
- Weeks 9–10
- Week 11
- Week 12
- Slides

E-mail me with questions

FIGURE 14–6   Homepage for HRD 512.

Motivation and Attitudes

This week we'll begin by asking. . .what makes people do the things they do? Pretty big question. Take a look at the slides for this week and see what a number of experts have to say about this question. Then check out the following websites for additional information:

Motivation and the workplace (make sure to check out the audio interviews. . .they're good!)
Systems thinking about workplace problems
Making sense out of chaos

This week's discussion questions:

1. Think about people you work with (or have worked with). Use the slides and this week's readings to consider why people sometimes appear to behave in ways that seem counterproductive. Provide some examples and insights.
2. What's the difference between intrinsic and extrinsic motivation? Why is this distinction important?
3. What recommendations would you make in your organization to use the information gained in the slides, websites, and readings?

Search for and post one additional resource related to this week's topic in the discussion area.

E-mail me with questions

FIGURE 14–7   Week 2 Course Materials Page.

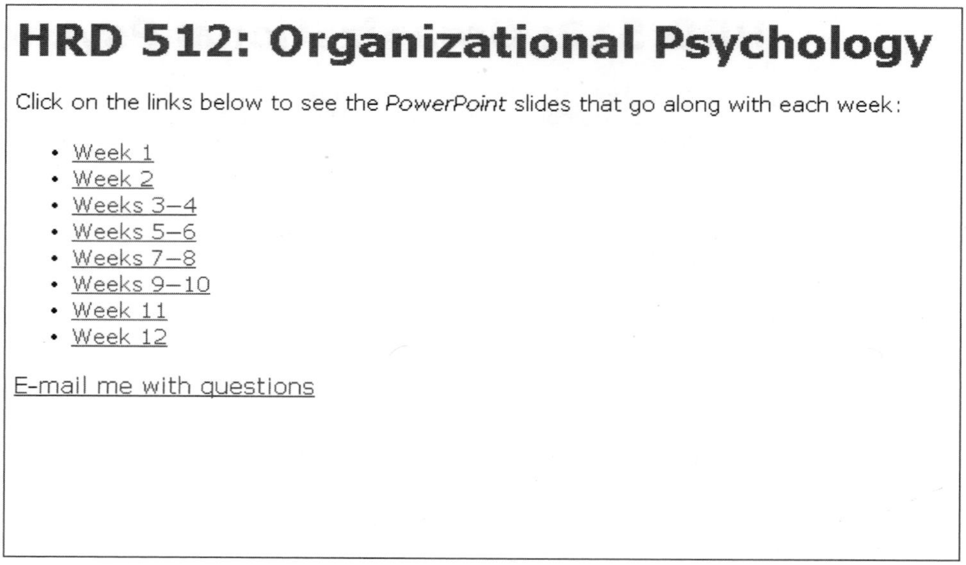

HRD 512: Organizational Psychology

Click on the links below to see the *PowerPoint* slides that go along with each week:

- Week 1
- Week 2
- Weeks 3–4
- Weeks 5–6
- Weeks 7–8
- Weeks 9–10
- Week 11
- Week 12

E-mail me with questions

FIGURE 14–8   "Slides" Page.

"Dr. Bates, if I'm a student in your course and it's Week 2, is everything I need to do for Week 2 here?" Ricardo asked. "No, my slides for the week are available on the "Slides" page, which is accessed from the homepage," she explained. She went back to the homepage and clicked on the link to the "Slides" page to show him how the slides for each week were accessed (see Figure 14–8).

"Any place else students need to go other than the Week 2 link and the "Slides" link?" asks Ricardo. "Hmm," Georgina thought for a moment. "They should go to the readings link, too—that's also available from the homepage." She returned to the homepage and clicked on the link to the "Readings" page. "And," she added, "they get to our course discussion forum from the "Readings" page, too" (see Figure 14–9).

With Georgina's help, Ricardo checked out the materials for the other weeks and saw that they were all accessed the same way: a general page that started off the week, readings listed on the "Readings" page (and a link to the discussion area), and *PowerPoint* slides accessed from the "Slides" page. "I'm thinking that students just aren't finding the information they need," explained Ricardo. "Does this hunch make sense, given what you're experiencing?" Georgina asked, "It's all there on the site, isn't it?" Ricardo clarified, "It's there, but, in my line of work, we assume that, if the learner can't find it, it really *isn't* there." Georgina considered his statement and then nodded her head in agreement.

Ricardo then asked Georgina to show him where the information that Sharonn and Kent needed was located. Georgina went back to the homepage and clicked on the "Introduction to the Course" page. "Here's where they find detailed assignment instructions and due dates," she said, pointing to the link to the "Assignment Instructions" page (see Figure 14–10).

HRD 512: Organizational Psychology

Below are the readings from your text for each week of the course.

Go to the discussion forum

Week	Reading	Focus questions
Week 1	Bradley and Moore, introduction and chapter 1	• What are the most critical organizational issues in organizations today? • How urgent are these issues? • Compare these issues to the issues of the mid 20th century. What has changed? Why?
Week 2	Bradley and Moore, chapters 2, 4 Tomlinson, pp. 15–45	• What does motivation mean? • How do the authors recommend that you think about intrinsic and extrinsic motivation? • What understanding does Tomlinson want you to have regarding the Cole case?
Weeks 3–4	Bradley and Moore, chapters 3, 5 Tomlinson, pp. 46–112	• In what ways are cooperation and conflict alike? • What were the main issues in the Ferana case?

FIGURE 14–9 "Readings" Page.

HRD 512: Introduction to the Course

The following information will help you gain the most from this course.

Welcome!

This three-credit course is a survey of the field of organizational psychology. We will cover theory and application in the following areas: work attitudes and motivation, group dynamics, organizational communication, organizational structure, and organizational culture. I want students to actively participate and highly encourage you to interact with me and your classmates in the discussion area.

Course Structure

Each week starts on Sunday and ends on Saturday. You'll notice that sometimes two weeks are together, on the same topic. Each week (or double week), we will have readings from the text, online activities, and *PowerPoint* slides. We will discuss these items in the discussion forum.

Assignments

Click here to get information about each of the assignments, including a rubric for completion and due dates.

All assignments are due on or before the due dates unless alternate arrangements have been made beforehand.

FIGURE 14–10 "Introduction to the Course" Page.

"I think we can take some of the frustration out of this for both you and your students, Dr. Bates," Ricardo suggested. "Let's make a flowchart of how your site currently works, and then we can determine what arrangement might work better, OK?"

Preliminary Analysis Questions

1. What is causing the frustrations Georgina and her students are facing?
2. Develop a flowchart of Georgina's site as it currently exists. Develop another flowchart with your recommendations of how to solve the current problems.
3. What other improvements would you recommend for the existing pages in order to decrease student frustration?
4. If you were Ricardo, how would you work with Georgina to fix these problems?
5. What options are available for salvaging this course at this point? Which course of action do you recommend?

Implications for ID Practice

1. Discuss the impact of interface and information design on the usability of online courses.
2. How can problems such as those that arose in this course be averted in the development of online course materials?
   a. How can instructional designers work with faculty members to address these issues?
   b. What overall guidelines might you provide to the faculty to avert these problems?
3. Develop a set of guidelines to help the faculty address the issues of interface and information design.

Beth Owens
Addressing Multiple Perspectives and Constraints in ID Practice
by Michael L. Wray and Brent G. Wilson

Charge from the Dean

It's a rainy day as Beth Owens arrives to meet with Dean Carlton Jacobs. Stepping into the dean's suite, she laughs as she shakes the remaining water from her raincoat. "I always enjoy the rain, especially in the West. We don't get enough of it!" Beth has lived the past 10 years in Colorado, first as a stay-at-home mom, more recently completing a master's degree in instructional design at a nearby state university. Eight months ago, she accepted a faculty consulting position at State College, a four-year, open-enrollment college in the downtown metro area. State's academic programs are always changing and faculty members appreciate the instructional design support that Beth provides. At any given time, Beth is consulting on 12 to 15 projects, with only an occasional need for in-depth analysis and evaluation. Technology leadership is a part of the job, but she sees her primary role as helping faculty members make the transition from traditional teaching methods to more constructivist kinds of teaching activities.

Dean Jacobs welcomes Beth into the office. "Thank you again for meeting with me. Your study of our programs is one of my highest priorities right now, and I know your findings will make a big difference to us." The School of Consumer Technology was recently divided, with the always growing Management Information and Office Systems moving out to create their own school, leaving the remaining half of the students in a wide array of service-oriented programs: cosmetology, fashion merchandising, hospitality management, and culinary arts. The dean is anxious to develop a growth plan for his remaining programs and to make improvements at all levels. His first goal is to review the culinary arts program, the smallest within the school.

"As you know," the dean continues, "Information and Office systems was something of a cash cow for us, to some extent subsidizing our smaller programs. Now every program has to stand on its own legs, both quality-wise and by the raw numbers. We're starting our analysis with culinary arts. The program is small but self-sustaining. We're having a few problems, which I'd like you to look at."

Beth is looking forward to jumping in on this project but just a little anxious about the prospects. In her eight months at State, she has heard occasional rumors about the program director. Chef Gerhard Reiner is known to be something of a taskmaster and disciplinarian. Beth turns to the dean, "I understand that the program director of culinary arts, Gerhard Reiner, teaches both the introductory class and the upper-level culinary classes. His teaching and leadership must be important to the program."

The dean responds, "Yes, he's a major figure. Reiner gets very good teaching ratings, although you'll always find the occasional student who can't stand him. He is well known within the school for being a challenging instructor. He maintains strict rules in his lab; any student can tell you that!"

"What kind of rules?" Beth is curious about this instructor. She doubts that this chef has even heard of such things as constructivist teaching methods.

The dean leans toward Beth. "I've had a couple of students in my office in tears, feeling overwhelmed by the demands of the program. They feel Chef Reiner is too strict. With enrollments more of an issue now, I don't want to lose any students unnecessarily. It's all about including all students and growing enrollments."

The dean leans back in his chair, continuing, "My problem is complicated. I want the program to produce quality graduates, but I also want to retain students and grow the program. I'd like you to figure out how we can be more inclusive, improve retention, and maintain a quality program at the same time!"

"Piece o' cake!" Beth jokingly replies. "Thanks for your time, Dean Jacobs. I think I would like to see the classroom and visit with Chef Reiner." The dean smiles, "I'll give you much more than that. How about a personal tour and lunch in our student dining room?"

Beth agrees, "I think that would be wonderful; please lead the way." Dean Jacobs shakes hands with Beth and escorts her from his office to the culinary labs.

Tour and Lunch

Beth is eager to see the students in action. Dean Jacobs shows her the student culinary lab, where students are preparing the meal before service. She is impressed to see everyone in crisp uniforms, each busy and involved in food production. It is easy to see who is in charge. Chef Reiner, in his tall white hat, has an air of authority, his name clearly embroidered on his starched chef whites, with his culinary title and a patch from the school he attended prominent on his breast pocket. The students rush from their work areas, receiving instructions from the chef. She notices him sampling the students' work, tasting and checking temperatures.

Following the tour, the dean and Beth take a seat in a small dining room adjacent to the culinary lab. The room is filled with administrators and staff members, who pay a small fee to attend the luncheon. The dean explains, "The restaurant serves meals three days per week, offering a sample of the students' accomplishments. It continues to be a popular event on the campus and attracts the general public." Beth smiles as she is served an inviting meal of roast chicken with a light cream sauce. "The plate is so elegant," Beth remarks. The garnish on the plate captures Beth's attention: roasted tomatoes pierced by rosemary stems. Beth sighs, "It smells wonderful." The dean nods in agreement as they both begin their meals.

During lunch, Beth begins to think about her approach toward advising the chef. She wants to introduce constructivist teaching principles but thinks it may be difficult to convince Chef Reiner of the benefits of constructivism. Reiner's approach to teaching seems antiquated and somewhat confrontational.

Beth declines the dessert, although it does look delicious, a five-layer chocolate cake with a rich frosting and mint leaves—decadent, indeed. Beth keeps imagining how nice the dessert would have been as she watches other guests enjoy it. But she settles for coffee and enjoys the pleasant service by the students.

After the meal, Beth concludes her tour with the dean and is anxious to get a chance to meet Chef Reiner and talk to him about the course. She thanks Dean Jacobs for his time and shakes his hand firmly.

Meeting the Chef

Beth knocks on Chef Reiner's door with a sense of anticipation. What is he like, really? As the door opens, Chef Reiner extends his hand, saying, "Good morning, I'm Gerhard Reiner. I've been looking forward to meeting you." Beth is relieved to see a tentative smile on his face. Stepping into the office, the two engage in conversation aimed at breaking the ice.

When Beth takes her seat, she is immediately impressed by the order of the room. The desk is clear, all items in their places. Beth's eyebrows rise as she notices that the books on the shelves are in order of height, smallest to the tallest, and the edges of the books are in line with the shelf. She smiles and thanks Chef Reiner for a great lunch. "It was a true pleasure," he returns. "I'm glad you had the chance to see the students working."

He gets to the point. "When the dean told me that you were coming, I immediately thought of how you could help us increase program enrollment. I'm looking forward to our work together. How can I help you get started?"

Beth reflects for a moment and responds, "Perhaps you could start by telling me about the successes the program has had. Tell me about your history with the college and what you consider the strengths of the program to be."

Chef Reiner begins a lengthy recital of his qualifications and the program's strengths. He has been at State College for five years, following a career as an executive chef for a major cruise line. He had also worked in fine dining in France and Germany. He speaks several languages and has had the opportunity to work with many fine chefs. He is also the president of the local chapter of the American Culinary Federation. His students have a chapter as well and participate in local competitions. The program's greatest accomplishment is the quality of the graduates. Before his arrival, the prior dean was concerned about the reputation of the program. They hired Chef Reiner to develop prestige for the school and produce quality graduates capable of obtaining high-level chef positions throughout the metropolitan area.

"Since I arrived," Chef Reiner explains, "I have instituted a student dining room, which produces meals three days a week, as you saw today. Before that, we had no outlet for the student work; most of the food production was in the classroom only. I have found that students like to see the public enjoy the meals they create."

Beth agrees, "I certainly enjoyed it!"

Chef Reiner continues, "We have had problems with student professional standards, and I have worked hard to reverse that problem."

"What do you mean, 'professional standards'?" asks Beth.

"We are in a metropolitan area," Chef Reiner explains. "Our students don't like to wear uniforms and maintain hygiene standards. We have had problems with long hair, nail polish, jewelry, and body piercings, which are not part of a professional and sanitary kitchen."

"How have you solved that problem?" Beth asks. Chef Reiner shows her his culinary laboratory evaluation sheet (see Figure 15–1). "Following each class, the students are evaluated on their appearance, quality of work, attendance, and so forth."

Beth studies the performance criteria and behavioral categories. Something in this grading sheet conflicts with her constructivist principles. Beth ponders how effective a point system like this would be. She sees the value of meaningful experiences, such as the student lunch, but wonders how such strict behavioral monitoring can be effective.

Beth looks up from the sheet. "Hmm. Neatness, organization, teamwork, ability to follow instructions. Does this work? How do the students respond to this evaluation?"

"It is quite effective," the chef explains. "Before our daily evaluations, I would get frustrated with student uniforms and professionalism in class. They would not behave professionally and respect uniform standards. I would give them low grades and they would get angry and not understand why they got bad grades. It is almost as if they expected to get an *A* for just being here."

Beth's mind is racing with ideas and conflicts as she asks, "How does the checklist evaluation change that?"

Chef Reiner is resolute in his response. "I get better performance from the students because the evaluations tell them what I expect. If they don't behave professionally, they can see how many points they will lose for not meeting standards. It is also less stressful on me."

"How do you mean?" Beth wants to understand what's going on in the chef's mind.

"At first, I would do the same as I was taught in culinary school. If a student didn't show up in uniform or behaved unprofessionally, I'd send him or her home, with a zero for the day."

Beth chuckles, "How did that go over?"

Smiling, Chef Reiner responds, "Not well at all! Students got frustrated, and I quickly realized I'd lose most of my students, so the daily evaluation gives them more immediate

Timeliness

On time
Stays entire time
No idle time

Uniform

Hat
Clean whites
Black slacks
Nonskid shoes
Closed-toe shoes
Ironed

Appearance

Hair clean, pulled back
Fingernails trimmed 1/4"
Hands and nails clean
Jewelry: two rings, watch, stud
earrings only

Equipment

Chef's knife sharp
Paring knife sharp
Apron
Kitchen towel

Production

Listens well
Tastes all food
Takes direction well
Displays knowledge
Observes others, stays involved
Respectful of speed, timeliness
Quality of food production
Respectful of waste and food cost

Sanitation

Aggressively cleans
Cleans/sanitizes well

Teamwork

Volunteers to work
Is supportive of leader
Offers suggestions
Provides constructive criticism

FIGURE 15–1   Chef Reiner's Behavioral Checklist for Student Performance.

feedback on my expectations. They can choose to change their behavior on their own, knowing the penalty. I'd say the daily forms are less forceful than how things were before."

Beth is skeptical. "Less forceful?"

Chef Reiner explains: "Most students actually like getting a grade each day—and they don't blame me as much for their grades. At least they know where they stand. The bottom line is, my students now wear their uniforms and act like a team. I do have some who still don't respond, but overall it's much better."

Beth is trying to process this approach. "Do you think the evaluation is causing some students to drop out?"

Chef Reiner sighs, "No, they make this decision themselves. I view my role as preparing them for success in the industry. Kitchens require a distinct chain of authority and rules. The students need to learn how to survive in that environment while in school. If not, they won't succeed in business. I'd rather they fail here than later on the job."

Raising her eyebrows, Beth responds, "Are you saying, if they can't stand the heat, get out of the kitchen?"

"Exactly!" Chef Reiner continues, "I realized that these students had never learned to take school or work seriously and professionally, so I created a performance system that takes me out of the picture, almost entirely. Instead of blaming me when they don't get the grade they want, they look at the point totals and see where they can change."

"Sounds as if it worked," Beth admits.

Chef Reiner continues with enthusiasm, "You wouldn't believe the difference. Before, I had students refusing to complete a cooking assignment, afraid it would wreck their nails. Nail polish, clothes, hairdo, whatever the excuse, I had students who were not doing the work. Now, everyone shows up on time, in uniform, ready to work. And word has spread around campus. The students take a great deal of pride in their accomplishments. Employers see the difference, too. We have a 96% placement rate, with starting pay up 60% in five years."

Beth stands to leave. "You've given me a lot to think about. Let me get back to you with some notes and observations; then we'll figure out where to go from here."

"That sounds fine," answers Chef Reiner as he stands to see Beth out. "If I can be of further help, please feel free to ask." Shaking hands, Beth leaves the office with a lot to think about. "Maybe I should have had that dessert!" she muses, returning to her car, umbrella in hand. The rain is gone and the sun is shining again.

On the drive home, Beth continues to turn over these ideas in her mind. She is unsettled about the strict behaviorist approach used by the program, but it seems to be working. She had wanted to suggest more constructivist ideas but didn't quite see where they would fit. In fact, the situation is something of a challenge to Beth's beliefs about good teaching.

Preliminary Analysis Questions

1. Identify the problem in this case, as perceived by Dean Jacobs, Beth, and Chef Reiner.
2. What is causing the conflict within Beth? How do her preexisting ideas about constructivism and behaviorism relate to her observations of the culinary arts program?
3. What suggestions do you have for Beth for how to deal with her perceived conflict between constructivist and behavioral approaches to instruction?
4. Beth has only begun her review of the culinary arts program. What further data should be gathered to address the dean's concerns and provide suggestions for improving the program?

Implications for ID Practice

1. Constructivism and behaviorism are often presented as competing philosophies, yet many designers seek to include elements of both approaches in their practice. How can that be done while maintaining some underlying integrity or cohesion in philosophy?
2. Professionals such as Beth develop their expertise by paying close attention to both theory and practice. What kinds of conflicts have you experienced between textbook approaches and everyday concerns of practice? How can instructional design professionals learn to respect both sources of knowledge and incorporate them successfully into their outlooks and practice?

Frank Tawl and Semra Senbetto*
Designing Curriculum for Southeast Asian Trainers
by Peggy A. Ertmer and Walter Dick

About 10 years ago, the government of a Southeast Asian country (referred to here as SEA), in cooperation with a major U.S. electronics corporation, began to plan the development of a training design center in SEA, in which participants would be trained to design instruction using a systems approach. The hope was that SEA would obtain the long-term capability to determine the need for, and then to develop, appropriate training programs for its workforce. At the time this decision was made, there were no instructional design (ID) training programs being offered in SEA, although there were various training institutes in operation (e.g., the Teacher Training Institute, the National Training Center, and the Vocational Education Center) and numerous government employees who provided training for local businesses. Although these employees served as trainers, they themselves had received little, if any, formal instruction in design theory or practice, and, furthermore, they had never participated in a curriculum that used a systems approach to the design and development of training. Although SEA trainers often delivered instruction on specified content, they had no formal experience with, or knowledge of, adult learning principles or the use of interactive teaching strategies. The instruction they created typically depended on their own content expertise or revolved around instruction that had been imported from the United States and then adapted.

---

*Based in part on a 1991 article by Walter Dick, which appeared in *Performance Improvement Quarterly, 4*(1), "The Singapore project: A case study in instructional design," pp. 14–22. Used with permission of the author and publisher. Note that information from the original case was altered in order to increase its educational value for our readers. Readers should not consider this case to be a true representation of the Singapore government.

A pair of U.S. designers was hired to plan and develop a curriculum for preparing SEA instructional designers. One of these designers, Frank Tawl, was a university professor and a noted expert on the use of the systems approach for designing instruction. Frank had developed a number of courses at his U.S. university that related to ID topics and issues, and he felt fairly confident that these could be modified to fit the SEA learners' needs. Frank's teammate, Semra Senbetto, was a private consultant who had worked with Frank on a number of previous projects and was noted for her ability to recognize and address culturally relevant issues in situations involving learners from diverse backgrounds.

As part of their front-end analysis, Frank and Semra conducted interviews to determine the current perceptions of professors at the national university, as well as training staffs at the Teacher Training Institute, National Training Center, and the Vocational Education Center, regarding the proposed ID training curriculum. Among other things, they were interested in determining the following: What kinds of training experiences were currently in place at the existing training centers? What procedures did SEA trainers follow when designing and presenting new instruction to their colleagues?

In these initial interviews, it became clear that the professors at the national university were supportive of whatever the U.S. Americans thought best—teaching whatever content Frank and Semra thought was appropriate, as well as using whatever strategies the Americans typically used. During follow-up interviews, they posed virtually no opposition to Frank's and Semra's ideas; after a suggestion was made, the professors would simply nod in agreement. Although Frank and Semra made a concerted effort to uncover any culturally sensitive issues that should be taken into consideration in the design of the curriculum, they identified almost none. If the SEA professors had any culturally related concerns, they didn't acknowledge them.

Additional interviews were held with potential students for the ID curriculum—namely, the current trainers. Frank and Semra asked questions to determine the following: What did the SEA trainers already know about the design process? What beliefs did they hold that reflected possible acceptance of the systems approach and/or findings from current research regarding the teaching and learning process? What beliefs seemed contradictory to these current theories about teaching and learning? How motivated were they to participate in this new training program? Although, on the surface, these potential students seemed to accept Frank's and Semra's ideas about interactive delivery strategies and alternative assessment measures, they were obviously unclear as to what was expected of them. They wondered how similar this training would be to the imported training they had become accustomed to modifying. Was this instruction going to be more or less effective with their students?

The SEA trainers indicated that they preferred lecture-based instruction and memory-based assessment measures. Interestingly, it was discovered during the interview process that SEA trainers had been modifying "imported" instruction by *eliminating* the built-in interactive activities and changing the assessment techniques to be more memory-based, as opposed to performance-based. The SEA trainers indicated that, although they "mostly" liked these training programs, they were concerned that their students would be uncomfortable performing in front of their peers and mentioned that losing face was something to be avoided at all costs. There was an additional concern that students over 40 years of age may not be sufficiently motivated to perform under the nontraditional conditions advocated by the imported programs. These students would be retiring when they turned 55 and mentioned that the time spent learning new skills, at their "mature" age, was "a real waste."

The majority of the trainers interviewed expressed little motivation to attend this new training when it became available. Those who were interviewed mentioned the following concerns:

- Additional time commitments involved in completing a degree program (all worked full-time)
- A need to learn a new way of designing and delivering training
- The lack of job advancement, salary compensation, or other rewards or recognition being tied to the completion of the program
- A lack of confidence in convincing clients to let them use these new skills

If these concerns were adequately addressed, the trainers indicated, perhaps, they would participate.

Frank and Semra decided to observe a few training programs currently being offered by the National Training Center. Additional time was spent with the instructors of these courses to determine how their training courses had been developed. In essence, the observations supported what had been suggested in the interviews. SEA trainers were accustomed to presenting and attending instructor-led training. They did not like being put on the spot (performing or responding in front of their peers); they liked assessment measures that provided a quick indication of how much they had learned. Also noted was the fact that they used very few media during instruction and did not engage in either needs analysis or formative evaluation procedures when developing instruction. It was difficult, if not impossible, to determine if any of the training being offered was making a difference on the job.

In contrast to the opinions and preferences mentioned by the SEA trainers, the SEA government strongly supported a move to more "modern" training—it was more than eager to imitate the U.S. Americans' approach to the systematic design of instruction. Although Frank and Semra agreed that appropriate teaching methods, such as simulations, role plays, and case studies, should be used when such methods supported the instructional objectives of the ID curriculum, they were concerned about motivating the learners to engage in these activities.

Frank and Semra realized that the typical ID competencies needed to be included in a way that fit the needs of the SEA students. Some modifications to a typical ID curriculum would be required. Finally, the question of who should teach the new courses, U.S. or SEA trainers, needed to be addressed. There did not seem to be any easy answers to the many questions facing this experienced design team.

As Frank and Semra labored to design a blueprint for the ID curriculum, including the identification of the strategies and approaches that should be used, they were faced with a number of difficult decisions:

- How to help the students master factual information and develop intellectual skills and positive attitudes regarding the systems approach to ID
- How to motivate the students to use effective learning strategies, including interactive techniques, when appropriate

- How to design and evaluate alternative assessment measures (e.g., project-based assessments, simulations, role plays, etc.)
- How to teach the students to use mediated instruction effectively
- How to get buy-in for the use of needs assessment and formative evaluation methods
- How to build the students' confidence to respond and perform in front of peers when appropriate
- How to motivate the older employees
- How to build confidence to work effectively with clients

Preliminary Analysis Questions

1. Make recommendations for the design decisions facing Frank and Semra.
2. Discuss the trainers' rationale for modifying existing programs. How can their concerns be addressed? Can you suggest modifications that are culturally sensitive?
3. Discuss the previous training experiences of the students in the new design program. What will their expectations be for the new curriculum? What kind of adjustments will they have to make? How can you facilitate this?
4. Provide a recommendation and rationale for selecting instructor(s) for these courses. How much should the instructor(s) be involved in decisions affecting classroom instructional strategies and assessment techniques?
5. Consider evaluation as a sensitive issue in this case. How should the effectiveness of the methods, materials, activities, and media be assessed? How should the students be evaluated?

Implications for ID Practice

1. Describe how an instructional designer might deal with issues related to the use of interactive instructional strategies in contexts where such strategies are not common and might not be welcomed.
2. Describe strategies for meeting the needs of older employees, as well as students who work full-time.
3. Outline strategies for promoting needs analysis and formative evaluation techniques.

Elizabeth Ward and Catherine Peterson

Repurposing a Course for Online Delivery

by Christine L. Thornam and Lauren Clark

Background

Preparing to teach Culture in Health and Healthcare during the upcoming winter intersession was going to be a new and exciting challenge for Dr. Elizabeth Ward. The Office of Extended Studies (OES) at the university asked her to offer the course to students living in remote parts of the state using the interactive video conferencing system. Elizabeth didn't have much experience with telecommunications but had a passion for teaching and was an expert and a leader in her field of specialization within nursing. The technical aspects of connecting with students at the remote classroom locations was something new to Elizabeth, but she was consciously making an effort to improve her technology-related skills and was up for the challenge. The OES provided support to faculty members who were teaching for the first time with the video conferencing system, and Elizabeth planned to avail herself of that assistance. Elizabeth contacted the OES to set up a meeting with its faculty support and instructional design personnel to discuss the necessary adjustments to her course delivery by video conference.

The meeting went well. Elizabeth realized that reaching students in the remote classroom was more than switching cameras and talking to students on a television monitor. She would need to extend her current ability to facilitate a psychological connection among students and between the students and herself. Following the meeting, minor logistical modifications were made to the course syllabus and assignments to accommodate the students located in the remote classrooms. Also, in an effort to reduce the psychological distance, lectures and teacher-led activities were modified to include more student discussion and small-group activities. The result was a clearer description of learner outcomes and the possibility of a higher level of student interactivity. Elizabeth enjoyed scrutinizing her teaching practice and course design in preparation for delivering her course by video conference because she could see how it would benefit her students. Her early reluctance to teach via video conferencing out of fear that it might reflect poorly on her teaching skills or that she might risk losing her status as an expert in her content area was soon replaced by enthusiasm for the process.

When the registration period for the winter intersession ended, the enrollment in the course was adequate to offer the course locally but was insufficient to support the delivery of the course to students in rural areas of the state. Elizabeth felt disappointment at the missed opportunity to test the changes to the course and to test her confidence in teaching with technology. However, given the option to teach the face-to-face course in the technology classroom, specially designed for video conferencing, Elizabeth decided to turn disappointment into opportunity. She used the technology classroom to teach the course locally as a way to acquaint herself with the equipment and to test changes to the course with students in the face-to-face classroom. The course went well, and Elizabeth and the students both enjoyed the experience. Elizabeth's appetite for teaching with technology was whetted; there was no turning back.

New Possibilities

After the initial disappointment of not teaching on the video conferencing system wore off, Elizabeth began to wonder about the feasibility of ever offering the course on the video conferencing system. Elizabeth wanted to maintain a low enrollment in the course to optimize student–student and teacher–student interaction. However, this desire for low enrollment, combined with the fact that the course was not required, made the possibility of future video conferencing look rather bleak. Elizabeth started thinking about other delivery methods as a way to offer the course to students in distant locations.

The second repurposing of the course began with an opportunity to apply for a small grant. Elizabeth called Catherine Peterson, the instructional designer in the OES and said, "You know, the Office of Education has these grants called *Innovations in Education.* The grants help the faculty develop new ideas, especially related to teaching with technology. Since we have a start on adapting this course for video conferencing, why don't we take the next step and redesign it for the web? The two of us could apply for one of those grants and use the money to build on the ideas we developed for video conferencing last semester."

Catherine was very excited about Elizabeth's phone call. Catherine's experiences related primarily to multimedia development and telecommunications, including video production and video conferencing. She designed online courses with other professors but typically met resistance when proposing anything but a text-based approach. The excitement she perceived in Elizabeth's voice struck a positive chord with Catherine. Still, she wondered if her experience with Elizabeth would be any different from her experiences with other professors. Was teaching with technology a brief romance for Elizabeth, or was it a reality she was meeting head-on? Was Elizabeth looking for techno-gimmicks, or was she trying to strengthen her instruction through technology? Did Elizabeth want to use technology simply to deliver the course, or did she want to use it to provide advantages that learners would not have in face-to-face instruction?

Elizabeth had a few questions of her own. How could the course be designed to enhance students' personal growth with respect to their cultural identities? Would students be equipped with the necessary hardware and software, as well as the technical skills necessary to access web-based instruction? Or would redesigning this course for delivery on the Web be an exercise in futility, just as the video conferencing experience had been? Still, after talking about the possibilities, both Catherine and Elizabeth agreed that, although there would be bumps in the road ahead, they were both ready for this adventure.

While they were putting the proposal together, the university administration decided that all courses delivered through OES would be repurposed for delivery on the web. In addition, all courses would be required to replace current course goals with performance-based competencies. This meant that Elizabeth and Catherine had to find a way to assess students' performances in cross-cultural patient encounters in a web-based learning environment. Determining whether learners could perform the expected competencies at the end of the course would be difficult, especially since most of the students in the course would never set foot in the same city as Elizabeth. However, Elizabeth and Catherine decided to apply for the grant funds. The application for the *Innovations in Education* grant was written, accepted, and funded for $5,000.

The Course

Elizabeth was eager to make a clear distinction between this course and other cultural competency courses she had reviewed. She did not want the course to be a laundry list of "do this, don't do that" when encountering a patient from another culture but, rather, a more respectful, fuller understanding of how culture influences one's health care practices—including the personal cultural influences health care providers bring with them to their practice. Elizabeth explained to Catherine: "I want students to think about how cross-cultural encounters with their patients are *crucial* to their nursing practice and to the delivery of safe and effective care. How can we get the students to really experience the beneficial effects of care delivered by culturally competent health care practitioners and, just as important, to grasp the potentially damaging effect of care that is *not* culturally competent? And, oh, yes, we need to design something that provides evidence of students' ability to perform competently in a cross-cultural patient–provider encounter."

Elizabeth wanted students to arrive at an understanding of the influence of cultural variation on clinical nursing practice and to use a culturally informed theoretical framework when considering patients' symptoms during a cross-cultural patient–provider encounter. The course addressed theory derived from medical anthropology as a basis for interpreting patients' construction of illness and eliciting patients' symptoms.

Based on Elizabeth's clinical observations and expertise, her experience teaching the course, and previous course evaluations, she wanted to sequence the course conceptually as expressed in the expected learner outcomes: (1) Recognize the broad cultural variation in clinical nursing practice and (2) Apply a culturally informed theoretical framework when communicating with patients. The early part of the course emphasized the discovery of one's own cultural heritage. The second part of the course emphasized theoretical perspectives and the application of these perspectives to clinical cross-cultural patient encounters.

Six broad topics were identified and later molded into modules:

1. Introduction to health care in multicultural environments (demographic trends, diversity vocabulary, common clinical challenges in multicultural health care environments)
2. Genogram (a picture of the relationships within a family) skills (self-disclosure, benefits of self-awareness, skills needed to assess patients' heritages)
3. Self-awareness (self-identity exercises, skills needed to assess patients' culture)
4. Theoretical frameworks in nursing practice (advantages of a theoretical approach to nursing care, including cultural assessment)
5. The viewing of symptoms through a theoretical lens (symptoms as merely symptoms, explanatory models, idioms of distress, semantic illness networks, folk illnesses, and the analysis of illness narratives)
6. Cross-cultural communication standards and skills (outcomes of provider–client [mis]communication; implications of differences between patients and providers in terms of language, semantics, and disease classification; and the elicitation of illness narratives cross-culturally)

Design Issues

Beginning early in the design process, Elizabeth was eager to make the online course visually appealing and media-rich. She had observed many online courses that were heavily text-based and had heard student criticism of those courses. She took pride in students' positive evaluations of her face-to-face teaching and wanted to avoid designing an online course that might lead to poor reflection on her teaching practice. Furthermore, her face-to-face teaching strategies consisted of interactive small-group collaborations, so why should her online course consist of lecture notes?

For example, activities such as drawing one's own genogram were deemed effective in the face-to-face classroom and, so, were redesigned as interactive graphics for the web-based course (see Figure 17–1). This allowed students to construct and culturally code a genogram of their own families.

Existing audio and video recordings that demonstrated cross-cultural patient-provider encounters were located and digitized for use in the course. These recordings approximated the high degree of interpersonal relatedness inherent in cross-cultural communication and assessment (see Figure 17–2). In addition, an excerpt of a lecture by a noted theorist in the field of medical anthropology added special interest to the module that introduced theory.

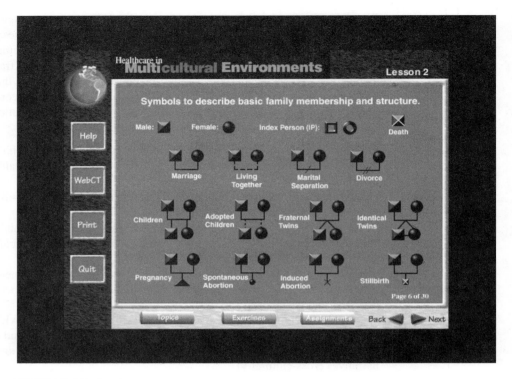

FIGURE 17–1   Genogram Development Tool.

Finally, Elizabeth took great care to design visually appealing screens throughout the course (see Figures 17–3 and 17–4).

However, because of the large, digitized audio and video data files, and the graphically rich nature of the interactive course material, download times would be extremely slow if added to the web-based course. Therefore, Elizabeth and Catherine decided to develop a CD-ROM. This was hyperlinked to the Web-based course, which also housed the text-based materials, the student discussion area, and course-management tools. Students could purchase the CD-ROM in the bookstore, just as they would buy a textbook.

Elizabeth was quite pleased with the progress toward the redesign of the course, which was renamed Healthcare in Multicultural Environments. However, she still had a few things to resolve. One of the shortcomings of the face-to-face course, as it was taught in prior semesters, was lack of exposure to, and participation in, real-world, cross-cultural issues faced by nurses. Elizabeth wanted to make up for that deficiency when redesigning the course and believed that information about current issues could be accessed on the web. However, harnessing all of the information on the web into something meaningful to clinical practice would be a challenge. As with planning for the video conference delivery of

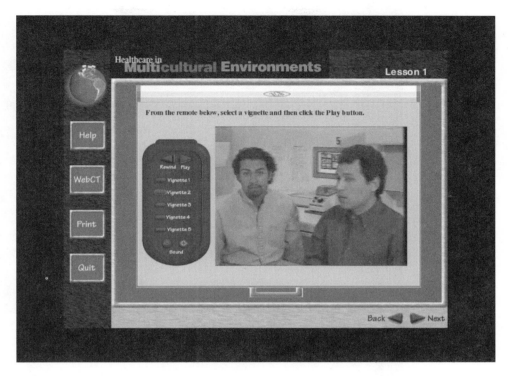

FIGURE 17–2   Video of Cross-Cultural Patient Encounter with Interpreter.

the course, Elizabeth was concerned about facilitating a psychological connection among the students and between the students and herself. On a broader scale, she wondered if she would be able to create a learning environment in which students could truly experience the affective elements of the course.

Elizabeth also knew that an understanding of the health care practices of other cultures begins with understanding one's own cultural heritage. For this reason, the redesigned course had an early emphasis on the student's journey of self-discovery. She recognized, however, that this could be dangerous if a student discovered painful family facts while isolated from a supportive group of peers or a supportive teacher. Also, Elizabeth worried about what to do if a student used the discussion forum as a soapbox to express a new found personal cultural identity.

Another concern centered on the school's shift to performance-based, competency assessments of learning. Elizabeth needed evidence of students' abilities to communicate cross-culturally to satisfy the school's new requirements. This meant finding a way to evaluate students' performances in cross-cultural patient encounters.

Pondering all this, Elizabeth developed a list of questions to ask Catherine when they next met. Although she was not sure how to solve all the potential problems, she certainly felt excited about the possibilities ahead.

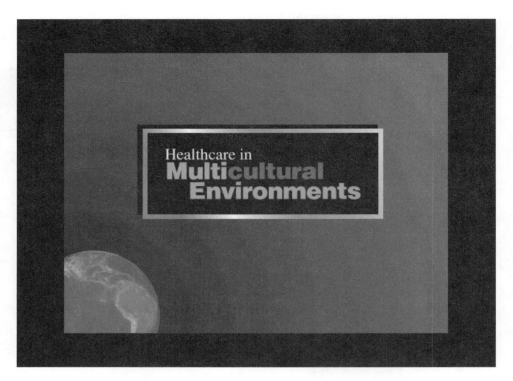

FIGURE 17–3   Course Title Screen.

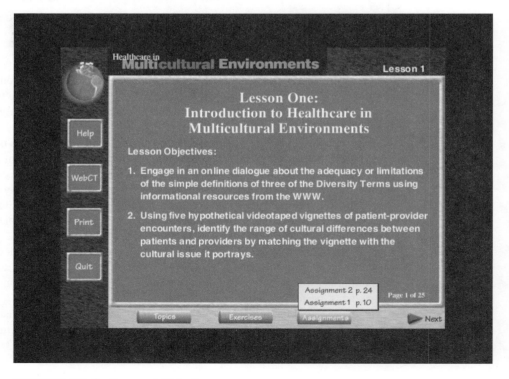

FIGURE 17–4   Lesson 1 Title Screen.

Preliminary Analysis Questions

1. Given Elizabeth's passion for teaching and her expert knowledge of the course content, how is this course redesign likely to affect Elizabeth's interaction with her students?
2. What support could you provide in this environment to protect students who might make painful discoveries about themselves? What strategies could be used to deal with inappropriate and excessive disclosure of personal information?
3. Given the content and the learners, develop a course outline that will enable learners to achieve the course goals.
4. Suggest appropriate methods for assessing learner performance.

Implications for ID Practice

1. What are the advantages and disadvantages to using the web to deliver a course with a high level of affective subject matter?
2. What are the benefits and challenges of offering a course in cross-cultural communication via the web?
3. Discuss when and how it might and might not be appropriate to use the web to implement authentic assessment strategies.

Case Studies

Section 3: Corporate Audience/Context

Abby Carlin
Documenting Processes in a Manufacturing Setting
by Monica W. Tracey

Just a few short months ago, while sitting in her final graduate instructional design course, Abby Carlin, a master's student in instructional technology, believed that she had found her life's profession. However, now that she had graduated and was standing in the middle of the floor of the Fritz David Manufacturing (FDM) Steel stamping plant, she began to have doubts. FDM, a company that manufactures large steel car parts, had hired Learning Together Through Training, Inc. (LT3), the instructional design firm where Abby's former instructor, Dr. Joyce Abbott, was vice president of design. The contract was for the design and delivery of training on the use of steel blanker machines. These were large, 60-year-old machines used to stamp out car parts from flattened steel. Abby, who had never been in a manufacturing plant before, received a call from Dr. Abbott, asking her to come work with her on this project. "Abby, you will be perfect for the job," she explained, "and this will be a great experience for you." These words gave a nervous Abby little comfort as she approached her first real instructional design job. Abby wanted to make sure she followed all of the necessary steps and completed the project successfully.

Abby's main contact, Andrew Thomas, the plant manager, met with Abby while Dr. Abbott was wrapping up another project. Watching him approach, Abby recalled what Dr. Abbott had told her. "You will have to approach Andrew carefully," she had warned. "He is somewhat skeptical of the training process, since he has never had a reason to use it before. Most of his senior employees have been working these machines for the past 30 years, and he has never had to train anyone. However, now that they are all retiring due to the incentives offered by FDM, he is faced with hiring new employees who have no idea how to operate this equipment. Andrew is just beginning to realize how much help he needs in this transition. That's why he's called us. He knows something must be done to keep production on track."

Andrew approached, holding out his hand. "Welcome to FDM," he said. "Why don't we go to the break room to talk?" They headed toward the break room located on the plant floor, and, after settling down with a cup of coffee, Andrew laid it on the line.

"This is the situation," he began. "Over the next 90 days, I have three shifts of employees retiring and being replaced by young, inexperienced operators. All of my guys have been with me for 30 years and have never needed any training to operate this equipment. The way I see it, the only way to learn how to use this equipment is while you're using it, and we've always had a new guy follow an old guy. But this time it's different, since there are so many new guys. We have to figure out a way to get them trained so I don't lose productivity."

"I'd like to begin by asking a few questions, if I could," Abby said. "Fire away," Andrew replied. "First of all, can you tell me a little bit more about the plant floor where the blanker machines are located?" Abby asked. Pulling out a notebook, Abby began to take notes.

"I'll take you on a tour in a minute, but, for the most part, it's a typical plant. All employees are required to wear safety equipment, goggles, hardhats, earplugs, and hard-toed shoes. The noise levels are pretty high down there, so there isn't much talking, and the lighting is bad. If the employees need to talk, they use this break room." He pointed to the wall, where a large bulletin board was filled with papers. "There's a board over there. They all know to check it for messages and announcements at the beginning and end of every shift."

"Can you tell me more about the current employees who operate the machines?" Abby then asked. Andrew replied, "For the most part, my guys are ready to retire. They are a good group of men, but, once they knew they were leaving, that was it. They aren't really interested in training the new guys. The problem is, they are the only ones who know how to operate the equipment. I came in as the foreman from another plant. Abby, I don't even know how to operate a blanker machine the entire way through. I have watched, but a lot goes on there that I just can't understand. We also don't have anything in writing on how to operate them."

"Can you tell me about the new employees who you have hired?" Abby asked. Andrew informed her, "For the most part, the new guys don't have a clue how to operate the blanker machines. Some have been in plants before; we even have a few transfers from other departments at FDM. They don't know what they have to do, even though all of them want to be here. We've had many applications, and we were able to pick the best of the best, which was great. The pay is good. We offer a lot of overtime and this is known as a great plant to be in."

"Is it possible for me to meet one of the retiring employees now?" Abby asked. Andrew, pleased with Abby's eagerness to learn more about the plant, replied, "Sure, let's go down to the floor now." The first stop was the safety area, where Abby received a pair of safety goggles, earplugs, and a hardhat. After putting on all of the equipment, she had difficulty hearing Andrew as he directed her to the stairway to the floor. Everything sounded muffled and looked darker due to the safety glasses.

The first stop on the tour for Abby and Andrew was the blanker machine operated by "Big Jon." She glanced at his name on his hardhat and began, "Hi, my name is Abby Carlin and I am in charge of training the new employees to operate these machines. I was wondering if I could ask you a few questions." Big Jon stared and shrugged. Andrew signaled to Abby that he couldn't hear her. "My first lesson learned," Abby said to herself. "It's instinct to talk to the worker to get information, but I can see that's not going to work here." Abby decided to just observe what Jon was doing. "I'm going to have to come back and really watch him," she thought to herself, "but he's moving so fast I'm going to have a hard time writing down what he's doing." Andrew signaled it was time to move on.

An hour later they finished their tour of the plant floor. As Abby took off her safety gear, she commented, "Well, Andrew, that was an eye opener. This is going to be a bigger job than I first realized. I'd like to come back tomorrow to observe Jon and try to document the process." "That's not a problem," Andrew told her. "Keep your safety glasses, earplugs, and hardhat and, when you come in tomorrow, stop by my office and I will give you the proper identification to get on the floor."

As she was walking to her car, Abby recalled that one of the things Andrew had mentioned was that the only way the learners could really learn how to operate the equipment was on the equipment. "Where do I begin?" she thought on her way back to LT3 headquarters.

The following day, Abby was back at the plant, watching Jon as he operated one of the blanker stamping machines. She tried to write down the steps he was taking but had difficulty seeing the buttons he was pushing. In fact, she had problems seeing at all with the poor lighting and the safety glasses. Abby also felt frustrated, since she couldn't talk to Jon as he worked, and he showed no interest in slowing down or demonstrating the steps for her. "I can see now how the trainees need to learn on this equipment, but I can't even write down the steps they need to follow, let alone create classroom training here on the plant floor," she thought. "I can't believe I have to train everyone while keeping up production," she said to herself. "Boy, do I need to talk with Dr. Abbott." Abby left the plant after stopping by Andrew's office, where he reiterated the tight deadline. "Don't forget, Abby, we need three shifts of employees trained in 90 days," he reminded her. "You can count on us," she assured him. As she made her way to the parking lot, she didn't feel as confident as she sounded.

On her drive to LT3, Abby had a comforting thought, "I think the blanker operators hold the key to making this training a success. I must figure out a way to document the steps they take in operating the equipment and how to talk to them where they can hear me. Then, I have to figure out a way to train the new employees on the equipment. I'm sure I can do this. I just need to figure it out."

A short time later, while in conversation with Dr. Abbott, Abby began to feel more confident. "The most important thing for you to do, Abby, is to think outside of the box. I brought you in on this project because you didn't seem to be stuck in a certain design or delivery mode. Let's take a minute and list what we know and all of the needs and constraints we have to work with. Once you write down what you know, that will help you define our needs and constraints. Then we can develop our plan. Let's begin with our list." Dr. Abbott wrote the words "Our Needs" on one sheet of flip chart paper and used a second one to write "Our Constraints." "Let's begin here," said Dr. Abbott, pointing at the first flip chart.

Preliminary Analysis Questions

1. What should be included on the two lists that Abby and Joyce are creating?
2. How can Abby work with the current employees to document the steps of operating the blanker stamping equipment?

3. What did Abby observe while on the plant floor that can help her in creating the training?
4. Given the constraints in the case, what instructional strategies can be used to deliver the training?

Implications for ID Practice

1. How can designers perform a task analysis in situations where it is difficult to capture and document task components?
2. What are some of the challenges and advantages to delivering training in a manufacturing environment?
3. How can instructional designers gather task information from subject matter experts who are unable or unwilling to provide all the required information?

Iris Daniels

Cross-Cultural Challenges in Designing Instruction

by Timothy W. Spannaus and Toni Stokes-Jones

Prototype Review Meeting

Finally, the project was coming together! Iris Daniels and her team had just agreed to create a prototype and present it to the seven-member consortium of software users. The prototype would show both the instructional and technical approaches of the computer-based training software program that they wanted to see developed. Iris was hopeful that the prototype would be positively received by all of the consortium members and would enable development to proceed. Iris had worked for Jim Huggins on many projects with their client, Hill Industries, and knew the importance of prototyping to communicate design, instructional approach, or feasibility. But getting to this prototype had taken longer than anyone had expected. This was Iris's first time working with an international team and, in addition to having to reach consensus regarding the prototype, she had to learn the corporate cultures of the organizations who made up the consortium.

Two Years Ago: Initial CBT Design

Hill Industries depended on a complex suite of manufacturing management software products used by thousands of engineers and product designers within Hill and its suppliers. The software was developed by French software developer, Lapin. For years, all of the training on the software had been in the classroom, led by a trainer. Several years ago, Hill Industries joined a consortium of large companies from several countries. About two years ago, the consortium members began to push Lapin to offer computer-based training (CBT) for the software. That request fit with Lapin's business strategy, so they began developing the CBT.

The initial version Lapin produced had disappointed some members of the seven-member consortium, especially the U.S. Americans. The CBT was attractively designed and very well written, especially considering that the developers were all working in a second language. However, it was not very interactive. For example, a lesson about designing a piston consisted of descriptions for the learner to read, followed by step-by-step exercises to be completed using the software. Because the lessons were not written in an interactive authoring system but in a word processor, there was no feedback. In fact, the learner could do anything or nothing in the exercise and the lesson did not respond at all. Learners had little control; they could only access a menu or click "Next" or "Back."

CBT Review Meeting

The Lapin development team had demonstrated the CBT at a consortium meeting. The consortium members were happy to have something with which to work. However, the U.S. Americans pushed for a more interactive designs, with simulations, case studies, and feedback to help learners improve their performance. Still, Lapin believed that there were technical constraints, beginning with the requirement that the CBT run on a wide variety of operating systems and hardware, sharply limiting what development tools would work. The consortium members agreed that the technical issues would work themselves out over time, as training moved to a web environment and the development tools improved. Far more difficult, it seemed, were the expectations of which training approach made sense for the users. The design that Lapin had produced was one with which it was comfortable. The U.S. Americans, influenced by their instructional design training, were expecting something more task-oriented and interactive.

Iris began the discussion by raising questions about practice, feedback, and transfer. The blank stares from the French and German participants were a surprise to the U.S. Americans. Jonathan Naik, a U.S. American engineer from another large Lapin software customer, described some of the CBT with which he was familiar. "In the past, we have demonstrated the procedure, then had the learner practice it, decreasing the amount of help and reinforcement as he or she continued to practice."

"Are you sure that's what learners want or expect now?" was the polite but incredulous response from Jacqueline Colbert, the lead training developer from Lapin. She had never used such a design and wasn't quite sure what to think of it. "I think they might want a theory section, and then a problem to work on, don't you? Maybe we could run a screen capture video to demonstrate the task. That would take care of it." For the rest of the afternoon, the consortium talked through various design approaches, without coming to any agreement. Not only could they not agree, but it seemed that, though everyone was speaking English, they were not communicating.

Iris and Jacqueline left the meeting together, talking about the design of Lapin's CBT. Back in Jacqueline's office, Iris showed her some CBT and web-based training her company had developed for other large clients. "We have always tried to avoid any long sections where the learner is just reading. We've used a couple of case studies, walking the learner through the first one. The learner is always doing something, maybe clicking or filling in a field to respond to a question or problem, but it's always related to the task or procedure. That way, from the beginning, the learner is practicing," Iris explained. Jacqueline went through a portion of Iris's demo, then responded, "To me this seems as if it might work, though I think some users would think it's too simple. I'd still like to have a theory section to explain what it is we want the learner to do, and why."

When the user consortium met again the next morning, there were two agenda items—one on design, the other on technical standards. They decided to start with design. Dieter Hoffman, the engineering representative from a German aircraft company, asked if he could speak. Dieter spoke only rarely at the consortium meetings but was always well prepared and worth listening to whenever he did speak. He plugged his laptop computer into the projector and began what appeared to be a prepared presentation. Very thorough and nuanced, he restated everyone's positions on the design, including both theoretical and practical viewpoints. He observed, as no one else had, that instructional design language and thinking pervaded U.S. American, but not French, training. Indeed, French universities generally do not have anything like instructional design in their programs. "So yesterday's discussion," Dieter observed, "did not move us forward, but only around each other."

As the meeting continued, Iris observed that some of the things she had said to Jacqueline in their private conversation yesterday were coming out in the meeting. Jacqueline shared with the group that, after some consideration of the U.S. American approach to having practice and feedback as part of the CBT, she felt it was appropriate. The consortium didn't come to any agreement on design, but at least they understood each other's positions a little better, thanks to Dieter.

The afternoon session dealt with technical standards, about which there was little disagreement. The only reasonable way to achieve the cross-platform compatibility necessary was to adopt Internet and web standards, avoid plug-ins, and use the two major web browsers. The decision not to use plug-ins took a while to sort through, but the objective was that the CBT should run the same on Windows NT® or 2000 PCs and several varieties of Unix®. Plug-ins might not exist for all those platforms, or they might not work identically. With a little better understanding on design and agreement on technology, the consortium members headed home from the meeting, agreeing to meet again in three months in the United States.

Back in the Office

Once back in the office, Iris debriefed with Jim Huggins about the plans for meeting with Hill Industries in a day or so. Jim thought the technical decisions made at the consortium meeting were good, but the design decision (or lack of it) baffled him. Then, when Iris talked about the way the meetings went, a thought struck him. "OK, let me see if I understand.

During discussions in the meeting, you and Jacqueline didn't seem to connect. She basically used the meeting to report on what she had decided. Discussion seemed to go nowhere." "Right," Iris replied. "Then, when we talked outside the meeting, we had a good exchange of ideas. However, the next morning, she reported some of our discussion as her ideas."

"Got it. So maybe what you want to do is make sure you have more one-on-one discussions with Jacqueline. You might also want to meet individually with the other French people, hash out ideas, then use the meetings as a forum where people can bring decisions to be ratified," noted Jim. "I think we might find that different cultures view the purposes of meetings differently. As I recall from my business trip to France last year, the French are more comfortable making decisions outside of public meetings. The U.S. American idea of coming to a meeting for the purpose of discussing and deciding is quite literally foreign to them," continued Jim. "Meanwhile, why don't we prototype a short learning module that demonstrates our design ideas and that incorporates elements of the French approach? Let's talk it over with Hill and see if we can build something that will communicate our ideas better than the discussion did."

A Meeting at Hill Industries

The next day, Jim and Iris met with Kimberly Mooney, their client at Hill Industries. Kimberly was the project leader of the group that trained the prospective users of the Lapin software. Kimberly thought the prototype would help communicate the design approach the U.S. Americans had in mind and would show that the technical approach the consortium agreed on would work. Jim agreed that they could show feasibility with the prototype, but it would be a challenge. After all, they needed to simulate a complex system, with just a browser and no plug-ins. Jim, Iris, and Kimberly agreed to create a prototype to demonstrate the design they wanted and to demonstrate that it could actually be done, given the technical constraints.

The design would need the following segments and would need to allow the user to modify an existing part with and without assistance:

- A theory section, which they called "logic," that explained the procedure and showed which functions of the software were used
- A demonstration, which used a screen capture video to show the procedure, with a voice-over narration; they decided to call this one "show me"
- A guided simulation, in which the learner completed all the steps in the procedure, with step-by-step prompts; they called this one "try it with a little help"
- An unguided simulation, in which the learner completed all the steps but without the prompts; they called this one "on your own"
- An assessment, in which the learner used the Lapin software to complete the procedure and then compare his or her result to the result in the lesson, using a checklist to highlight important measures of accuracy; they called this one "putting it all together"

"This is a good start," said Jim. "Now the hard part begins. Let's get to work on developing our prototype."

Preliminary Analysis Questions

1. How was the design process from the initial design of the CBT to the proposed elements of the prototype influenced by the different backgrounds of the consortium members?
2. Evaluate Jim and Iris's approach to handling cultural differences among consortium members.
3. Critique the elements of the prototype proposed by Iris, Jim, and Kimberly. What would you add or eliminate, if anything?
4. What outcomes might Iris expect from the demonstration of the prototype?

Implications for ID Practice

1. What steps can a designer take in preparation for working on a cross-cultural team?
2. Discuss the importance of bringing to the surface assumptions about teaching and learning among members of an instructional design team.
3. In what ways can the development of a prototype help or hinder further design and development work?

Sam Gonzales
Measuring Learning and Performance
by Brenda Sugrue

Atlantic Airlines was expanding and was about to hire 200 new flight attendants. The existing corps of flight attendants had been working with the airline for an average of five years and, based on current evaluations (customer satisfaction and supervisor ratings), was doing a very good job. The director of Human Performance Technology, Sam Gonzales, wanted to increase the consistency between the criteria used to evaluate performance at the end of training and the criteria for judging on-the-job performance.

He decided that asking trainees to answer questions about videotaped situations would increase the authenticity of end-of-training assessments. He planned to try out his idea with one group of 20 trainees for 2 of the 18 performance goals included in the basic training. He selected the goals of "performing preflight checks" and "dealing with difficult passengers" from the job map of level 1 flight attendants (see Figure 20–1). For each goal, he asked his instructional designer, Linda McMillan, to do the following:

1. Write a performance goal to represent each task in the job map
2. For each goal, make eight short video clips. Two should show a flight attendant performing the task correctly in frequently occurring situations. Two should show a flight attendant performing the task with errors in frequently occurring situations. Two should show a flight attendant performing the task correctly in unusual situations. Two should show a flight attendant performing the task with errors in unusual situations.

Thus, 16 video clips, each lasting about two minutes, were produced. Half of the clips were to be used as practice activities during the training, and half were to be used as end-of-training assessments. The end-of-training clips were embedded in a computer program that asked students related questions.

Sam thought that the ability to identify errors in the performance of the attendants in the video clips would predict the ability to perform well in situations similar to those portrayed in

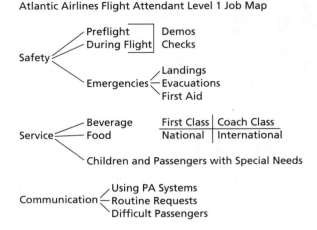

FIGURE 20–1   Simplified Job Map for Level 1 Flight Attendants.

the videos. He was convinced that this type of assessment would be more valid than the previous end-of-training assessments, which were pencil-and-paper tests. The pencil-and-paper tests had a variety of types of questions, including 1) multiple-choice questions asking trainees to select the correct sequence of steps for performing various tasks and 2) questions that depicted situations and asked students to write short answers describing what should be done in the situation.

Sam also thought that short-answer items were too time-consuming to score and that the new multimedia assessments should have only multiple-choice questions, administered by computers to permit automatic scoring and immediate generation of data. The items related to a video clip would typically ask students to (1) identify what job task was being performed in the video, from a list of choices; (2) decide if the attendant in the video made any errors in performing the task; and (3) if there were errors, identify what they were, from a list of choices; or (4) if there were no errors, identify the most critical aspect of the attendant's performance in the video, from a list of choices. Scores for any one video scenario could range from 0 to 8. An example of the questions that accompanied one "difficult passenger" video is provided in Figure 20–2.

Once selected, the trainees completed their training in groups of 20, each with a different instructor, with one group of 20 using the new assessments (instead of pencil-and-paper tests) on the two selected performance goals (preflight checks and dealing with difficult passengers). This group received the same assessments as every other group on all other performance goals. Some of the trainees in this group were concerned about how the new assessments would affect their overall end-of-training scores, but they were not allowed to switch to another group. When the end-of-training results came out, the overall results of this group were slightly lower than the other groups. Two students (students 1 and 17 in Table 20–1), who got particularly low scores, were upset and blamed their low scores on the new assessments. They wrote a letter to Sam, stating that the new assessments were unfair and that they should be allowed to complete the old set of questions for

1. Which of the following job tasks is illustrated in the video?
   a. Serving dinner on an international flight
   b. Responding to a common passenger request
   c. Dealing with a difficult passenger
   d. Dealing with a passenger with special needs

2. Did the attendant in the video make any errors?
   a. Yes
   b. No
   c. I'm not sure.
      If yes, question 3 would be displayed.
      If no, question 4 would be displayed.
      If not sure, question 5 would be displayed.

3. Which of the following errors did the attendant make?
   a. She did not ask the passenger to go to the back of the cabin so that she could discuss the problem.
   b. She did not smile.
   c. She did not promise the passenger that she would mention the problem to the supervisor.
   d. She did not repeat the passenger's concern in her own words.
   e. a and b
   f. b and d

4. Which of the following actions was the most critical aspect of the attendant's behavior in this situation?
   a. She isolated the passenger from other passengers.
   b. She talked to her supervisor.
   c. She repeated the passenger's concern back to him.
   d. She did not appear annoyed.
   e. a and c
   f. b and c

5. Which of the following makes you unsure?
   a. The situation appeared to be resolved.
   b. You did not spend enough times studying this aspect of the course.
   c. The attendant in the video did not follow the procedure you learned exactly and that confused you.
   d. The situation did not appear to be resolved.

FIGURE 20–2   Sample Multiple-Choice Questions to Accompany a Video Clip.

TABLE 20–1 *Scores of End-of-Training Video Assessments for Two Performance Goals*

| Trainee | Performance Goal 1:
Preflight Checks | | | | Performance Goal 2:
Dealing with Difficult Passengers | | | |
| | Frequent
Situations | | Unusual
Situations | | Frequent
Situations | | Unusual
Situations | |
	Clip 1	Clip 2	Clip 3	Clip 4	Clip 5	Clip 6	Clip 7	Clip 8
1	4	4	6	2	2	4	6	4
2	8	8	6	4	6	8	6	6
3	8	8	2	0	8	6	4	2
4	8	4	4	4	8	8	4	4
5	2	4	4	2	4	6	6	6
6	8	8	2	0	8	6	4	2
7	6	6	6	2	8	6	6	4
8	8	8	8	4	8	8	6	6
9	6	8	4	0	8	4	4	2
10	6	6	6	4	8	6	6	0
11	6	6	8	2	6	6	6	4
12	8	8	2	0	8	6	4	2
13	4	4	6	2	4	6	6	6
14	8	8	6	6	6	8	6	6
15	8	8	4	0	8	8	6	2
16	6	6	8	4	8	8	4	4
17	2	4	4	2	2	6	3	2
18	8	2	6	0	8	6	4	2
19	8	6	6	6	8	6	8	8
20	8	8	8	4	6	8	8	2
Mean	6.5	6.2	5.3	2.4	6.6	6.5	5.35	3.7

the two performance goals that had brought down their overall scores. The instructor who taught the special group also complained that the new assessments were more difficult than the pencil-and-paper tests for those performance goals and that the new assessments made it look as if he were not a good instructor. He suggested to Sam that the multimedia assessments be abandoned.

To make an informed decision, Sam asked for a complete breakdown of the data for the 20 students on the multimedia assessments. He also asked for the on-the-job evaluation data for this group of students on tasks related to the performance goals measured by the new assessments. During the first two months after training, the performances of trainees were evaluated on the job. Scores on each on-the-job task evaluation could range from 0 to 6. The checklist used to evaluate performance in dealing with difficult passengers is shown in Figure 20–3.

Table 20–1 shows the scores for all 20 students on end-of-training assessments for the two performance goals. Figure 20–4 shows average performance across the eight end-

1. Did the attendant listen carefully to the passenger's complaint?	________
2. Did the attendant paraphrase the passenger's complaint back to him/her?	________
3. Did the attendant offer the passenger the simplest solution to the problem first?	________
4. Was the attendant polite during the entire interaction?	________
5. Did the attendant maintain a normal tone of voice during the entire interaction?	________
6. Was the passenger reassured and calm by the end of the interaction?	________
Total points (out of 6)	________

FIGURE 20–3 Checklist for Evaluating Performance When Dealing with a Difficult Passenger.

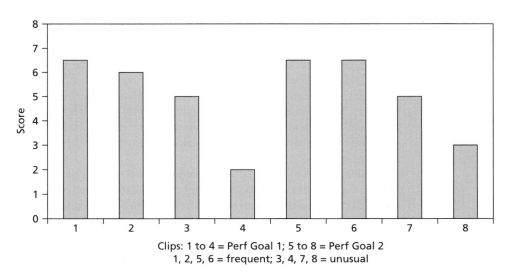

Score
0
1
2
3
4
5
6
7
8
1
2
3
4
5
6
7
8
Clips: 1 to 4 = Perf Goal 1; 5 to 8 = Perf Goal 2
1, 2, 5, 6 = frequent; 3, 4, 7, 8 = unusual

FIGURE 20–4 Average Performance on End-of-Training Video Assessments Across Video Clips.

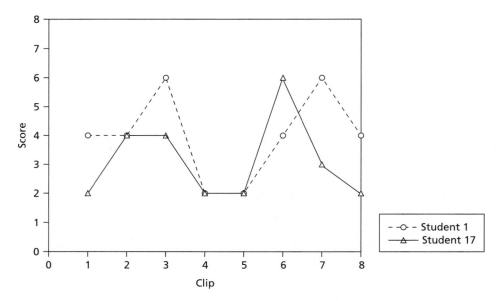

FIGURE 20–5   Profile of Scores of Low-Scoring Students 1 and 17 on End-of-Training Assessments

of-training video assessments. The traditional measure of reliability (Cronbach's alpha) was .49 if one considered the four end-of-training scores as a single measure of mastery of performance goal 1. If one considered the four video clips as measuring two different aspects of performance—ability to handle routine tasks and ability to deal with unusual situations related to that goal—the reliability coefficients increased to .72 and .75 for frequent and unusual situations, respectively. Cronbach's alpha for performance goal 2 (considering the four clips as measuring the same goal) was .32; when frequent and unusual situations are treated as separate subgoals, coefficients increased to .40 and .61, indicating that the two frequently occurring clips for performance goal 2 were not yielding comparable estimates for some students.

Figure 20–5 shows the performance of the two students (students 1 and 17) who complained that the assessments were unfair. Table 20–2 shows total end-of-training scores for the two performance goals and average performance in a situation on the job that corresponded to each goal. The correlation between end-of-training and on-the-job performance scores was .95. Typically, correlation between end-of-training pencil-and-paper assessments and on-the-job evaluations was .80.

TABLE 20–2 *Total Scores on End-of-Training and On-the-Job Performance for Two Performance Goals*

Trainee	Performance Goal 1: Preflight Safety Checks		Performance Goal 2: Dealing with Difficult Passengers	
	End of Training (max = 32)	On the Job (max = 6)	End of Training (max = 32)	On the Job (max = 6)
1	16	3	16	3
2	26	6	26	6
3	18	4	20	4
4	20	4	24	5
5	12	2	22	5
6	18	4	20	4
7	20	4	24	5
8	28	6	28	6
9	18	4	18	4
10	22	5	20	4
11	22	5	22	5
12	18	4	20	4
13	16	3	22	5
14	28	6	26	6
15	20	4	24	5
16	24	5	24	5
17	12	2	13	2
18	16	3	20	4
19	26	6	30	6
20	28	6	24	6
Mean	20.4	4.3	22.15	4.7
Correlation between end-of-training and on-the-job performance = .95				

Preliminary Analysis Questions

1. Determine the reliability and validity of the assessment instruments in this case.
2. What modifications (if any) to the new assessments would you suggest if Sam is to continue to use them as an end-of-training tool?

3. What weaknesses in the training program do the data suggest?
4. What weaknesses in individual students and groups of students do the data suggest?
5. How should Sam respond to the trainees and instructor who complained that the assessments were not fair?

Implications for ID Practice

1. Discuss the advantages and disadvantages of different types of instruments (pencil-and-paper, multiple-choice, multimedia multiple-choice, open-ended responses) in assessing performance.
2. Distinguish between using assessment information for the purpose of learner certification versus using assessment information for program evaluation.
3. Compare the usefulness of data collected at the end of training to data collected on the job to determine training effectiveness.

Craig Gregersen

Balancing a Range of Stakeholder Interests When Designing Instruction

by Stephen Dundis

Craig Gregersen kept trying to think of how he could see his way through what no longer seemed to be such a golden opportunity for his budding consulting practice. Five weeks previously, he had been hired by a large international corporation to design an important training program that would be delivered to its employees around the world. The assignment had seemed to be a perfect fit when the Electron Corporation asked him to be the lead designer for a course on product liability. He did, after all, have a law degree and had just received his Ph.D. in instructional design a year earlier. However, now it seemed that his name was going to be associated with a course with which no one would be satisfied and that would almost certainly not accomplish its intended goals.

Background

When Craig had originally spoken with the training project manager and the chair of the Safety Steering Committee at Electron, he had been invigorated by the prospect of using both of his degrees to educate people about an important issue and to increase the company's bottom line. The Electron Corporation was a leader in the design and manufacture of two-way radio systems, cellular telephones, pagers, and other communication devices, including accompanying software. Stan Neuhaus, one of the senior design engineers for the company and chair of the Safety Steering Committee, described how Electron took the quality and safety of its products seriously. Although product liability suits were not a large problem for the company, Electron was becoming aware of a number of situations that might produce liability—transmission systems interfering with the operation of other electronic equipment in hospitals, defective software causing shutdowns in police communication systems, battery disposal problems, and so on.

And, as Electron became more and more involved in the production of consumer-oriented products, it was becoming increasingly concerned about appropriate designs and warnings for consumers.

Both Stan and the training project manager, Louise Masoff, told Craig that the course was intended to provide a proactive approach to product safety—one that would prevent lawsuits from happening. Other than that, however, the content of the course was up to Craig—whatever he thought was needed to make employees more conscious of product liability in their daily behavior. Both Stan and Louise stressed that they wanted a course that would address concerns at every level of the company. In this regard, they presented Craig with a list of initial telephone contacts with line engineers and management at several installations across the country. He was also given free rein to make any other contacts that might prove useful.

Then, of course, the other shoe dropped. Craig was asked to start immediately because there was a lot of pressure to get a course up and running very quickly. Louise believed that two weeks of telephone interviews would be enough time to determine what content needed to be included in the course, then another three weeks to develop the course. The course itself could be only a day long, maximum. According to Louise, even though this was considered an important topic, there were just too many other demands on employees' time. And, of course, the legal department ("legal") would need to be consulted on everything. Louise was sure that legal would have plenty of ideas for him but that sometimes "they could be pretty unapproachable." Stan added that legal felt rather strongly that it should be carrying out the training in this area but that a prior course it had put together had not gone over especially well.

However, Craig was not discouraged. He was already used to quick turnarounds. Legal might be a problem, but, looking on the bright side, it could be very helpful providing content for the course, including pending cases that might be used as examples. After all, Craig was a lawyer, too. That should eliminate a lot of communication problems. After some initial research, he was ready to start contacting the names he had been given.

Gathering the Data

It didn't take Craig long to realize that there were more aspects to product liability at Electron than had been discussed in the original meeting. The basic law dealing with product liability was difficult for a layperson to understand, but, with Electron having plants in 16 countries and doing business in almost every other country, just understanding the international differences in liability would be a challenge. In addition, engineering issues were not limited to design considerations. There were also process engineers, who dealt with the manufacturing process and attendant safety concerns, and field engineers, who dealt with the construction and maintenance of large systems, such as transmission antennas and radio relay stations. There was also a multitude of concerns ranging from appropriate procedures for product recalls and risk evaluations to attempts at keeping up with the constant regulatory changes issued by various standards organizations.

The first person Craig interviewed was Richard Mull, the legal contact he had been given. However, if Craig had expected a willing ear for what he saw as the challenges in designing the course, he was mistaken. Although cordial, Richard didn't waste time making it clear that he believed legal should be handling the education on these issues, rather than an outside consultant. When Craig started talking about the various content issues, Richard interjected that, rather than worrying about all the details, engineers needed to develop a general sensitivity to the "legal realities" and that just designing a product to the best of their ability might not be enough. In response to Craig's request for relevant examples, Richard stated that he couldn't discuss ongoing cases and that using any of these as an example in a class would be out of the question. Statements made about these cases could possibly be used against the company. He ended the conversation by suggesting to Craig that he review the four-hour course that Richard and his colleagues had developed several years back—a course that he still considered would be perfectly acceptable with just a few modifications.

Somewhat chastened, Craig started interviewing other people in Electron. He found that his list of suggested contacts blossomed (or maybe "*exploded*" was a better term) as he spoke with more and more people. Engineering not only broke down into process, product, and field concerns but also included management concerns that often tended to differ considerably from the concerns of engineers on the line. Line engineers wanted to know how to fix specific problems, whereas their managers wanted to know how to make the correct decisions about protecting their areas of responsibility along a number of fronts, often international in scope. Marketing and sales were also making themselves heard. For instance, how far could they go in making claims about various products without these claims coming back to haunt them later? There were also the installation, servicing, and maintenance sectors. What effects on liability could occur from improper repair or installation? Who took customer complaints, and how should they be processed and documented? How should products be disposed of safely? And there seemed to be no one entity responsible for keeping employees current on all of the manufacturing and design standards that were being promulgated.

Complications

In a follow-up discussion with Stan Neuhaus, Craig became aware of an even bigger problem. Stan confided that many in engineering had believed for some time that product liability at Electron was much more a communication than a knowledge issue. He argued that, in spite of what legal thought, most engineers were already sensitive to product liability issues. What was lacking, according to these engineers, was a company-wide, systematic approach to these issues that addressed specific questions, such as the following: What was the chain of command for handling product liability issues throughout the company? Should there be a monitoring system for actively searching out potential product defects, and what should be included within it? What was the procedure for taking corrective action, such as a product recall, in a particular instance? How did one document the decision to warn rather than initiate a redesign, or should one do nothing at all? And what were the acceptable time frames?

Stan produced the draft of a company-wide product safety program that established a comprehensive organizational structure and detailed procedures for a number of the issues he had mentioned. He believed that a course that centered on building an understanding of these procedures would go a long way toward educating people about what they needed to *do,* instead of discussing these issues in a general way. Stan added that the prior course that legal had presented was too mired in such generalities. They had provided few, if any, concrete answers as to what to do in particular situations. Besides, it had been almost all lecture and, after the first hour of hearing about common law principles, "people had found it pretty hard to stay awake."

Although Craig recognized that many engineers had a propensity to see product liability in terms of black and white (which he knew, as a lawyer, was not always possible), he also agreed that providing them with a structured way of dealing with a variety of day-to-day problems made sense. The draft of the company-wide product safety program was extensive. It provided an excellent start for a content outline for what he now considered to be a major part of the training. However, when Craig ran his idea by legal, Richard Mull curtly informed him that the draft had never been approved and that it should never have been passed around, particularly to an outside consultant. Richard argued that the problem with internal standards and procedures, especially when they were more stringent than general regulations and the common law, was that they, in effect, became a new standard to which the company could be held in a court of law, regardless of their intent as only general guidelines. Providing training on specific procedures and policies could be regarded as being legally equivalent to a written standard because it evidenced the company's intentions as to those procedures and policies. When Craig countered that the alternative might be even less palatable, Richard replied that this was why Electron had legal to advise it. He reiterated that the course needed to stay away from details, although he did not object to "jazzing it up somewhat" to keep everyone interested.

Craig left the meeting with the growing realization that the project was expanding and moving in several directions. He arranged a meeting with Louise Masoff to brainstorm ways of coping with the scope of the project. But he soon discovered that Louise did not feel in a position to press for any changes to the course's one-day, all-in-one structure. She certainly did not want to get involved in a political tug of war with legal about the direction of the course. As he listened to Louise, Craig began to believe that he had been handed what many in Electron had probably already known was an instructional design minefield, with no readily acceptable solutions. In the end, he suspected, the prevailing wisdom had been to let someone from the outside take the fall.

What to Do Now?

Craig sat in his hotel room, contemplating a project that seemed to be unraveling in front of his eyes. He had more content than he knew what to do with and a rapidly expanding group of target learners with varying interests, all squeezed into a course "box" that seemed way too small. Worse yet, he was being told to go in a design direction that would probably result in little performance change in the company. There would be almost no difference between Craig's course and the older and instructionally ineffective one, except that now the course would have his name on it. His sense of pride, as well as his ethics, would not let him accept this without a struggle. Craig truly wanted to design a course that would make a difference for Electron and its employees, but, with all the conflicting demands that he faced, how could he do this?

Preliminary Analysis Questions

1. Identify the key issues Craig must consider as he decides what to do next. It might be useful to think in terms of types of issues—e.g., needs assessment, organizational development, and instructional content analysis.
2. For each issue that you identify, what solution(s) would you suggest? Then consider the *interaction* of these issues. What effect will these interactions have on your proposed solutions?
3. How would you go about dealing with the impasse between the desire for specifics (engineering) and the desire for generalities (legal)?
4. Do you believe it is possible to accommodate the varying content interests in a day-long course? If so, how would you design the course? If not, what changes would you advise?
5. If you could get no agreement from the various interests and it was decided that you would present essentially a "regurgitated" version of the previous course, how would you react? Provide a rationale for your reaction.

Implications for ID Practice

1. What organizational issues within a corporate setting can affect the success of an instructional design project?
2. Describe strategies for achieving agreement and buy-in for a training project when stakeholder groups have differing and opposing needs. How might an outside consultant go about making his or her voice heard within a large corporation when decision makers are unable or unwilling to break through an impasse?
3. Describe strategies for dealing with resource and time limitations that interfere with the adequate completion of an instructional design project. How does one make an objective determination of what is "adequate" under a particular set of circumstances?
4. What issues need to be discussed and made part of the consultant/client contract at the beginning of an instructional design project?
5. What are the ethical issues involved for an instructional designer when the client insists on something that the consultant does not believe is in the best interests of the overall project?

Case Study
22

Scott Hunter
Developing Online Assessment in an International Setting
by David L. Solomon

Scott Hunter. Vice President, Creative Director. Automotive Performance Improvement Consultants (APIC). There I was—staring at my business card minutes before a tough meeting—and the only insight I could seem to muster was that my title didn't really reflect what I did. I had no idea where I would begin when I approached my supervisor, Ken Young, with the most recent challenge facing the international training team. I remembered being thrilled about my international job assignment—a real opportunity to apply so much of my training in instructional design and technology—but frustration soon replaced enthusiasm.

We had confronted so many problems over the past year and we were now so close to launching the sales consultant certification program that everyone could taste it. One last hurdle remained and it was gnawing at me. I had to stop myself from saying what I truly felt when Ken asked, "Can you refresh my memory and help me understand what's going on?"

In the first few minutes of my meeting with Ken, I explained the turmoil that seemed to plague this project. First there was Katarina (Kat) Wilder, the abusive training manager at the client organization, Trans-Continental Motors (TCM), who once held the position currently occupied by Antoine Devereux (see Figure 22–1).

I couldn't believe it had taken so long for Bob Kelly, the senior manager, to do something about her constant diatribes, but there was an ocean between them and so much red tape. Kat was skilled at generating lengthy e-mail messages and creating a lot of "busy work," but she had no vision of the desired outcomes. We flew overseas for several meetings with TCM and found that "next steps" were always unclear and several disparate projects seemed to appear as each conversation with her unfolded. I remembered wondering if she even knew we were the training supplier or merely considered us to be another department in the advertising agency where we resided. Either way, it was clear to me that we were underused. Unknown to APIC, Kat had been working with Antoine, the training manager

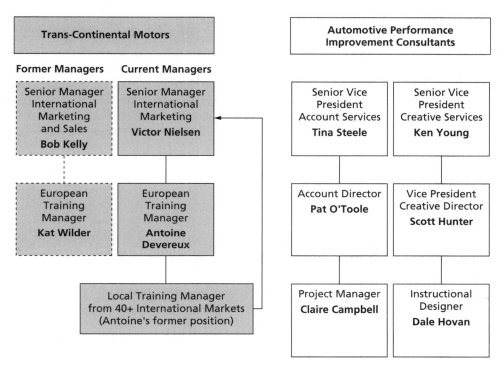

FIGURE 22–1 Client and Consultant Organizational Flowcharts for an International Training Team.

from France at that time, to create a certification test for sales consultants. She and Antoine were clandestinely working with a close relative of Antoine's to coordinate a pilot.

"So, Kat was working on a pilot program with Antoine, who hired one of his relatives to develop the certification test and no one from APIC knew about it?"

"That's right," I said to Ken, half-surprised that he was following this soap opera. "The certification test was the most critical piece of the certification program and we had a clearly defined strategy. But, there's more to the story and a few twists and turns along the way," I said as I continued with the saga.

"We've had our share of headaches, too. We lost about three or four months due to turnover on the account team. Pat O'Toole, the account director, had to move back to the United States from Europe in the middle of all this, and Claire Campbell, the project manager, didn't start working full-time on this project until about six months ago, so we basically put this entire certification program together in less than nine months."

Once the personnel issues were addressed, I explained other concerns that we had confronted. Many of the training managers at TCM had dual responsibilities for the same manufacturer, which included a large European luxury division and our American brand. The European luxury division had already launched a certification program, and there was pressure to adapt this program for the American brand.

"Makes sense," responded Ken.

"Well, it's true that there is this belief that whatever works for the luxury brand will automatically work for us, but in my experience, this is rarely the case," I explained. "We've got two very different types of cultures operating in this situation, with very different retail environments, product offerings, and customers. Plus, TCM wants everything to be administered online and the existing program for the luxury brand is mostly paper-based."

"But politically, it looks very good for *everyone* when we can borrow from the luxury brand. Management appreciates when costs can be shared across divisions. Why couldn't we do this?" asked Ken.

At this point, I handed over a copy of my notes from an early meeting of the Block Exemption Regulation (BER) Task Force and offered the following explanation (see Figure 22–2).

Automotive Performance Improvement Consultants

Block Exemption Regulation (BER) Task Force

Launch Meeting Summary

- Global training already has a certification process in place for a luxury brand.
- It has been difficult to adapt this existing program in international markets where the American brand is sold for several reasons:
  - The certification process is complex.
  - The competencies are robust and include more than 250 elements.
  - Behavioral styles and personality characteristics are integrated with the competencies and appear to be culturally specific.
  - The competencies have only been validated locally and may not generalize internationally.
  - The assessment process required a third-party evaluator which can cost up to 2,000 per individual.
  - The curriculum requires a minimum of 18 training days per individual (and does not recognize prior knowledge or experience).
  - The existing program does not include personal development plans, which is a BER requirement.
  - Product knowledge tests are complicated and costly. Multiple correct answer formats increase the cost of translating the number of answers from multiple-choice questions and the computer programming requirements are more complex traditional multiple-choice formats. This will also increase costs.

FIGURE 22–2   Scott's Meeting Notes.

"Well, the existing program was highly complex and required a third-party evaluator to assess each sales consultant, which cost about 1,200 euro per day. In addition, in some countries the evaluator had to be an industrial or organizational psychologist. This simply wasn't an option for the smaller markets, as the costs were prohibitive and the ability to pay varied from one country to the next. In addition, the product knowledge tests were multiple-choice with multiple correct answers that required a sophisticated scoring algorithm. Translation costs, alone, for the product knowledge test would be expensive because of the increased number of answer options needed for the multiple correct answer format. In addition, complex programming would be needed, which would require more time and money compared to traditional multiple-choice questions where only one correct answer is needed."

Ken's patience seemed to be wearing thin as he interrupted and asked, "So, what did you do?"

At this point, I pulled out the certification model (see Figure 22–3) for the sales consultant certification program and began to summarize some key points.

"We developed this model to explain the certification program to the local training managers. It begins with job descriptions and competencies," I explained. "For this, we *did* use the existing materials from the luxury division's certification program, but we basically edited and simplified the content and their competencies based upon our knowledge and expertise in the automotive industry. We later validated these materials, which I can explain in a minute.

"The next component is recruitment and selection, which is a collection of processes and procedures to ensure that qualified sales consultants are representing the brand, which

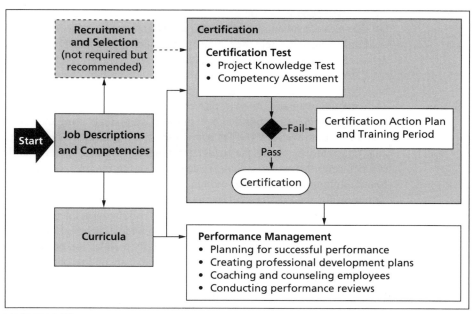

FIGURE 22–3 Certification Model.

is a mandatory requirement for the European luxury program. The American brand cannot legally impose recruitment and selection processes for international dealerships because the ability to pay for these activities varies among the different-sized international markets, so it's not required, but recommended, in our program.

"The certification component consists of a product knowledge test and a competency assessment. For the product knowledge test, we're writing basic, multiple-choice items that test a sales consultant's factual knowledge of our client's products. Depending upon the vehicles sold in a given market and the guidelines we've established, individual tests are generated using randomly selected items from the question pool."

"So how do you handle cheating in the local dealerships?" Ken asked.

"Well, we recommend that the tests are proctored by local training managers or by independent testing facilities, but we've also had to accept that we couldn't prevent cheating from occurring. We'd like to think that people would take the certification process seriously, but those who really want to cheat—or work collaboratively as a group—will figure out a way to do so. Now, that doesn't mean we make it easy for them either! The test items and the response options are generated randomly and every sales consultant is given a unique ID number and receives a unique test. If people work in groups, they'll have to complete a lot of individual tests, but they'll also learn a lot along the way."

Ken looked skeptical. "So, what's to prevent individuals from answering the test questions with the product reference guides right there in their laps or leaving their computer stations to look up an answer?"

"Well, we can't really prevent that from happening, but if sales consultants leave their tests for too long, they are automatically timed-out of their product knowledge tests. The website will bookmark where they left off, saving everything that had already been answered but the sales consultants will be required to log in again and a different test item will then be randomly assigned where they left off. Sales consultants will have to repeat this process over and over again until the test is completed."

"Okay so, what's up with the competency assessment then?" Ken continued.

"Well, this was our greatest challenge because we needed an alternative to the on-site evaluator and we had limited resources, both financial and human. We decided to conduct a job analysis with sales consultants in our top five markets using the simplified competencies as a foundation. We removed the parts of the test that assessed behavioral styles and personality characteristics from the luxury program and created operational definitions for eight competencies that would generalize across all of our international markets. For example, we found minimum standards for written and spoken communication and wrote an operational definition for the communication competency. It simply wasn't feasible for us to conduct in-depth evaluations of every sales consultant working in an international market. We decided to conduct the job analysis using the critical incident technique with a small sample of top performers. This approach allowed us to identify a collection of behaviors that were critical to successful job performance. We constructed an online competency assessment using authentic scenarios from the job analysis and, along the way we were able to validate the competency framework and job descriptions."

Looking impressed, Ken asked: "Great, so how does the competency assessment work?"

"We've aligned a series of questions with each of the competencies and each item has three response options. The best answer is assigned three points and it reflects what exemplary performers do in certain situations. There is also an acceptable response, which is assigned two points and a least-acceptable response, which is given one point. This type of scoring procedure was used to discriminate between acceptable performers and those individuals who needed to improve. Once the competency assessment was completed, a score was given for each of the competencies and the candidate either passed or failed. For those sales consultants who failed, a certification action plan had to be developed by the responsible sales manager to improve upon the weaknesses that were identified in the competency assessment. Then, the sales consultants were re-tested after a probationary period of time."

"So what's to prevent someone from cheating on the competency assessment?" Ken wondered.

"The website is programmed in the same way as the product knowledge test and there is a bank of questions that are scrambled for each candidate. Again, we won't be able to prevent cheating but we're confident that most sales consultants will recognize the benefit of receiving constructive feedback on their individual performances because it can directly impact their ability to generate sales.

"If they don't pass the required competency assessment, the certification action plan should help them prepare for the re-test. Remember, the competency assessment is only designed to discriminate between acceptable and unacceptable performance and the program is not intended to be punitive. Continuous improvement is the ultimate goal and once sales consultants become certified, they receive personal development plans when they enter the performance management phase of the program. From here, the only requirement for recertification is successful completion of product knowledge tests. The program can potentially help sales consultants earn more money if they are truly committed to improving their performance."

"Well, everything sounds great to me. So what's the problem?"

As I took a deep breath, I mentioned that TCM recently reorganized and several positions were eliminated or consolidated. Then, I explained that Antoine was now reporting directly to Victor Nielsen in Europe because Bob's position was eliminated.

"And the problem is . . .?"

"The problem is . . . Bob never felt a need to develop a certification test for vehicle delivery specialists. These are customer-facing employees who are only responsible for handing over the vehicles to customers after the actual sales transactions take place. They answer questions and demonstrate how to use certain features like the radios or air-conditioning systems. Bob just didn't think we needed to include them because there are only about 60 or 70 throughout the entire European Union. But Victor insists that the program must include vehicle delivery specialists and Antoine is demanding it but we've run out of time and money."

Ken probed further. "So, what was discussed at your last meeting with the client?"

"Here's a copy of the Call Report . . . I'm just not sure what to do" (see Figure 22–4).

"What are your instincts telling you about this one?" Ken asked as he skimmed through the call report.

Call Report

Client: Antoine Devereux
Author: Pat O'Toole
Participants: Claire Campbell
       Antoine Devereux (via telephone)
       Dale Hovan
       Scott Hunter
       Pat O'Toole
Purpose: Certification Program
Date: October 3rd

Purpose

The purpose of this meeting was to discuss the status of the Sales Consultant Certification Program.

Background

- All elements of the Sales Consultant Certification Program were reviewed and approved prior to launch, including:
    - Revised job descriptions and competencies
    - Interface design and functionality
    - Product knowledge test items
    - Competency assessment
    - Certification action plan and personal development plan
- TCM inquired about the status of the vehicle delivery specialist (VDS) certification. APIC informed TCM that Bob did not request VDS certification materials because there were less than 70 job incumbents throughout all international markets.

Discussion

- TCM informed APIC that VDS certification materials must be prepared by the first of the year so that the manufacturer will be compliant with block exemption regulation (BER) standards.

FIGURE 22–4 Call Report.

- APIC facilitated a brainstorming session to explore various options, which included:
  - Request quotation from competency assessment supplier to conduct critical incident interviews with top-performing VDS job incumbents
  - Check with domestic training team to see if they have any relevant materials to assist with VDS certification
  - Send e-mail message to all relevant training managers to request information on any existing VDS certification materials
- TCM explained that in most markets, sales consultants (SC) handle vehicle delivery and the VDS position is only implemented in very large markets, often in dealerships that sell both the luxury and American brands. The VDS position is often perceived as an entry-level job for the SC position and a VDS should be able to fulfill the basic functions of the SC position.
- TCM informed APIC that certification materials exist in the United Kingdom for the luxury division. A brief training program is delivered in the dealership, followed by a role-playing scenario where the training manager determines if the VDS should be certified.
- TCM also informed APIC that training support must be available for VDS candidates who fail the certification test.

Next Steps

- APIC to collect existing assets, which are currently known to include:
  - VDS certification materials from the United Kingdom
  - VDS and SC job descriptions and SC competencies
  - SC competency assessment (including approved items that were not used)
  - Domestic training materials for vehicle delivery including five-point vehicle walkaround positions
  - APIC to prepare request for quotation from competency assessment supplier

FIGURE 22–4 Call Report, *(cont.)*

"One thing I know for sure TCM does not have enough money to hire an outside supplier to conduct the critical incident interviews for vehicle delivery specialists in order to identify key behaviors critical to their successful performance."

"And how complicated do you think this task would be?"

"Generally, my instincts are telling me that vehicle delivery specialists need to be familiar with basic product features, just in case questions arise at delivery. They need to know which product features to present or demonstrate at various interior and exterior positions around the vehicle, and finally, there are some typical situations that might occur during vehicle delivery that require basic common sense and any customer-facing employee should be able to act accordingly."

"Like what's a typical situation that occurs at delivery?"

"Sometimes the customer is in a hurry and doesn't allow enough time for delivery or the vehicle may not be prepped when the customer arrives."

"Do you think Dale Hovan will have any time to work on this?" (see Figure 22–1).

"It's a possibility, and he was very involved in the sales consultant certification program, but I guess it depends upon whether or not we can find any existing training programs that can be repurposed for vehicle delivery specialists."

"I see. Makes sense. Well, it looks like we've got about a week to come up with some recommendations."

At this moment, Ken glanced at his watch and then pointed to a framed quotation on his wall by M. Scott Peck, which stated:

> The truth is that our finest moments are most likely to occur when we are feeling deeply uncomfortable, unhappy, or unfulfilled. For it is only in such moments, propelled by our discomfort, that we are likely to step out of our ruts and start searching for different ways or truer answers.

"I know you're very frustrated with all this, but maybe the certification test for vehicle delivery specialists will be one of *your* finest moments on this project. By the way, whatever happened to Kat?" asked Ken.

"Well Kat was dismissed and Antoine was promoted to European Training Manager," I answered matter-of-factly.

Confused, Ken muttered, "But I thought Antoine was. . . . "

I continued with, "Yes, Antoine established an inappropriate working relationship with his relative, but he also seemed to get things done and TCM gave him the promotion with the understanding that his relative could complete the pilot but could not work on any other international business."

"So typical," Ken said as he shook his head and started gathering some papers for his next meeting.

"Thanks for your time," I replied as I found myself thinking that truth is sometimes stranger than fiction. Then I realized that I was the one who would have to fix this mess. One more deliverable, little time, and no budget. "So typical," I echoed as I headed back to my office.

Preliminary Analysis Questions

1. Given the complexity of the existing certification program, critique APIC's approach to the sales consultant certification program it developed.
2. What are the advantages and disadvantages of using a third-party evaluator compared to an online competency assessment?

3. Scott Hunter states, "If people work in groups . . . they'll also learn a lot along the way." What do you think about this statement, given the strategies used to handle cheating in this case?
4. Evaluate the options that resulted from APIC's brainstorming session (see Figure 22–4). Suggest other approaches to the certification of the vehicle delivery specialists.

Implications for ID Practice

1. Discuss the design challenges associated with working in volatile client environments where turnover, restructuring, and/or job rotation strategies can impact ID projects.
2. What type of communication strategies would you suggest for global project teams that operate in different countries, especially if English is a second language for many members of the team and/or audiences?
3. Propose a range of strategies for addressing performance improvement needs when the intended audience is very small.
4. Discuss the issues involved in implementing online assessment in real-world settings.

Margaret Janson
Developing Learning Objects for Adult Learners
by Rod Sims and Naomi Waldron

Simon Wilcowsky reflected on his career at Third Eye Media. Although his original background was in graphic design, he had worked on teams with other professionals on instructional design projects over the past several years and had risen to the position of e-learning production manager. So far, he'd been very successful in managing the needs of his clients while meeting deadlines and making a healthy profit for the company. He had a great team under his supervision: instructional designers, programmers, illustrators, animators, even video producers. Most clients had been happy with the quality of the e-learning materials that the company had produced; Third Eye used high-quality graphics and illustrations that were easy to read and animations that illustrated difficult concepts. The company had won numerous awards for its e-learning products and was one of the most successful companies in the country.

But this latest client was different. The Australian Vocational Network (AVN) had very clear ideas about the development of learning objects that were at odds with what previous clients had requested. Simon wondered again about AVN's request for a Proof-of-Concept that required approximately 40% of the final product—that was some "proof"! But now the client was threatening to pull the project and cancel the contract. Somehow the design practices that had built Third Eye Media's reputation were not working with this very important client. Simon had just spent 20 minutes on the phone with his boss, Caroline Porter, about the memo he'd sent her first thing this morning, trying to explain what went wrong and why he'd almost lost the $100,000 project. She was not at all pleased, but he assured her that he would save the project. But how? Simon knew that other perspectives often helped shed light on difficult issues, so he decided to talk to Margaret Janson, one of Third Eye's more experienced instructional designers, about the problem.

Margaret was sitting at her desk, feeling relaxed as she had just completed a major project and was looking forward to meeting her university friends for tea. She'd just enrolled in a master's program in e-learning and she loved the challenge. Her instructors had encouraged her to compare the theories she was learning with the practical knowledge she'd gained from working on projects with Third Eye Media. Simon poked his head around the door—"Got a minute?" he asked. "Sure," responded Margaret, "Come on in."

"We have a problem," said Simon. "What do you know about deep-sea oil exploration?"

Margaret shrugged and grinned. As an instructional designer for Third Eye, she was used to unusual projects and the thought of a new and challenging assignment was exciting. "Nothing," she replied, "but from the look on your face, I think I'm going to find out very soon!"

Simon continued, "You know that $100,000 government contract we won to develop competency-based training in deep-sea oil exploration? The brief required us to develop a set of e-learning objects for the accreditation of new employees and to re-accredit those with experience."

He gulped. "The entire project is at risk: we're at the Proof-of-Concept phase, and unless we can figure out what went wrong and fix it—fast—then, we stand to lose $100,000 of work, not to mention our company's reputation. Our client is the Australian Vocational Network. As you know, AVN is the premier vocational organization in the country. They have a designated project manager as well as an industry-appointed oil exploration expert assigned to this project. So we have a lot of stakeholders to impress here. The AVN and project manager are setting our technical specifications and project requirements but don't know anything about deep-sea oil exploration. On the other hand, Joe Strickler, our oil exploration expert, is very familiar with the needs of the industry, but doesn't really understand the technical limitations with which we are working. So, the design that we created needs to be negotiated to suit both parties, as well as achieved within the time and budget we have available."

Simon continued, "They're also very specific about what they mean by a learning object. Have a look at this." He removed a page from the project folder and handed it to Margaret (see Figure 23–1).

Simon also handed Margaret the internal memo he had sent his boss earlier (see Figure 23–2). "I had to send this to the Head Office this morning to explain the situation. Maybe you should have a read. I'll be back shortly—I have to go call the AVN project manager now. I'll be back with an update shortly."

Margaret finished reading the specifications and memo and began to speculate on how the project might have gotten to this stage. She began to ponder how Simon's team had missed the requirements for interactivity and active learning that were so clearly specified. She wondered if the main reason were related to the fact that previous clients had requested products that were graphical and fun to use, but rarely had they been so specific about using a preferred learning approach.

When Simon returned, he asked Margaret for her thoughts. "Well," she began a little hesitantly, "you seem to have completely misunderstood the client's requirements. Surely the specifications document you handed me earlier can't be all you were given to work from. How did you go about the instructional design task and sign-off with the client?"

"The first thing that happened," responded Simon, "is that we were invited to a briefing meeting in Sydney. Our lead instructional designer, Janet Smith, went on our behalf.

AUSTRALIAN VOCATIONAL NETWORK
MEMORANDUM

To:	LEARNING OBJECT CONTRACTORS
FROM:	LEARNING MATERIALS DIVISION
SUBJECT:	LEARNING OBJECT SPECIFICATIONS
DATE:	12 JANUARY 2005
CC:	DIRECTOR, TECHNICAL TRAINING

TO ALL DEVELOPERS:

THESE SPECIFICATIONS SHOULD BE USED FOR ALL LEARNING OBJECT DEVELOPMENT. PLEASE CONTACT YOUR ASSIGNED PROJECT MANAGER FOR FURTHER INFORMATION.

Desired Characteristics of AVN Learning Objects:

Excerpt from the Tender Guidelines for AVN Learning Objects—Series 3 AVN Project Manager, 5 June, 2004

Learning object structure

1) Each module is to be designed as a learning object so that it is:
   a) SCORM compliant
   b) Self-contained (i.e., no explicit links between modules)
   c) Deliverable through a learning management system

2) Each module is to contain an associated work-based context that immerses the learner in a realistic, problem-based environment that engages the learner to use the content objects (described in point 3) to solve the problems

3) Within each module there are to be smaller learning objects that cover single learning objectives. These objects are to be repurposable, content-rich, and include a self-test at the end.

Teaching and learning approaches

The modules must exhibit effective teaching and learning approaches as demonstrated by the following features:

- an educational model that recognizes an active, constructive role for learners

- learning activities that engage the learner in active processing rather than mere knowledge acquisition

- resources that are visually attractive, motivating to use, and organized logically

- representations of authentic, real-life settings in preference to textual descriptions

FIGURE 23–1 Australian Vocational Network Memorandum.

Third Eye Media

Suite 65,100 Spotty Gum Lane
Eucalyptus Business Park
Gooneellabah NSW 2480
AUSTRALIA
P: 61-2-6623-4567
E: support@3im.com.au

CONFIDENTIAL

TO: CAROLINE PORTER, CEO
FROM: SIMON WILCOWSKY
SUBJECT: AVN E–LEARNING PROJECT
DATE: 23 JULY 2005

BACKGROUND
The Australian Vocational Network (AVN), through its funding body the Australian Education Committee, commissioned Third Eye Media to develop a suite of web-based learning objects for deep-sea oil exploration and underwater drilling.

During initial consultations it was emphasized that a critical element and measure of functionality for the learning objects would be active learning contextualized in a problem-based environment. The AVN specifications required the materials to integrate interactivity for engagement and learning, although there was no definition or examples of these terms.

The key personnel identified for the project were the project manager (appointed by AVN), the subject matter expert (appointed by the Oil Exploration Industry Committee), and the instructional designer and multimedia software developers employed by Third Eye Media.

Based on our understanding of the requirements, and following our development of what we considered a Proof-of-Concept, the AVN has recommended the contract be terminated.

KEY FACTORS
The following represent the key factors and issues that have impacted delivery of the desired outcomes and placed the overall project in jeopardy.

- The project start date was delayed due to disagreements between the AVN Project Manager and the Industry Committee on the selection of content.
- We encountered initial delays to the commencement of the instructional design phase due to the resignation of our instructional designer.
- We experienced difficulties in obtaining and identifying content resources. One reason for this was that the units had previously only been taught in a face-to-face apprenticeship model, with no written content available, apart from high-level textbooks.
- The specifications for the Proof-of-Concept appeared consistent with our prior experience with the production of a sample product and we used this knowledge as the basis for the initial deliverable.

This combination of factors meant we were challenged to meet the requirements of the initial Proof-of-Concept.

CURRENT STATUS
Our initial instructional design for a sample learning object and the accompanying Proof-of-Concept was not completed to the satisfaction of the AVN Project Manager. Two reasons were provided in their feedback report: First, the Proof-of-Concept did not demonstrate what they considered to be the key components of problem-based and exploratory learning; secondly, the Proof-of-Concept was not consistent with their expectations for style and layout. With respect to the overall design, the initial determination from the AVN Project Manager was that the content was poorly structured, there were no clear pathways through the content, and that the interface design was rudimentary.

In retrospect there was a conflict between our understanding of the Proof-of-Concept and that of the client's; our expectations were that it represented a rough work in progress, while their expectations, determined only recently, were that 40% of the learning objects would be complete. This was certainly well beyond the Proof-of-Concept requirements for previous projects.

It is my recommendation that we propose redoing the Proof-of-Concept at no cost to AVN, and within the agreed time frame. I have since spoken with our primary contact at AVN and they have agreed to speak with us later this morning.

The income from this project is $100,000 with the expectation of further work next year if the project is successful. It is my opinion that given the influence of the Australian Vocational Network, any concerns about loss of profit from redoing the Proof-of-Concept should be weighed against the potential loss of reputation from the project's failure.

Yours sincerely,

Simon Wilcowsky

FIGURE 23–2   Simon's Memorandum to Caroline Porter.

However, she resigned shortly afterwards and we had to put Trevor Adams on the project instead. Trevor's a great guy but because he missed all the lead-up briefing meetings, we were behind from the start. And while he's fantastic at designing the kind of training materials that we've done before, he was a bit lost when faced with issues related to authentic learning contexts. As you know, Trevor's been trained on the job and doesn't have a background in education. I didn't pick up on that gap until recently and this Proof-of-Concept is the first sign-off point we've had with the client.

Margaret skimmed Simon's memo to Caroline again. "Forty percent completion for a Proof-of-Concept! That's a bit much isn't it?"

"Sure is," agreed Simon. "Based on our previous experiences, we assumed a Proof-of-Concept wouldn't need to be so complete, and with the change of staff and Trevor's inexperience with this level of development, we somehow didn't pick up that the AVN expectation for Proof-of-Concept meant we had to complete nearly half the work! We haven't worked for AVN before, but apparently that's just what they expect."

Margaret was silent for a while, then carefully added her own perspective. "You know, this project is quite different from most of the others we've completed. That would explain why you overlooked some of the requirements. Most of our clients just want an "electronic textbook" solution—they want classy-looking information presentation. For this project though, we were clearly asked to work at a much more sophisticated level, and to engage the learner with the content through structured interactive activities."

She paused. "Let me see if I understand the situation correctly. We won this project and, after some initial staffing issues, in our effort to meet the submission requirements, we just did what has worked for us in the past."

Simon shuffled in his seat looking uncomfortable. "That's one way of looking at it. Margaret, I just got off the phone with AVN and they have agreed to continue with the contract. However, we must identify and assign a new instructional designer to the work. Since Trevor doesn't have an education degree, I'd like you to take on the project. We have exactly three weeks to develop a completely new Proof-of-Concept at our own cost. If it's successful, then we'll be paid for the whole project. If not, we'll be out of pocket for the extra work."

Margaret laughed nervously. "Three weeks! That's ridiculous. A project like this should take months. Can't you talk them into giving us a few more months?" Simon looked at Margaret gravely. "You don't know how hard it was for me to convince them to give us another chance. They were adamant that we couldn't have any more time. The only reason they're giving us three weeks is because I convinced them that we had the production capacity to pull it off."

Margaret took a deep breath. "So who else is on the project, then?" Simon was quick to answer. "You can have whomever you need—the whole team, if necessary. Just don't let me down."

"Wow. This is going to be some project," thought Margaret to herself. "Where are the learning outcomes and content?"

Simon replied, "There are some industry-based underwater exploration competencies, but because it's such a specialized field and very skills-oriented, there is no written training material at all. Until now, training has all been apprenticeship-based. There is one expert,

Martin Howe, who's been training people for years. However, because he lives in Tasmania and was off-shore on an oil rig for a lengthy period of time, Trevor could only contact him briefly by phone and by e-mail. I believe he is back now and if you want, I will approve a flight for him up here and have him spend dedicated time with the team. Anyway, have a think about what you'd like to do and come back to me with a plan of attack first thing in the morning."

Contemplating three weeks of hard work and little sleep, Margaret returned to her desk and reviewed the client's feedback from the initial Proof-of-Concept (see Figure 23–3) that Simon had left with her.

AVN | AUSTRALIAN VOCATIONAL NETWORK
MEMORANDUM

To: SIMON WILCOWSKI, THIRD EYE MEDIA

FROM: L.J. SMITH, DIRECTOR, LEARNING MATERIALS DIVISION
SUBJECT: PROOF-OF-CONCEPT FEEDBACK
DATE: 20 JULY 2005
CC: DIRECTOR, TECHNICAL TRAINING

Dear Simon,

We have received and reviewed the Proof-of-Concept for the Deep-Sea Oil Rig learning object.

Attached please find the formal assessment and feedback.

As you can see, we have serious reservations about the ability of Third Eye Media to complete the project.

We advise that you contact your AVN project manager to discuss the status of the project.

Yours sincerely,

L J Smith

L.J. Smith
Director, Learning Materials Division

Enclosures: Assessment and Feedback Report

FIGURE 23–3 AVN Assessment and Feedback Report. *(continued)*

Third Eye Proof-of-Concept: Assessment and Feedback Report

Teaching and Learning Approach	Rating (1–5)	Comment
The learning object is based on an educational model that recognises an active, constructive role for learners.	1	The product does not appear to be based on any known educational model.
Learning activities require learners to process the subject matter, rather than mere knowledge acquisition.	1	The activities do not engage the learner, and use of interactivity is at a low level.
The learning setting and tasks encourage meaningful communication (among learners as well as between teachers and learners).	2	There is no direct reference to communication among learners or between teachers and learners.
The learning setting represents real life in preference to textual descriptions.	1	The learning environment is very plain, and does not suggest the environment of deep-sea oil exploration.
The product is visually attractive, motivating to use, and organised logically for ease of navigation.	1	Navigation is very confusing; there is no logical pathway through the product and the appearance of the product is poor.
Product Functionality	**Rating**	**Comment**
The product uses non-proprietary development software.	3	The product is developed in HTML and Flash, but is very unappealing.
Content that is likely to be changed is represented in HTML or Word.	4	Most of the content is represented in HTML text or is in a Word document.
The product allows for multiple pathways through the material, although a suggested learning sequence may be appropriate.	1	Navigation is confusing, and there are no directions for learners on different pathways.
The product can be easily split into a series of reusable, independent learning objects.	2	Although the technology supports it, there do not seem to be any sections that would lend themselves to being separate learning objects.
Compliance with Standards	**Rating**	**Comment**
The product complies with W3C Priority-1 Web Content Accessibility Guidelines.	5	Most content is represented in plain HTML.
Conforming to the above guidelines should not result in any loss of desirable qualities in the features of the product.	2	The product needs to be made more engaging.
The product is SCORM compliant.	3	The product is technically SCORM compliant, but the separate learning objects have not been defined.

FIGURE 23–3 AVN Assessment and Feedback Report. *(cont.)*

FIGURE 23–4   Course Opening Screen.

Even at first glance she could see there were some serious problems—the score on the Teaching and Learning Approach was 6/25, Product Functionality scored 10/20, and Compliance to Standards scored 10/15. It was clearly very fortunate that Simon had managed to negotiate a resubmission of the Proof-of-Concept. Looking at the review scores and comments more closely, Margaret reflected on why the Teaching and Learning Approach component had scored so much lower than the other criteria. From her university studies she was beginning to understand more about the importance of learning theory, interaction, and situated simulations and began to wonder the extent to which they were applying these ideas in their e-learning products.

"What went wrong?" she wondered again. "Hadn't the team seen the rubrics before they started development?" She then examined two of the screenshots (see Figures 23–4 and 23–5) and the flowchart (see Figure 23–6) for the design submitted to AVN for the proof-of-concept.

As Margaret proceeded through the modules, her suspicions were confirmed—the team had not really integrated the types of interactivity and authenticity that AVN had requested. Was this the missing link that had caused the project to be nearly lost? Were there some aspects of instructional design for e-learning that Third Eye was not integrating into its applications? It was then that Margaret remembered listening to a presentation by a visiting professor who had talked about the importance of designing engaging interactions and authentic learning experiences. Perhaps he would have some additional ideas that would assist them while completing the project.

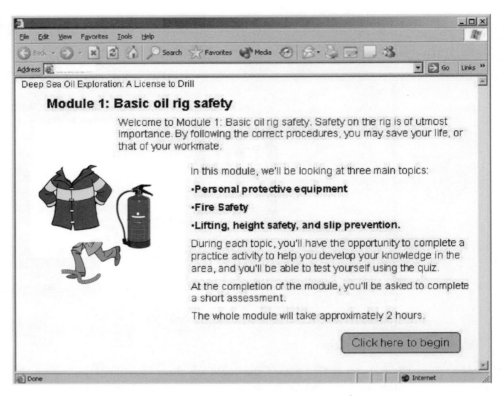

FIGURE 23–5   Module 1 Opening Screen.

The next day Margaret found the professor's business card. Geoff Charles was an e-learning consultant who had written widely on interactivity. When he spoke to Margaret's class, he was very clear about the importance of developing effective interactive learning experiences. Margaret picked up the phone and called Geoff and luckily he was free for a coffee that very afternoon.

"Tell me, Geoff," Margaret inquired, "how can we create an e-learning object that integrates interactivity for authentic engagement? We've got a project for training deep-sea oil explorers and I need some new ideas fast! I learned a lot from your presentation, but would really appreciate some further input."

Geoff thought for a moment and then replied carefully, "It seems you may have a context issue here." Geoff then went on to explain, in some detail, several projects he had worked on, describing different interactive strategies that had proven successful for different types of learners in a broad range of contexts.

After an hour of talking with Geoff, Margaret's suspicions about the reasons for the rejected Proof-of-Concept seemed to have been confirmed. For most of Third Eye's previous projects, the emphasis had been on translating some very dreary content into a more

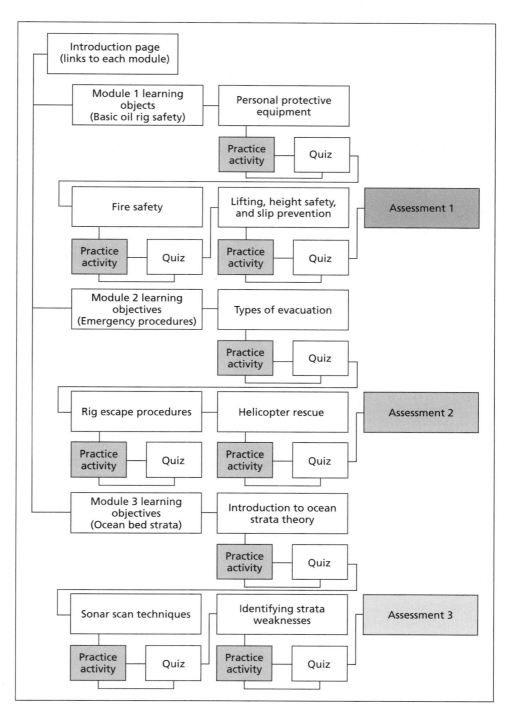

FIGURE 23–6 Course Flowchart.

accessible and presentable format—and the clients had been very happy with what they called their new "interactive" e-learning products. But this client had quite different expectations for interactivity, ones that were much more aligned with Geoff's ideas. It was not just about presenting attractive content, but engaging students in the learning material through their participation in authentic activities. As Margaret started back to the office, she now felt she had the basis for recreating a Proof-of-Concept that would meet the needs of AVN.

Preliminary Analysis Questions

1. Describe the differences between the learning objects required in the memorandum presented by AVN and the Proof-of-Concept delivered by Third Eye.
2. There were a number of misunderstandings and false assumptions made in this case. Suggest strategies for improving communication between AVN and Third Eye.
3. Develop an action plan for Margaret to present to Simon. Draw up a three-week calendar, with Project Briefing on Day 1 and Project Submission on Day 21.

Implications for ID Practice

1. The role of instructional design project managers has been compared to a juggler—they have to manage the often-conflicting requirements of different stakeholders within the constraints of time, money, and resources to design a quality product. What strategies might be employed to ensure that the client, the manager, and the developers are satisfied with the design?
2. Learning objects are intended to allow for maximum reusability; however, a common criticism is that they may lack a context to make learning meaningful and authentic. How would you respond to this criticism? What design considerations might you take into account to counter these criticisms?
3. Compare the approaches to achieving interactivity (student-student, instructor-student, student-content) in face-to-face and online learning environments.

David Jimenez
Performance Improvement of Engineers
by Martha Mann, Valerie A. Larsen, and Mable B. Kinzie

Carillon Productions is an instructional design firm that grew from a small team of instructional designers in the late 1990s to well over 50 employees in only a few years. Carillon became well known, among its clients of educational publishers, for its development of multimedia-based supplemental textbook materials. David Jimenez was an instructional designer at Carillon who had been specializing in the design of science and mathematics instruction for the past four years. His innovative and award-winning designs covered a wide range of applications from interactive problem-solving physics modules to 3-D calculus tutorials. David credited the successful design of his products to his skills as an instructional designer, to his programming skills, and to his 10 years as a secondary science teacher. His teaching experience provided him with insight into learners' needs and enabled him to serve as both content expert and instructional developer. In this way, he was able to work on his own as he designed and developed products for Carillon's clients. David had to modify his formula for success, however, when he was promoted to project manager and assigned to head up a project for Dragone Drilling Technologies, a leading manufacturer of petroleum analysis tools and extraction equipment. Due for market release in 90 days, Dragone Drilling's Odysseus System was being promoted as a cost-effective technology that had the potential to revolutionize natural gas hydrate exploration. The firm wanted a training module that would encourage the use of this new analysis, archiving, and forecasting system.

The Odysseus System project would be David's first experience as a manager and his first as a designer dependent on others for their content expertise. However, David was enthusiastic about these new challenges and saw this as an opportunity to expand his leadership and instructional design (ID) skills. Dragone had conducted a field test with the beta version of the Odysseus System, and it cited results that it thought pointed to a need for training among its users. According to executives at Dragone, this need was demonstrated by the engineers' resistance to using the product, a problem they thought was generally common to organizations introducing new technologies. In their report, they noted specifically that 17 engineers had been asked to use the technology for a period of two months in the field. By the end of the second month, the engineers had abandoned the new technology and had returned to their standard data-collection tools.

David's Team

Once Carillon had won the Dragone contract, its Department of Human Resources allocated one graphic designer, three software/interface programmers, and two entry-level instructional designers for the Odysseus System project, all working under David's direction. David thought it was important to introduce the client to his "stellar" team and arranged for the graphics designer and lead interface programmer to participate in their first face-to-face meeting with the client. David had each of them describe the variety of products they had produced as he pointed to the numerous awards their educational materials had received. A manager from Human Resources at Dragone Drilling and the marketing director for the Odysseus System represented the client.

After introductions, the marketing director for Dragone presented the promotions packet for the Odysseus System and described its functionality. He explained that standard methods for data collection were laborious, necessitating hours of manual gauge calibration, along with the manual recording of each data probe in the field, followed by lengthy analysis in an off-site lab. The Odysseus System streamlined this process, with automated calibration and on-site analysis: The system involved a three-stage, on-site digital system that collected data on compositional gradients and hydrate gases from potential drill sites. Multivariate analyses of the reservoir fluid properties were automated and integrated with satellite-networked databases, equipped with algorithms for forecasting site productivity.

According to the marketing director, the petroleum industry was facing a combination of finite, diminishing petroleum resources and increased competition. Those firms with access to new technologies for natural gas hydrate exploration, such as the Odysseus System, had the potential to maintain or increase their market share.

Representatives from Dragone Drilling explained what they were looking for from Carillon Productions: an interactive, self-study training module that would be ready for distribution with the final release of Odysseus in three months. Dragone wanted the engineers to experience the benefits of the Odysseus technology and recognize its ease of use. The goal was to ease the learning curve for the use of the Odysseus System in the field. Their thinking was that an effective training solution would lead to widespread adoption of the Odysseus System.

David shifted into high gear at this point in the meeting and segued into a discussion on the design process. He believed it was important to secure approval for a needs assessment, and, using examples from prior projects, he enthusiastically described how the process could pinpoint the needs of the field engineers and help match the training module to those needs. The Dragone Drilling representatives agreed that a needs assessment seemed to be a practical way to ensure that the training module resolved the problem of technology adoption. They emphasized that time was critical, however, and were reluctant to postpone development of the training module until the needs assessment was completed. As an alternative, Dragone Drilling suggested that David obtain any information he needed from the project manager of the programming team that was contracted to design and develop the Odysseus System.

After some discussion, David and his client agreed to a compromise: They brainstormed some initial ideas for the interface design and for the structure of the instructional module, including options for software or web-based materials. After the latter option was selected, David's team agreed to start development right away. To ensure that appropriate content was included in the module, however, David convinced his clients to approve an initial two-week time period for the collection and analysis of needs data from the Odysseus developers and potential users of the product.

Under David's supervision, then, his team members began to storyboard the instructional sequence, and he was pleased with his team's progress. He was impressed with the competence of his lead developers. Recognizing that he himself worked best when given wide latitude within general guidelines, he instructed them to proceed with the development of the interface components they'd discussed, designing the best interface they could for the anticipated content.

The Lompoc Technology Team

David made arrangements to begin the needs assessment with a visit to the software development company, Lompoc Technology Group (LTG), located in a Southern California beach community. There he met Bill Peters, the project manager of the Odysseus development team, who would serve as his content expert for the instructional module.

Bill greeted David with a coffee mug and a company tour, where he met everyone from the chief information officer (CIO) to the company's interns. The LTG facility provided a friendly work environment, with music playing throughout the "house," a large, open workspace for the programmers, and a conference/game room stocked with food and crash pads for those all-too-frequent times when programmers worked through the night. The programmers appeared absorbed in their work as they hammered away at their keyboards and stared intently at their monitors. David observed a small group of programmers congregated around a dry-erase board as they engaged in an active discussion about a glitch with the login form for the Odysseus intranet.

The tour of LTG concluded in the company's conference room with an overview of the intranet communications system that drove the Odysseus System and a striking visual display of the project's milestones. The first item on the display was a description of the guidelines that Dragone Drilling had presented to the Lompoc team in the form of a flowchart, which listed each of the required functions that the Odysseus System would perform. The last item was a chart displaying the final stage of revisions that began during the beta test of the product. Bill then led a discussion with David and the Odysseus software team about the product and its projected implementation. They walked David through the product demo on a laptop computer similar to those distributed with the Odysseus System. The software team, mostly young men and women averaging two to five years of experience in the software design industry, believed that Odysseus was vastly superior to the current manually driven analysis tools because it handled all of the data-collection and analysis tasks within a single product.

The programmers explained that Odysseus was a simple application to use once the user understood each of the screens and its functions. Also, given a user's guide that was accessible from within the program and a smart tool that defined functions when pointed to, they believed that a separate training module for the engineers would be superfluous. One of the lead programmers noted, "The field engineers who don't 'get' Odysseus are the ones too set in their ways to adopt new technologies at this point in their careers." Another programmer suggested that it might take a new generation of engineers to break a tool such as this into the market.

David left LTG with an Odysseus System laptop and a copy of the beta software. The project manager provided contact information for the engineers who had participated in the Odysseus System beta test and phone numbers for overseas field engineers whom they thought were representative of the potential Odysseus System user population.

Reservoir Fluid Property Analysis

Over the next four days, David was able to contact seven potential users of the Odysseus System. Six of the seven engineers whom David interviewed spoke English as a second language and practiced their profession in their home countries. They had earned their degrees from prominent U.S. schools of engineering, such as Texas A&M and Purdue University. They described their practice as 60% technical and 40% "a feeling of the gut." They had developed their skills under the guidance of experienced field engineers, and, although the standard equipment they used was old, they were comfortable with the process and found it to perform reliably under a variety of conditions. They claimed that they would embrace a tool that expedited the analysis and forecasting of hydrocarbon reserves, but it would have to perform the reservoir fluid property analysis efficiently and accurately. Four of the engineers were wary of using new technologies promoted by their superiors. They described previous tools that were supposed to "deliver the world," according to management. However, when the equipment failed, it was the engineers' performance that came into question, rather than the tools that management had adopted.

David spent his second week meeting with eight of the beta test engineers for the Odysseus System at various sites around the Houston area, four of whom were recent university graduates who planned to return to their native countries in the near future. David was able to observe the new data-collection methods and discuss the engineers' beta test experiences with them. According to the engineers, the first month of the beta test had focused on programming glitches. The intent was to resolve minor bugs and ensure functionality. The majority of the bugs identified involved intranet access (login problems) and problems with user input that caused the system to crash because it was not supported by the analysis algorithms. The engineers were then left to use the new technology in the field for a period of four weeks.

After taking Odysseus through its paces, the engineers reported that they had experienced some drawbacks, which one engineer described as "shining a new light on our old equipment, making the old methods seem like a model of modern perfection." They had found the Odysseus software difficult to navigate and described the multitude of screens that had to be set up for each drill site, with parameters specific to that site. The engineers explained that they often became lost in the system, which required them to start over with their data entry. Consequently, they did not feel confident using Odysseus and had elected to return to their standard tools to ensure accuracy. The beta test engineers remained reluctant to use the final release of the tool, explaining concerns about the functionality and the accuracy of their data entry.

Attitudes, Performance, and Beta Test Data

David returned to the Carillon office and spent the next few days compiling data from the interviews and his explorations of the Odysseus System. After several hours interacting with the software, its embedded user's guide, and job aid cards, he began to understand Odysseus's basic functions, as well as its drawbacks.

Meanwhile, David supervised his designers as they moved forward with a highly sophisticated and attractive interface for the learning module. When the needs assessment data were ready for a final analysis, David asked his instructional designers to take a break and help him review the findings. They found a complex series of problems (see Table 24–1 and Table 24–2), which seemed unlikely to be solved by attempts at "attitude adjustment" (suggested by the software company) or "performance training" (requested by Dragone Drilling).

TABLE 24–1 *Hardware Concerns Highlighted During Field Beta Tests of the Odysseus System*

Contrast/lighting

■ Laptop LCD screen presents significant lighting and contrast problems in direct sunlight. The earth tone colors are attractive but are too similar to differentiate between objects on the screen, especially in varying lighting conditions.

Pulley system

■ Data probes must drop up to 20,000 feet underground. A pulley controls the probe cables and organizes the different probes for each type of sample. The device also reduces the tension placed on the laptop connections. The pulley occasionally crimps the wires, resulting in a negative reading.

Setup of the data probes

■ Setup takes approximately three hours (the same as the standard system). The engineers are accustomed to calibrating their tools prior to each data-collection session and are not comfortable with the "self-correcting" calibration in the new system.

TABLE 24–2 *Software Concerns Highlighted During Field Beta Tests of the Odysseus System*

Navigation

- There are between 8 and 14 windows among which a user must navigate for data entry and analysis.

- The only way to determine if data are missing is to run the analysis, which takes several minutes. After the analysis, a screen prompts the user for missing information.

Online Help

- The three engineers who spoke English as a second language found the help screens inadequate. The screens did not define the steps needed to complete the task in question, and the engineers didn't know what terms to input when searching for navigation tips.

- The two engineers for whom English was the primary language thought the help screens were too simplistic and were cumbersome to access.

- The search engine did not cover all of the system terminology and provided simplified definitions of functions.

- The user guidelines often referred to links or buttons without directing the user to their location.

Functionality

- Several of the software functions were assigned names unique to the software, rather than names reflecting their physical counterparts.

Next Steps

As he reviewed these data, David wondered how he could move forward with a training module when it seemed the product itself needed to be revised. David needed his colleagues' input and a resolution for this dilemma. He had known all along that he could be compromising the effectiveness of the instructional design process when he had the team move directly into interface design before the needs were articulated. And, although he was aware of the potential problems that could result from beginning product development prior to the completion of a needs analysis, he was surprised to uncover problems that were not instructional.

In less than 24 hours, David and his team would present their findings and their progress on the development of the instructional module interface. David and his team members needed to determine how they should address the discrepancies between the needs analysis data and the module that was now under development. As he leafed through the data tables, he thought, "If only Dragone Drilling would allow me to close myself in a room for the next year, I could redesign the Odysseus software and make it the innovative solution that they envision."

Preliminary Analysis Questions

1. What information led the client to conclude that there was an instructional need? How might David have explored this topic in greater depth at the initial meeting?
2. How can David diplomatically encourage the client's consideration of problems in its own product, instead of just problems with the users' knowledge, skills, and attitudes?
3. Considering the time constraints placed on this project, what other options might David have pursued concerning the immediate development of a training module?
4. Given the situation at the end of the case, how might David proceed with Dragone Drilling?

Implications for ID Practice

1. How do you direct a client to consider all stakeholder perspectives when the client has predetermined an instructional need?
2. List and explain project management skills does an instructional designer need to have to lead a design and development team?

25

Davey Jones
Designing an Electronic Performance Support System
by Gary Elsbernd and Donald A. Stepich

Davey Jones had worked for WidgetMart for 10 years. He had begun as a technical writer, documenting procedures for the company's point-of-sale system, but had taken on a number of other responsibilities over the years. Because of his increasing knowledge of store operations and personnel, and the lack of formally trained instructional designers, Davey had been thrust into the roles of both instructional designer and stand-up trainer, responsible for teaching everything from new procedures to interpersonal skills.

WidgetMart was making a transition to an integrated electronic performance support system (EPSS) to replace its existing training and performance support materials. Existing materials were being repurposed and new information developed for online presentation. Davey's expertise in computer interface design made him a natural for the project, and he had been given the task of heading up the project team. It was a high-profile project, the kind of assignment that could be a real feather in Davey's cap. But it wasn't going to be easy.

Background

WidgetMart had grown steadily, from 1 store in 1956, to 800 stores in 1979, to 4,000 stores in 1991. At the time of this project, it was the nation's largest discount widget retailer, with 5,000 stores throughout the United States, Puerto Rico, the U.S. Virgin Islands, and Canada. Each year, the company sold more than 250 million widgets to nearly 150 million customers, with sales of approximately $3 billion. The company was actually made up of three related stores:

- WidgetMart—selling high-quality widgets at affordable prices in self-service stores
- Universal Widgets—catering to the upscale widget market
- BuyMore—a leased sales operation with department space in large retail stores

Throughout the company's history, an effort had been made to teach the associates and managers working in the stores the best practices of day-to-day operations. During the old days (prior to 1979), most of this took the form of "sit with Fred" training, in which new trainee managers spent 6 to 18 months with experienced managers and district supervisors, who carried best practices from store to store.

However, there were several problems with this kind of training. One was that the procedures varied from region to region and sometimes from store to store. The six regional management offices could rarely agree on the most efficient procedure for anything from processing an incoming shipment to handling customer returns to setting displays. This resulted in six different sets of best practices and difficulties in transferring associates from region to region. Another problem was that the information degenerated as it passed from person to person, much like a photocopy of a photocopy. The first trainer might understand the procedures and the rationale behind the procedures, but the next trainer might understand only the mechanics of the procedures. By the time the information had passed to the associates in the stores, the compelling business reasons were often lost and the procedures themselves were often changed, similar to the telephone game played by kids at camp. It's fine for the message to degrade in a game, but in business it leads to inefficient and ineffective performance.

These problems became more noticeable during the company's explosive growth in the 1980s. As a result, management had decided to make the information more formal and consistent. Company-wide standards were adopted, and a team of technical writers collected best practices throughout the stores and compiled them into an operations manual ("ops manual"). As an example, prior to 1979, merchandise displays were left to the individual store. Some managers displayed the best-selling widgets, hoping to extend the sales of those units. Others displayed the widgets with the biggest inventory to increase product turnover and free up shelf space. Still others chose seasonal widgets to match their concepts of fashion. To make displays more consistent, the ops manual included a standard for product displays, based on projected sales throughout the company and designed to present a consistent image to customers. Similar standards were developed for other store operations.

The ops manual became the foundation for a set of structured workshops and paper-based, self-paced training materials, which were made available to all store managers and associates. However, the ops manual and the training materials were organized differently. The ops manual was organized by functional area within the corporate office: leadership, human resources, store administration, merchandise administration, marketing, loss prevention, and store maintenance. The training materials were organized by position responsibilities for store associates: orientation, merchandise, customer satisfaction, sales transactions, store administration, supervisory skills, and management skills. Over the years, the ops manual and the training materials were updated, but more effort went into adding new information than into deleting old, obsolete information.

In 1994, a text-based online reference tool was added, consisting of more than 1,100 topics presented as ASCII text files in an indexed and searchable browser. This opened up the possibility of reusable, hyperlinked information. But the technology available at the time limited the online reference to one megabyte of information within a DOS environment, and the system was, at best, rudimentary. Beginning in 1995, the company began to replace its outmoded computers with more sophisticated equipment. This opened up the prospect of overhauling the training and performance support of the associates.

The EPSS Design Plan

The plan was to use the new, more sophisticated computer technology to update and replace the existing materials with a system that was entirely online. The online materials needed to be accessed easily and just as easily revised. They also had to include best practices related to all aspects of store operations—loss prevention, retail operations, merchandising, human resources, and so on. The goal was to embed the knowledge in the software as field edits, prompts, and error messages that provided the necessary knowledge or tools to perform the task on demand or in the background. This would radically redefine the work in the stores and would allow managers and associates to focus on tasks that required human intervention, rather than tasks that were more easily completed by the computer, such as looking up information or calculating numbers. One example was the scheduling system. Previously, the manager created work schedules manually, based on his or her knowledge of the workload, labor laws, and associates' requests. Under the new system, an EPSS scheduling function would take the current best knowledge of these factors and create a draft schedule for the manager to review and edit or approve, optimizing the scheduled work to the projected workload. As the manager made changes to the schedule, the software reviewed the change against workload, labor laws, and associates' requests and preferences, providing warnings or recommendations as necessary.

In tasks completed away from the computer, such as rack allocation, the EPSS software would present the necessary data (e.g., number of racks, inventory), the decision criteria (e.g., current and projected sales, seasonal promotions), and the recommended process (each rack charted by size and style) in an easy-to-use worksheet. The challenge was to create a system in which knowledge and best practices of every process were embedded in the EPSS software and support systems.

Some steps had already been taken. A thorough analysis of the performance environment had been performed to determine where and how information was used in the stores. Because WidgetMart was a self-service store, associates were rarely on or near the computer. They spent most of their time processing shipments in the backroom or stocking displays on the sales floor. Store managers spent only about 15% of their time on the computer, completing tasks such as scheduling and inventory tracking. Still, all managers and associates had access to the computer and used it for timing in and out. Based on this analysis, the EPSS would be made up of four functions:

- Applications with embedded knowledge—software applications for computer-mediated tasks in which data, best practices, and business rules would be embedded, negating the need to learn or even review the knowledge. For example, an inventory finder with embedded suggestions for cross-selling would support customer satisfaction.

- A reference function—a repository of knowledge, which could be accessed whenever needed. For example, if a manager needed to determine how many days off were provided to an associate whose uncle had died, he or she could access this information.
- A job aid function—a collection of printable worksheets and reminders, which would be used away from the computer to support performance. For example, the rack allocation guidelines would dynamically generate the optimal display guidelines and outline the process for changing the racks for new associates.
- A computer-based instruction function—structured information and guidelines designed to help associates internalize the information. For example, when an irate customer walks in the door, the associate needs to be able to react properly in the absence of any external support. Therefore, associates must learn how to deal with difficult customers.

With these functions in mind, the project team decided to meet to work on the design of the EPSS. The first meeting was arranged for a Monday morning.

The Project Team Meeting

After coffee and rolls, everyone settled down so that Davey could explain the next stage of the project. Looking around the table, Davey thought about the knowledge represented by the team. No one had formal training in instructional design, but each member of the team was an expert in different aspects of store operations. Ellen understood merchandising processes and had designed many of the business applications that would be incorporated into the EPSS. She would also take on some of the project's administrative responsibilities, allowing Davey to continue to build sponsor support and advocacy and to determine a long-range strategy for the system. Josie worked on the acquisition team for Universal Widget and was instrumental in defining the training system for BuyMore. She understood better than anyone else the variations in the information required for WidgetMart, Universal Widgets, and BuyMore. Tim was the translation expert. He understood the variations needed in the information from country to country to account for customs, language, and governmental requirements. Barry, the newest member of the team, had been brought in for his experience in management development and interpersonal skills. His focus would be on the internal marketing and change management aspects of the system, rather than the technical implementation. The team had a wide range of talents and the knowledge necessary to complete the project.

"You know the background," Davey began. "We're creating an online performance support system with four functions—applications with embedded knowledge, a reference function, a job aid function, and a computer-based instruction function. The problem is that there is a massive amount of information. Information has been accumulating in the ops manual and training programs over the years, and not much has been done to combine or weed out the outdated information. The information sometimes overlaps. Sometimes it's downright contradictory. And, sometimes, different employees get different information at different times in their careers, which confuses things even more. To make matters worse, there is a whole collection of new information that comes with the change we're making to a new system and new processes.

"In order to create the new online system, this information will have to be collected, sifted, and assigned to one of the four functions. The goal is to have a completely integrated system that presents accurate information in the most concise, reusable form possible. In other words, we have a big pile of information and four buckets—five, if you count the trash bucket. Our job is to figure out how to break down the information into the smallest usable bit, catalog it, and sort it. We'll have to come up with a way to decide what information to keep and a way to decide where each piece of information goes. We'll also have to figure out how to make sure that the functions support one another, without any inconsistencies.

"The challenge is to create a single, seamless package that includes everyone from entry-level shipment processors to district managers with responsibility for 20 to 30 stores, and it has to include variations of the information for our 3 stores—WidgetMart, Universal Widgets, and BuyMore—and the unique requirements for the various countries we're in.

"How should we start?"

Preliminary Analysis Questions

1. Outline a method (or methods) that can be used to gather all of the information. Describe how this information can be broken down into the smallest chunks that would be appropriate for the knowledge inventory.
2. Suggest a method that can be used to catalog the information into the five buckets mentioned in the project team meeting. That is, how can the team make consistent decisions about what information should be converted (vs. discarded) and about what information should be placed into each of the four established functions of the EPSS—maintaining the consistency of the information without making it unnecessarily redundant?
3. Describe a method that can be used to make sure the inventory is complete—that it includes all of the relevant information. Suggest a method or methods that can be used to maintain the inventory once it has been completed.
4. Describe a method that can be used to make sure the inventory is accurate.
5. Outline a plan for adapting the inventory for all the variations within WidgetMart (stores, countries, and languages).

Implications for ID Practice

1. Electronic performance support systems are not appropriate for every situation. When can (and should) an EPSS be used, either in conjunction with or in place of traditional training?
2. What can be done to help ensure the successful adoption of an EPSS throughout an organization?
3. What criteria and methods might be used to assess the effectiveness of an EPSS and its value to an organization? How might such an evaluation be built into the design and implementation of the EPSS?

Diane King
Rapid Design Approach to Designing Instruction
by Ronni Hendel-Giller and Donald A. Stepich

Diane King, a seasoned instructional designer with IDEAL Solutions, a performance consulting group, hung up the phone. Stan Smith, her client from the automotive insurance division of Delta Financial Group, had called to tell her that he would like her to design and develop training materials for team leaders ("leads") in the collections departments of Delta's branch offices.

Background

About a month earlier, Diane had completed a course for Delta's phone representatives ("reps"), which covered issues associated with customer handling. The audience for this course had been reps who were new to Delta and had limited experience with collections work. These new reps needed to develop an approach to customers that was assertive without being aggressive and alienating. Most new reps had difficulty finding the right balance. This balance was needed to help customers find ways to bring their accounts current and to show them the importance of doing this.

Diane and her team developed a model for handling calls and designed a three-day course that helped participants achieve the desired balance in their calls through the use of this model. The "soft" skills required to support the model (listening skills, negotiation skills) were developed and practiced, using very specific role plays and case studies. Diane had been excited about the work she'd done—she had a great team of designers and knew the course was well designed. She had received great support from her subject matter experts (SMEs) and she knew that the course was built from a deep understanding of Delta's business challenges and priorities.

Early on in the project, however, Diane and Stan began to realize that the ultimate impact of the course would be limited. While new and recent hires were being trained to be appropriately assertive when handling calls, their colleagues and managers were not aware of what was included in the training. And, to make matters worse, most of the current supervisors and team leads had learned their jobs by trial and error. According to Diane's SMEs, the team leads and the more veteran reps were generally too aggressive or too passive with customers, which was one reason that Delta had a problem with delinquency. It was clear that the new reps would not be supported in implementing what they had learned in the course.

To complicate matters further, the team lead job was relatively new. Recently, the entire collections function had been redesigned and the team lead role established. The team leads had been promoted from the ranks of advanced reps. Now, instead of being responsible for handling the difficult calls themselves, their job was to coach and monitor a team of reps. A new system had been installed that tracked measures, such as call time. Until now, no tracking devices had been used. In addition, a call monitoring system was put in place that allowed team leads to record and listen to calls and provide feedback to reps. When the new systems were rolled out, Delta provided about two hours of systems training for the team leads, but no training was provided on how to use the data that the systems generated to give feedback to the reps.

Diane and Stan had asked to develop team lead training concurrently with the development of training for the reps. At the time, however, Stan had been unable to convince members of the operations group to make this investment. The rep training had already been budgeted, and the team lead training didn't fit into anyone's budget. The restructuring and new systems had been expensive, and there just wasn't any money left.

The Present Problem

When Stan called to ask Diane to design a team lead course, they both almost had to laugh. Finally, the organization had realized that it had to start with the team leads. It was apparent, in every Delta branch, that the team leads were not performing their jobs as they had been defined. They were reluctant to give feedback to people who had only recently been their peers, they weren't sure how to use the data they received, and they didn't necessarily handle the calls in the most effective ways themselves. Most team leads had slipped back to their previous behaviors and were spending the majority of their time taking the hard calls and ignoring their leadership and management roles. Their supervisors were at a loss—they really weren't much better than the team leads at managing the new processes and tools. Most supervisors had minimal guidance, support, and training in their own roles as coaches and leaders.

Stan and Diane, although frustrated that it had taken this long, were excited that they finally had the opportunity to "do it right." They even hoped to include supervisors in the training process and start from the top down. At the same time, there were a number of challenges that would make this project difficult. Delta was now concerned about what was happening in its branches and had determined that this training was a high priority, meaning the timeline would be very aggressive. It needed to be deployed as soon as possible. Also, Delta had a minimal budget for this effort.

Stan understood that this meant that they'd need to find ways to speed up the ID process. IDEAL Solutions had previously prepared materials for Delta that were robust—participant guides that were graphically impressive and facilitator guides that were highly detailed. Diane knew that Stan would have trouble with any materials that were less than polished and with any approach that appeared to short-circuit the design process. IDEAL Solutions was known for the quality of its process and its deliverables. "Fast and cheap" was *not* its motto.

Nevertheless, Diane was not discouraged. She knew the work environment at Delta, had met with several team leads during the design of the customer rep training, and thought that she understood the organization's culture. She also knew that a quicker, less labor-intensive design process was something that IDEAL needed to develop. More and more clients were emphasizing speed, and more and more vendors were developing training to support organizational change initiatives that were being implemented at a rapid pace. If Diane could succeed with this project, she'd be helping IDEAL become more competitive in the marketplace, as well as helping her client meet its goals.

The Existing ID Process at Ideal

Diane decided to try to figure out ways to speed up the existing ID process at IDEAL and to reduce labor costs. The existing process consisted of the following steps:

1. A commitment to a thorough needs analysis: IDEAL told its client that analysis was key to training effectiveness and that a thorough analysis was critical. Typically, IDEAL spent three to four weeks conducting research, including interviews, focus groups, and surveys of the training audience. An assessment report was generated and discussed with clients before proceeding to the design phase.
2. Development of a detailed design plan with clear and well-defined performance objectives was a must. The time line for design plan development was usually about two weeks (for a two-day workshop), with a week for client review and a full-day client review meeting. Another week was allotted for revision to the design plan and final sign-off on the design.
3. First-draft development was allotted about a month, with a full-time designer assigned to the project; Diane served as primary client contact and occasionally did some development herself. This included the development of participant and facilitator guides. Role plays and case studies were very detailed, incorporating specific work situations to ensure better transfer to the job. When necessary, the designer talked with SMEs to gather additional data.
4. The first draft review and pilot draft development usually took about three to four weeks and included walkthroughs of activities to gain formative feedback from SMEs, accuracy checks by SMEs, and the involvement of a desktop publishing team to develop a polished product for the pilot.

5. A pilot was held with a representative sample of end users. Once the pilot was held, about a month was allotted for pilot revisions and the production of the final materials.

Based on this process, a 2- to 3-day course, such as the team lead course, would take about 20 weeks or 5 months, from start to finish. In some cases, IDEAL could speed up the process by increasing manpower—which reduced the time line but did not impact the cost of the project.

Rapid ID Strategies

Diane had heard about rapid design and decided to do some research. She wanted to develop some strategies for reducing the time and cost of the design and development process while continuing to deliver training that would meet the needs of the learners and would achieve the desired organizational results. From her research, she learned that there were several key assumptions underlying traditional design and that many of these assumptions were being challenged by those suggesting rapid design strategies. Key assumptions included the following:

- All components of the design process are required to deliver a robust product.
- Design is a linear process, in which each component of the design model appears once and is not reconsidered unless revision is required.
- Effective design requires a commitment to the full execution of each component of the design process.
- Failure to complete a component of the design process will reduce the effectiveness of instruction.

Diane recognized that these assumptions were at the heart of IDEAL's design process and were assumptions that she herself had made in her work as an instructional designer. She also knew that these assumptions were often hard to live by. There had been times when she had tried to short-circuit the traditional design process and had often felt as though she were "cheating." She discovered that proponents of rapid design methods were challenging these traditional assumptions and suggesting new approaches and strategies. Some of the rapid design principles that Diane discovered included the following:

- A belief that instructional design is a nonlinear process and that there is no one right way to design. Different stages can be completed in tandem and then revisited in an iterative manner. Initial budget constraints can result in an initial set of lean materials, which can, if necessary or desired, be enhanced at a later stage.
- Analysis and design are thought of as a collaborative process. Designers work with key stakeholders to quickly complete the analysis and design work. The end user is often a key player in the design process, both contributing to the development of materials and testing prototype materials as they are developed and refined.

- Analysis is completed rapidly by making full use of extant data and by limiting the quantity of data collected with a limited but targeted analysis.
- Budget and time constraints are addressed by focusing on content and instructional strategy, rather than on level of production. Minimalist facilitator and participant materials can be developed—especially for an initial pilot. If necessary, these can be expanded and enriched at a later stage in the project.
- The use of participant input in the actual training session can eliminate some of the need to develop full-blown role-play and case-study scenarios. Sharing real issues and concerns in an action learning type of model, in which participants work with real issues and concerns, can reduce design time and increase value and relevance.

Using these strategies, Diane set out to define a project plan that would allow her to conduct the first training of the team leads within two months of the start of the project and, then, be able to train the rest of the team leads within two weeks after that.

Preliminary Analysis Questions

1. Review each step of IDEAL's instructional design process in light of the rapid design principles described in the case study. What suggestions can you make to speed up the process and reduce labor costs?
2. How receptive do you think Delta might be to these suggestions? What concerns or objections might be raised by the client? What might you do to sell your rapid design strategies to the client?
3. How can Diane ensure that the training she develops using a rapid design methodology is consistent with the quality for which IDEAL Solutions is known?

Implications for ID Practice

1. In this case, the use of rapid design is important because of a request to speed up the process used to design and develop instructional products. What other factors might push instructional designers either toward or away from the use of rapid design?
2. What are the risks and benefits of a rapid design approach? In what kinds of situations would rapid design be most useful? Are there situations in which rapid design should be avoided?
3. How does using a rapid design approach change the knowledge and skills required of the designer?

Austin McGwire and Ken Casey

Managing the Development of Blended Instruction

by I. Andrew Teasdale and Sean R. Tangney

Brian Joseph, manager of a newly restructured engineering department in a major manufacturing company, initiated a request to his company's training department for a new course. Brian's department was charged with building large dies for manufacturing-formed sheet metal. The dies range in cost from $1 million to $3 million. The training was intended to update the die engineers on information they needed to perform their jobs, to provide guidelines for keeping projects on time and within budget, and to provide recommendations for managing projects that had time or cost overruns. There were two principal reasons for Brian's request. First, the restructuring had caused significant changes to the department's tools, people, and processes. Second, several projects managed in his department had significantly overrun their allotted budgets. Brian had identified some causes for these overruns and wanted to present solutions to the cost overrun problems.

Austin McGwire worked in the training department and was the lead designer assigned to the project. The training department had traditionally focused on developing classroom training. Now the management of the company was encouraging "e-business" (i.e., using the company's intranet and the Internet to make work processes more efficient); Austin was charged with integrating web-based components into interventions developed by the training department. The plan was that Austin would have primary responsibility for the instructional design as well as contribute to interface and content design. Ken Casey would be the developer for this project. His principal role in the project would be to develop all paper-based and online materials. Ken had experience developing classroom-based courses but was new to web-based development. He was completing his master's degree in training and development and was contracted to the manufacturing company from an outside firm that specialized in training.

Week 1

Ken and Austin learned about Brian's training request from their director who wanted an intervention that would implement some of the corporation's e-learning initiatives (the corporation seemed enamored with anything "e"). These initiatives included a push to reduce the amount of class time by delivering content asynchronously over the company's intranet as well as a move toward blended approaches—interventions that combined classroom-based instruction with other delivery methods, such as intranet-based and video-based delivery. The director had scheduled a strategy meeting for the following week between representatives from the training and engineering departments to sketch out a rough plan for the intervention.

Week 2

The meeting consisted of Austin, Ken, Brian, and three subject matter experts (SMEs) from Brian's department: a program timing expert, responsible for overseeing the events and deliverables associated with the various stages of the die development process; an investment report expert, responsible for managing the spreadsheet that tracks spending on a project; and a part management system expert, responsible for tracking various parts in a die.

In the meeting, Brian agreed to an intervention that blended classroom-based instruction with an intranet-based performance support system. The classroom portion would serve dual purposes: (1) provide instruction on the new tools and processes and (2) introduce course participants to the performance support system to which they would have access on the job. The performance support system would have all the content necessary for the course, plus additional information that could be accessed back on the job as needed.

Austin and Ken pressed for access to the die engineers to conduct a preliminary needs analysis and to identify a few engineers who could become part of the development team. Brian's response was that, essentially, he already knew what they would say and that their participation would not add any value to the project. He also added that there weren't any engineers who had time to participate. Ken and Austin emphasized that the intervention would be successful only if it addressed actual needs. Brian assured them he knew what the engineers needed and commented, "The process is new to many in our organization, and we need to tell them how to do their jobs."

Ken and Austin feared that there were other factors, not related to a lack of knowledge or skill, that were significantly impacting the performance of Brian's department. For example, Ken asked Brian what an engineer should do if he or she learned that a project was exceeding its budget. Brian's response was, "Manage the project better." When pressed for more detail, Brian responded that he would deal with project management issues elsewhere.

Ken and Austin expressed other concerns during the meeting. Foremost was their concern about Brian's aggressive project time line. He wanted an intervention ready several weeks earlier than they had estimated would be possible. They told Brian they could meet the deadline he proposed only if a strict schedule were developed for Brian's team to deliver content and if the team adhered to the proposed schedule. Brian assured them that this would happen.

Ken and Austin also had additional time line issues, which they did not express in the meeting. They were concerned that the time line didn't allow for technology problems that could be expected to surface with an innovative (for their company) approach that included a web-based component. In addition, they were concerned that Ken, an untested designer/web developer, would not have ramp-up time to learn web technology. Finally, they were concerned that the nature of the development environment would cause too many delays in transferring information among members of the team. As a contract employee, Ken did not have access to the company intranet and would have to rely on other team members to shuttle information back and forth between Brian and his team.

Given the short project time line, Austin suggested that the development team use a rapid prototyping approach to designing the intervention. Brian, Ken, and Austin had agreed that weekly meetings would be necessary to review the progress, and this meeting schedule appeared to Austin to be a perfect scenario for rapid prototyping. In addition, Austin believed that a rapid prototyping approach would have two significant advantages. First, it would reduce the risk of spending time on a design that was not satisfactory to the client, since the client would have the opportunity to review the design each week. Second, rapid prototyping would allow the client to be more involved in the design, leading to a corresponding feeling of ownership in the intervention.

Week 3

Austin was beginning to think about the project in terms of the two main components: design and content. He believed that both parts would evolve as the project continued, with a heavier emphasis on design toward the project's start and more attention to content as the project progressed. Ken and Austin were working on the design of the classroom instruction as well as the design of the performance support system.

Ken had already roughed out a prototype of the performance support system organized around timelines, tools, and supporting information (see Figure 27–1). The time line sections ("Program Timing" and "Event-Based Procedures") were intended to help the learners understand project flow, key milestones, and the deliverables. The tool sections ("Investment Report" and "Part Management System") were designed to provide information on using the tools necessary to perform project tasks. The supporting information section included an FAQ (frequently asked questions) page and course outline. In the weekly meeting, Brian reacted enthusiastically to the preliminary design, making suggestions on how content could fit within the different areas. The discussion around the performance support system occupied nearly all the allotted time, so not much was said about the classroom component.

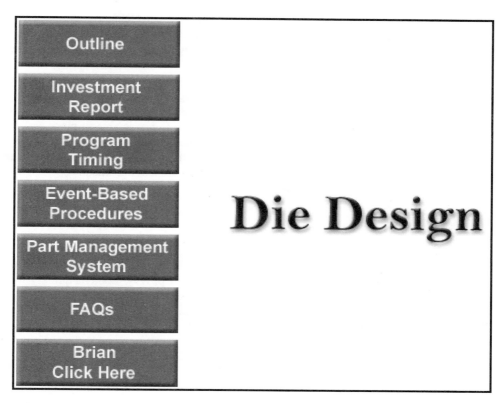

FIGURE 27–1   Preliminary Design for the Main Page of the Performance Support System.

Week 4

Austin and Ken both brought laptops running the performance support system to the weekly meetings. Austin displayed the performance support system and led the presentation. Ken also had a copy of the performance support system on his laptop. As changes and suggestions were made, Ken made updates on the fly. At breaks and when conversation shifted to noncontent discussions, Ken provided Austin with the updated content, allowing the meeting to continue with the changes already active. In addition, they audiotaped each meeting. The tapes proved to be very useful in developing the participant guide for the classroom component.

Austin and Ken experienced some unexpected benefits to their approach. Due to the time pressures on the project, they never made the effort to fully develop a content document and accepted the risk of some possible gaps in the content because of this lack of attention. As the project progressed, they realized that the performance support system was functioning as a pseudo-content document. In the weekly meetings, the review of the performance support system provided a structure for identifying missing content and refining the existing content. When missing content was identified, assignments were given to the various SMEs. They provided the content to Austin; then he entered it into the performance support system for the following meeting. Ken also added a button to the main page of the performance support system: "Brian Click Here." Since the performance support system was available on the company's intranet, Ken was able to place preliminary designs for Brian to review. This allowed Ken and Brian to communicate about ideas between the weekly meetings, so the initial work on the design of the performance support system was, in some respects, analogous to framing a content document.

Week 5

By week 5, the excitement of the initial project launch had faded. In the initial strategy meeting, Brian committed his people to provide content quickly to Austin and Ken. Now, however, already late on delivering the content they had promised, Brian and his team were beginning to realize the scope of their commitment. During the previous week's meeting, Ken and Austin reemphasized that, considering the aggressive time line, they could not be responsible for identifying and gathering content and that a late delivery of content would postpone the course pilot and the roll-out of the performance support tool.

In this week's meeting, Brian acknowledged that the initial project time line was unrealistic and that the project time line would slip (i.e., the course pilot date would have to be pushed back). Austin and Ken were both relieved. Both had suspected a slip in the time line, but allowing Brian to come to that realization on his own worked much better than Austin or Ken telling him. Ken whispered to Austin later in the meeting, "We just need to be sure that we aren't the cause of any delays later in the project!"

Even with the delays in getting content, the development of the performance support system was moving along fairly smoothly. Ken was becoming much more comfortable with the web development and graphics software. He hadn't had the opportunity to take formal classes on using the software but had learned from experience and a never-ending flow of questions to other web developers in his building. Ken's technical prowess was improving, but he had to deal with other problems somewhat out of his control. Because he was a contract employee, he did not have access to the company intranet and had to receive messages by way of other team members who were employees of the company. For example, once Ken learned that someone had sent content to a co-worker (usually, the content was sent as an attachment to an e-mail message). He needed to figure out a way to get the information from his co-worker's computer to his own. If the file was relatively small, he could save it on a disk and transfer it to his own computer. However, if the file was significantly larger (which was commonly the case, due to PowerPoint™ files with large graphics), he had to either compact the file or resend the e-mail message to one of the other employees in his building who had both access to the company intranet and a larger-capacity drive. Transferring of data was very cumbersome in this organization.

Ken and Austin left the weekly meeting feeling a little better. They were waiting on the SMEs to provide the needed content. The performance support system was reviewed and Brian was happy with the progress. The performance support system was functional, but it still lacked a great deal of content.

Week 6

From a development perspective, this week was very productive. Ken and Austin made some changes to the performance support system that considerably enhanced its usability. One enhancement was a new method for navigating. Ken and Austin browsed the Internet for a few hours and considered ideas from other sites. In the previous version, users had to navigate to the main menu (review Figure 27–2) to get from one area of the performance support system to another.

Based upon designs they saw on the Internet, Ken and Austin created a navigation bar, which appeared on most pages. The navigation bar contained tabs that allowed the user to navigate from one area to another with one click (see Figure 27–2). The framework for the performance support tool was nearing completion, but there remained considerable content gaps.

This week's meeting took a slightly different tone. The SMEs had been slow in providing information to Ken, and the delivery deadline was again pushed back. In addition, for the first time, Brian began trimming the material he wanted to include in the performance support system and in the classroom instruction.

Ken and Austin were comfortable with the changes in the time line. After all, this only made their work easier, allowing more time for design, for changes, and for Ken to learn the technology. However, the reduction in scope that took place this week was troublesome. Austin and Ken were already worried that they might not be addressing the real (or complete) problem. Now that the scope had been reduced, they became even more concerned that the intervention would not address the problem that Brian presented initially.

FIGURE 27–2   The Redesigned Navigation Bar.

Week 7

Several times during the meeting this week, Austin displayed content that was not the current version, and Brian expressed some frustration. Somewhere in the process of getting content from the SMEs to Ken, there had been problems, and either Ken didn't get the proper version or something unknown had happened. Ken realized that they were too informal in defining how they wanted content sent to him. In their after-meeting debrief, Ken and Austin decided that on the next project they would be sure to develop a process for communicating content and make that process explicit to their client(s). They even went as far as to rough out a spreadsheet they would use to track content as it moved through the development process.

Nevertheless, the performance support system was functioning well, and the gaps in content were being filled. The classroom component was nearing completion and would be ready on time. Ken and Austin tested the performance support system on the computers in the classroom. There were a few small problems, which were quickly corrected. Brian was pleased with the progress. This week, he admitted that he initially had some serious reservations about the performance support system, but now he believed that it would provide real benefit.

Week Before Pilot

In the meeting this week, the team decided that Ken would drive the performance support system during the pilot (i.e., run the computer that is projected to the front of the classroom). Brian would be the instructor for the pilot. He wanted to personally gauge the reaction of the audience he had selected. He also wanted to answer any questions and determine the changes to be made for the subsequent classes. Brian was comfortable with the content, and, given the circumstances, Ken and Austin were satisfied with the design.

Somewhat surprisingly, Ken and Austin were not in a panic over last-minute technology problems. Early in the development, they had put together an implementation plan and had identified most of the areas needing attention. They had tested the support tool in the classroom before the pilot, and it had worked as designed. They even went as far as to create a CD-ROM version of the performance support system to load onto individual computers in the classroom in the event that the company's intranet was not functional.

Pilot

The pilot was completed two months later than Brian initially desired and, interestingly enough, precisely when Ken and Austin predicted. Brian was frustrated with the delay but recognized the source of the problem. The pilot went well. The technology worked flawlessly. The only problem was that Austin forgot to put together an evaluation form for the participants. The training department had a standard evaluation form, but Austin wanted to target some specific areas dealing with the performance support system. He hastily created an evaluation form (with no time for testing) and had it ready on time. However, the evaluation form suffered from the lack of testing and refinement. Austin made a mental note to be sure to add an evaluation section to his implementation plan and to review his implementation document more regularly in future projects.

Twenty students registered for the pilot (many were handpicked). The pilot was held in a computer classroom, each student with his or her own computer. Ken drove the performance support system during the pilot and encountered only one glitch (a bad hyperlink). With Ken driving, Brian was free to elaborate and move somewhat at will in response to questions and other feedback from the audience. The design of the performance support system was such that Ken had no problem keeping up with unscripted changes in course flow. Most content could be accessed with three mouse clicks.

While Ken was driving, Austin was surreptitiously observing the audience and their interaction with the support tool. Several people refused to touch the computer. They gave their full attention to Brian and viewed the content as Ken displayed it. The majority followed Ken's lead and clicked through the content on their own computers. A few spent a portion of the class exploring the entire site (not paying much attention to Brian's lecture). Austin noted that the elements that seemed to generate the most interest were the support tool's visual areas: graphic representations of the major processes.

The class participants' responses to the performance support system were, for the most part, what Ken and Austin had expected. However, they were surprised that some refused to touch the computer. The results from the smile sheet evaluation forms (a series of questions about the classroom experience) placed this course on par with other courses. The questions on Austin's supplemental form specifically addressed the performance support system and its future applicability to their work. The responses were favorable but not outstanding. Several participants wrote that the tool should not be used in lieu of a paper-based guide.

Brian was satisfied with the intervention. He felt the pilot went well and enjoyed the discussion the class generated. He had several recommendations for improvements, which he promised to send to Ken within a few days.

Six Months Later

Things were quiet, too quiet. The classroom instruction was going well. Every other week, 20 students took the course. The evaluations remained consistent with other courses hosted by the training department. The performance support system continued to serve its purpose in the course. The course instructor had only positive things to say about the performance support system, and all of the links were still working. The course instructor had received some feedback from students that there had been some process changes that need to be reflected in the support system. He promised to assemble the suggestions and forward them in a few weeks.

However, the feedback from the instructor was the only feedback Ken and Austin were receiving. There had not been any requests for additional information. There had been no requests for clarifications or corrections. Austin suspected one of two things might have been happening. Either the performance support system was designed so well that it was functioning perfectly, or no one was using it. He suspected the latter. Without the ability to speak with the engineers, Austin and Ken had worried that the intervention would have little value. The lack of response to the performance support system seemed to confirm their fears. The silence was almost deafening. A spider web is as good as a cable if no load is placed upon it—and they feared there was no load on the performance support system.

Preliminary Analysis Questions

1. Early in the project, the instructional design team was denied access to the target audience. What would you do in that situation? If you had the choice, would you have continued with the project? Why or why not?
2. Ken and Austin were concerned about Brian's aggressive time line. Placing the responsibility for meeting the deadlines on Brian worked, in their case. How might they have handled the situation differently?
3. As Ken and Austin realized the project time line was going to change, what might they have done differently?
4. Austin found some class participants unwilling to use a computer in a learning situation. What are some strategies he could have used to help those in the target audience who were not comfortable learning from computers?

Implications for ID Practice

1. Ken and Austin were asked to provide a blended intervention: one that combined classroom instruction with a web-based component. What do you think would be important in designing such an intervention?
2. Ken and Austin used a new (for them) instructional design approach in this project. What might be the benefits and drawbacks to trying new approaches?
3. Often, people or organizations see a need for training only after a problem has been identified—often with a need to have the training completed immediately. How might ID practice be made quicker and more responsive to customer demands in such situations?
4. Many organizations now outsource their development and delivery of training to companies that specialize in training and e-learning. Ken found some disadvantages to his situation as a contract employee because his client had not provided sufficient technology support for his activities. What do you think are some of the benefits of outsourcing training? What might be some drawbacks?
5. If you were asked to implement a new technology in a training intervention, what would you do to ensure a smooth transition to using the technology?

Natalie Morales
Managing Training in a Manufacturing Setting
by Krista D. Simons and Shanna M. Salter

Natalie Morales started her day at Chipex Manufacturing with nervous excitement. It was her first consulting job after having recently earned a master's degree in Instructional Technology (IT). When one of her former professors alerted her to this opportunity, Natalie jumped at the chance. Natalie had previously worked for this professor on a number of IT jobs in manufacturing settings and both felt this would be right up her alley—in a large, semiconductor organization that manufactures electronic microchips used in everything from computers to traffic lights to cell phones. While this particular factory was in the Southwest, Chipex was a large manufacturer with factories all over the United States and the world.

Natalie arrived promptly to her 8:00 A.M. meeting with Rich Davis, a human resources representative, who gave her more information about the task at hand. "We have a training problem," Rich explained. "I'll give you the basics until you can meet later with Michelle Griego for the details. We're hoping you can identify some solutions. We've noticed a problem in the factory with our technician certification process. The technicians are the people who actually work on the floor moving the wafers through the line. They are responsible for obtaining and maintaining their own certifications, but it's come to our attention that the supervisors have been prioritizing the certifications differently and there's not a standard process."

Natalie was writing as quickly as she could, but the look on her face must have betrayed her confusion. Rich stopped himself. "OK, let me back up a bit and give you some more information. The training culture at Chipex can be summed up in one phrase, 'You own your own development.' In other words, employees are expected to maintain their own training and development. In particular, technicians are responsible for obtaining and maintaining various certifications. Some certifications are required for every technician, such as compliance with safety procedures. Others are area-specific or job-specific. The more certifications a technician holds, the more highly his or her skills are valued, which is a strong factor in promotion and yearly raises."

Natalie nodded, continuing to write while Rich went on. "It was Michelle who brought to our attention an ongoing problem with certifications. She's a supervisor of one of the process areas in the factory and manages a team of technicians. You'll be meeting with her later today, and she'll actually oversee your work. The basic problem is that we don't have a standard process in place for managing and prioritizing certifications. Every supervisor prioritizes differently; so, for example, in one area, some technicians hold numerous certifications, but these may not be the most strategic ones based on shift needs. In another area, the technicians might not hold as many, but they are the strategic ones for the area. At any rate, Michelle will explain all this to you in more detail. You'll meet with her at 7:00."

Natalie looked at her watch—8:15 A.M. "Seven o'clock?" she asked.

Rich clarified, "This is a 24/7 factory, meaning we run shifts 24 hours a day, seven days a week. Michelle is on the night shift. You'll meet with her at 7:00 P.M. In the meantime, I'll have you meet with my administrator, who can get you set up with the paperwork, an ID badge, and a temporary e-mail account. I'm looking forward to your final report and recommendations in a few weeks."

Natalie left a short time later feeling challenged by the complexity of the task facing her. She decided to organize her notes and make a list of questions for Michelle. Everyone here seemed to be in such a hurry, and she wanted to make the most of her time.

After organizing her notes, she came up with a list of questions for Michelle:

- What is a "process" area?
- How many technicians are in an area? How many areas are there?
- How exactly are certifications obtained?
- How long does it take to obtain a certification?
- How do technicians maintain their certifications?
- Who else should I speak with?
- When can I speak to some of the technicians?

Natalie also used the time before her meeting with Michelle to learn more about Chipex. She went online to learn about the electronic microchip manufacturing process, and found out that the chip starts off as a silicon wafer. It goes through layering phases, called process steps; at each step, something is applied to the wafer, such as a chemical, metal, or ultraviolet etching. The wafer goes through numerous processes and is built, literally, from the bottom up. At the end of the fabrication, it is cut into hundreds of microchips.

Natalie connected the information to some statements Rich had made earlier, and concluded that when he made reference to a "process area," he was talking about one of the areas that applied a chemical, metal, or etching process to the wafer. She noted that each process area must, therefore, consist of a supervisor and a team of technicians. She was happy to cross the first question off her list.

Before she knew it, Natalie's research had taken most of the day. Remembering Rich's statement about the 24/7 factory, she anticipated it may be a late night. Natalie took a nap and then grabbed dinner before heading off to her meeting with Michelle, who smiled warmly and welcomed Natalie by saying, "Thanks for coming on board to work on this project. It's something important to me because I think a lot of shift frustrations can be addressed by tackling this issue."

Natalie smiled in return, relieved that Michelle didn't seem as frantic as Rich. "I'm glad to be here, and I'm anticipating a productive experience. I made a list of questions based on my meeting with Rich. I'm familiar with what is meant by a process area, but can you start by telling me more about the process area and the certifications? How many people are in an area and how does someone become certified in that area?"

"OK, let's start there. Each process area consists of about 20 to 30 technicians and one supervisor per shift, but numbers can fluctuate. There are about 17 areas for my shift. Technicians are responsible for earning certifications, meaning they have gone through official training and can perform the skill. Factory-wide certifications, such as those related to compliance with safety procedures, are required of every technician. These are usually obtained through taking a class, though there are exceptions. Those that are job-specific or area-specific involve demonstrating skills with a tool that applies a process to the wafer. Do you know what I mean when I refer to the wafer process?"

Natalie nodded, and was pleased to note that she did.

"Good. As I was saying, there are large tools that actually apply the process to the wafer. When I say 'tool,' keep in mind these aren't small tools like you'd find in your garage. In fact, some tools are so large they couldn't fit in your garage! So, becoming certified on a tool is a two-step process: (1) taking a class or working one-on-one with a peer trainer, and (2) obtaining a sign-off from the trainer after demonstrating skill proficiency. And, depending on the complexity of the tool, a certification can take up to 18 months to complete, but most only take a few months and some can take only a few weeks. When a new tech is hired, he or she shadows a trainer until the certification has been earned and the technician can work independently. In effect, the longer someone has been an employee, the more certifications they should have. Are you with me so far?"

Natalie nodded, and continued to write as Michelle proceeded with the explanation. "For a given skill, there are also 'levels' of proficiency: 1, which represents basic operational skill, through 4, which represents an expert level. A Level 4 could perform complex preventative maintenance on a tool or repair it if something goes wrong. Trainers for the various tool certifications are technicians who hold at least a Level 3 certification and a 'peer trainer' designation. Finally, if someone needs a certification but no one on the shift can train, the technician has to schedule training with someone on another shift.

"So," Michelle continued, "now that you have the background on this, let's move on to some of the problems. For one thing, this is currently self-monitored by the technicians and the trainers, though supervisors like myself are expected to manage technicians' certifications and make sure shift needs are met. For example, it doesn't make a lot of sense for me to have a bunch of Level 1 certifications among my technicians without balancing this with higher levels. Similarly, it's a waste of time to have a bunch of Level 4s, since that skill takes so long to master but is rarely needed. But it's not as if there's a magic ratio of lower to higher levels because every process area is different. The supervisor just has to know the needs of the area intimately, and work with technicians accordingly. Unfortunately, this can be difficult, especially because some technicians and supervisors are short-sighted. They take a 'more-the-merrier,' shotgun approach, and try to rack up as many Level 1s as possible.

Some technicians are awarded with raises in this manner. Plus, it's difficult to obtain higher levels, which involves more long-term goal-setting."

Natalie took a moment to think, realizing she would need to speak with some of the technicians as soon as possible, and probably some other managers as well. "We certainly have a lot to think about," Natalie reflected aloud. "I'd like to speak with some of the technicians, if possible. How can I go about getting their perspectives?"

"Yeah, I figured you'd want to speak with them, and I've got to go to another meeting. I don't really know the best process for setting up interviews since they're in the factory. The best I can do is set you up in a conference room and send some technicians your way during the next few shifts. It might involve some late nights, and the interviews might be short and intermittent. Can you handle that?"

"Sure, let's get started tonight, if possible."

"Great. I've got two people in mind that I'll send to you shortly—Hector Madrid and Tran Nguyen. They've both got a wide range of certifications, they're both peer trainers, and they've been here for a number of years. They'll probably be able to give you some key information. Any more questions?"

Natalie looked over her notes for a moment. "I'm not sure I understand the difference between a job certification and an area certification."

"Well, that's a good question. A job-specific certification deals with operations; in other words, operating the tool that moves the wafer through the line. An area certification means the technician has to understand the process of the wafer in the area. It's an advanced skill, and technicians with area certifications understand more about the priority of the product and how to most efficiently move the product through based on where the wafer is coming from and where it will go next.

"Oh, and that reminds me . . . I made a simplified matrix for you that should help you understand the certifications on my shift (see Figure 28–1). I've only been supervising this team for a few weeks, so I put this together to see the current status myself. This includes the names and length of employment in descending order down the left. There's a list of certifications across the top, but I used simple names because you wouldn't really understand our codes and it's not important anyway. Skills and their related proficiency levels are listed below. The numbers 1–4 indicate the level of certification, but you'll notice that safety is required of everyone and there aren't levels. In addition, process skills are only two levels. Finally, a 'P' means that the technician is in the process of getting that certification. Also, keep in mind that this matrix is a only a sample of a few tools and a few process certs."

Natalie studied the matrix briefly and then filed it among her materials for later reference.

One hour later, Natalie was sitting with Tran and Hector at one end of a big conference table. She asked them about their perspectives on the certification process.

"Well," began Hector, "the certifications are an interesting approach to training. I, for one, like being in the role of trainer, but I hated when I was the new guy trying to get the Level 1s. For one thing, it involves trying to schedule time with someone. If they're in a hurry, you won't get quality instruction. That's why it can take so long—the training can be intermittent, and you might forget things in between the sessions. I try to be really sensitive to this fact. If I know someone needs certification, I really try to work with that person."

Name	Length of Emp.	Safety A.1	Safety A.2	Tool A L1	Tool A L2	Tool A L3	Tool A L4	Tool B L1	Tool B L2	Tool B L3	Tool B L4	Tool C L1	Tool C L2	Tool C L3	Tool C L4	Tool E L1	Tool E L2	Tool E L3	Tool E L4	Tool F L1	Tool F L2	Tool F L3	Tool F L4	PCMT L1	PCMT L2	Ops L1	Ops L2
Hector*	>6 yr.	X	X	X	X	X	X					X	X	X										X	X	X	X
Tran*	>6 yr.	X	X					X	X	X						X	X	X	X	X							
Rod*	5 yr.	X	X	X	X															X	X	X					
Phuoc	4 yr.	X	X					X	P							X	X	P									
James	4 yr.	X	X	X	X	X						X	X	X	X												
Tinh	4 yr.	X	X													X	X	X	P								
Mario	4 yr.	X	X	X	X	X																		X		X	
Angela	3 yr.	X	X	X	P			X				X	P			X				X	P						
Carlos	3 yr.	X	X	X	X	X						X	P													X	P
Carmen	3 yr.	X	X	X	P							X	X	X													
Phuong	3 yr.	X	X					X	P							X	P										
Gregg	3 yr.	X	X	X	X																						
Pete	3 yr.	X	X	X	P			X				X				X				P				P			
Tong	2 yr.	X	X					X	P							X											
Amato	2 yr.	X	X	X								X	P														
Rachael	2 yr.	X	X	X				X												X							

*Indicates peer trainer designation

FIGURE 28–1 Status of Employees' Training Certifications.

"Yeah," Tran remarked, "but things are a lot easier for them now. Back when we were getting our first certifications, there were *external* certifiers who would actually watch you perform the skills and sign off. Now, because they've cut back on staff, it's the trainers like us that certify a person. You can imagine that it's easier to get signatures now. Even if the person can't perform it right then and there, I can think, 'Well, I know I taught that skill, and I saw the person perform it at that time.'"

That didn't seem appropriate to Natalie, but she nodded anyway. "Wait a second," exclaimed Hector, "you mean to tell me you're signing off on techs who you haven't seen actually *perform* the entire skill?"

"Well, I didn't say that," replied Tran. "I just said that if techs skip a step or two but I know that I saw them do it previously, I'm going to let it go. I'm saying it's better that we do the sign-offs, because we know what we taught them. Besides, the more people I can certify, the more highly I'm rated in my effectiveness as a trainer."

"Are you serious?" Hector appeared furious. "Here I am being painfully thorough, only to find out you're handing out certifications like Halloween candy so you can get higher ratings for yourself."

"Not like Halloween cand—"

"OK," Natalie interrupted. She knew she had to do something before this went further. "This brings me to another question. How do you decide who to train?"

She could tell Hector was still angry, but Tran jumped right in. "Usually they come to us. But hopefully the supervisor is working on a plan with the techs, and helping them to know which Level 1s to get, and when to start getting the Level 2s and up. We just figure if people are asking, they know what they need."

"Well, what Tran's saying is not entirely accurate," added Hector. "Sometimes, it can depend on other factors. For example, I speak Spanish and Tran speaks Vietnamese. When we get techs in here who can't speak English very well and they're from Vietnam, they go to Tran and get training. Now we've got a number of Vietnamese techs, and their skill sets are limited only to what Tran can train them on. Over time, their English will get better, but until then . . ." Hector drifted off before adding, "It's the same with me and those who speak Spanish but not much English."

Natalie nodded, making a note to refer to the matrix at a later time to see if there was a pattern there.

"What does a typical supervisor do to address all of these issues?" Natalie directed the question to Hector.

"Well," began Hector, "it can really depend on the supervisor. Some supervisors want to look like their technicians are really productive, so they've got them obtaining all these certifications left and right. The problem is, when are these technicians doing their actual *jobs*? If they've got time to get all these certs, they aren't doing their jobs or they've got too much staff on the shift. But then again, it's also a problem if a shift has too few certs."

"Well," added Tran, "I'm not sure I agree with Hector about too many certifications being a problem. Is there a problem with 'too many skills' on the team? For me, there is a bigger issue. Managers tend to get shifted around on a yearly or bi-yearly basis. What one supervisor said was important may not be what the new supervisor prioritizes. It's hard to know, and we're sometimes stuck in the middle. I mean, techs like Hector or myself aren't in jeopardy, but the newer techs aren't always able to set goals and make a plan, so it really throws them when supervisors change."

"For once, I can say Tran and I are in agreement on that issue," said Hector, "but we don't have time to go into all that. We've got to get back to the factory."

That left Natalie not quite knowing *what* to think herself. She recognized that the project incorporated numerous issues, each of which seemed equally important. Though she was exhausted, Natalie decided to take another hour to study the matrix, make a list of what she had learned so far, and develop a plan of work.

Preliminary Analysis Questions

1. Identify the factors that are affecting the training certification process at Chipex. What other information do you think Natalie needs to help her address these factors?
2. List the ways in which language impacts workers' performance and ability to get ahead in the situation described in this case. What are some potential strategies for addressing this issue?
3. Hector and Tran have different motivations and approaches to training technicians. What problems do these cause for Chipex?
4. Suggest a strategy for standardizing certifications at Chipex and obtaining buy-in from all stakeholders.
5. Develop an overall plan that Natalie can present to the company that provides a strategic solution to the problems presented in this case. Explain how your plan addresses each of the constraints in the case.

Implications for ID Practice

1. How can contextual factors affect how trainers manage the implementation of training in an organization? How can instructional designers account for these factors when providing guidelines for the implementation of training?
2. List and discuss the legal and ethical issues involved when employees don't have equal opportunities for training.
3. Discuss the benefits and challenges of one-on-one peer training. Suggest a set of guidelines for implementing and managing one-on-one peer training in an organization.

Catherine Nelson
Managing Processes and People in an Instructional Design Project
by Linda Lohr and Laura L. Summers

Insulware, a major manufacturing company, had awarded Instructional Media Solutions (IMS) a contract to redesign a two-day, instructor-led course for online delivery. As part of the contract, IMS was asked to convert supervisory skills training to web-based instruction for Insulware supervisors worldwide. Because this first course conversion was successful, a bigger contract between IMS and Insulware had been awarded to develop an entire web-based university for 66 Insulware facilities.

The lead instructional designer for the Insulware project was Catherine Nelson, a confident young woman in her mid-thirties, who was one of the five managing partners of IMS and one of the company's four vice presidents (see Figure 29-1). However, Catherine wondered if IMS would actually be able to fulfill the bigger contract. Although IMS had completed the project successfully, the entire development of the first Insulware course was fraught with internal problems. Catherine thought back through the project history.

Early April

At the start of the project, Catherine was full of positive thoughts regarding her work at IMS. Though long-term job security wasn't a given in a start-up multimedia learning company like IMS, the excitement of potential success more than made up for the risk of working there. Every day was new and exciting. Catherine remembered the thrill of walking into the conference room when Carlos Martinez, the chief operating officer (COO) and project manager for the Insulware project; Dan Layton, the computer programmer; and she, had first met Patricia Morrison, the Insulware training director. The room was bright and cheerful and

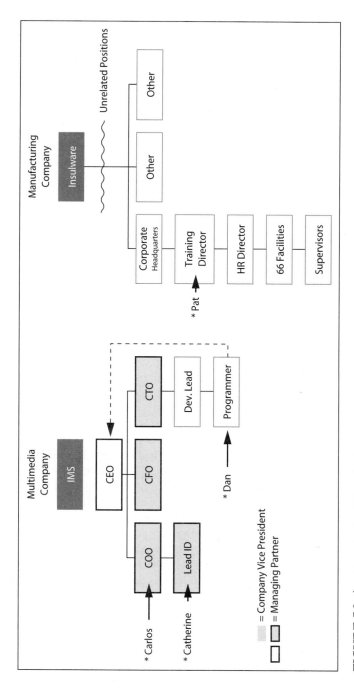

FIGURE 29-1 Organization Flowchart.

the mood relaxed. Dan was wearing jeans and had his feet propped up on the edge of a nearby bookcase. Catherine and Carlos were dressed in casual business attire.

When Carlos introduced Pat, Catherine stood up and extended a courteous handshake. Dan simply nodded his head to acknowledge Pat. At the time, Catherine was mildly annoyed at this subtle disrespect toward Pat, but she was too interested in the project to think much about Dan's behavior. As she reminisced, though, she realized his behavior was a red flag that should have alerted her to problems ahead.

Prior to the meeting that day, Dan had sneered when Catherine mentioned one of her classes in her Ph.D. program in instructional technology. Dan commented, "In our field, education doesn't mean a thing—it's what you can do that counts. I was self-taught; I didn't need a Ph.D." Catherine thought that the way he said "Ph.D." mocked her and her efforts.

Dan's confidence was somewhat understandable; his father was the CEO, and at the age of 23, he had just been offered a six-figure salary to join another highly successful technical company in the Pacific Northwest. Everyone, Catherine included, didn't want Dan to leave IMS, so the company let him get away with behaviors that wouldn't have been tolerated from others. Dan believed that his technical skills gave him the right to be condescending and often rude.

There were other red flags that day as well. Carlos started the meeting with his usual charismatic flair. He put everyone at ease and had a magnetism that made people feel confident in his abilities. He passed out a tentative project schedule, listing major dates and deliverables. He mentioned to Pat that he didn't want unnecessary detail to clutter their first meeting, since the objective of the meeting that day was to discuss the big picture and to make sure that the overall goals for the project were identified. He assured Pat that she could expect to see a comprehensive project plan sometime the following week. The red flag, Catherine thought now, was the lack of detail in the project plan. Looking back, Catherine now realized that she, Dan, and Pat never did receive a more detailed project plan.

The final red flag was Pat's attitude toward any type of instructional analysis. "I just want you to put our existing training online. You really don't need to change the training much. It should be easy; everything is right here," she said, pointing to a stack of training manuals. "Besides, I don't want to go over budget here. We need to keep the costs of this project down. I'm really concerned about that," she added with emphasis.

Catherine persuaded Pat to consider a front-end analysis of the existing training. "Pat, we want to give Insulware a high-quality learning experience. We try to shape your training to fit the needs of your learners and the special requirements of web-delivered instruction. Although your training is probably very good now, we will try to discover if we need to add new information or change any of the existing information. I'll be able to do that by visiting some of your facilities to talk with the very people who will be using this training."

Pat hesitated, clearly not excited by this news. She responded, "I really doubt you'll find much need for any visits. This training has been very successful in the past. Besides, it is important for me to keep costs down."

"Well," Catherine responded with a warm smile, "you have already paid for the site visits. It was part of our contract, so that shouldn't be a problem."

Pat half-heartedly agreed to go ahead with the site visits. "OK, I'll set those up for you next week," she said, making a note in her calendar.

One Week Later

A short time later, Catherine stopped Carlos in the hall. She was concerned with the aggressive deadline shared in the initial projected plan. She wanted to check out how he had arrived at his deliverable dates.

"Based on my calculations, Carlos, a 150:1 development ratio has been used to estimate the time it will take to create and test the Insulware training," she said. When Carlos looked confused, she added, "You know, 150 hours of development time for every hour of deliverable instruction. In my experience, I've found a 300:1 ratio to be more realistic."

Carlos motioned Catherine into his office and asked her to take a seat. "I know it is probably not realistic, but I really wanted us to get the Insulware business, so I bid low. If we do a good job on this project, we are almost assured of many more projects in the future. We essentially use this to get our foot in the door. In a way, you can consider it a marketing expense."

"I understand," Catherine responded hesitantly, thinking that she would be the one putting in the extra hours. The next four months would be long ones for her. "I'm just wondering if we could call a meeting and talk about what needs to be done in order to work efficiently with the time we have."

Carlos smiled at Catherine and said, "Catherine, you didn't get our communication award for nothing. Why don't you set up the meeting?" he suggested.

After jotting down several dates that worked for her and Carlos, Catherine entered Dan's office to ask him to identify the dates that would work for him. Dan replied, without looking up from his book, "Just e-mail them to me." However, Dan never returned the e-mail, so Catherine met only with Carlos. During that meeting, they created the design document, the storyboards, and a rough schedule designating deliverables for the site visits. Catherine remembers thinking that Dan's lack of communication wouldn't hold her up for a while at least.

Mid-April

Catherine had been excited about being the lead instructional designer for this critical project because it would finally prove to Dan that she really knew what she was talking about and that her education was an asset to the company. Dan commented frequently on the futility of her degrees in instructional technology. Just last week, he told her at the water fountain, "If I had more education, I would be laughed at by my co-workers."

In mid-April, Catherine traveled to Insulware headquarters to meet with Pat. After waiting in the lobby for a few minutes, Pat appeared behind the security-glass doors. She wore a navy blue suit and briskly walked down the narrow hall to her office overlooking the city. Catherine listened to Pat talk about the 100-year history of the company. In a male-dominated industry, Pat felt lucky to be one of nine women at the corporate managerial level. Pat had visited the installation facilities often and knew most of the managers, who had been in the company since high school.

Catherine's first site visit would be to Miami, Oklahoma, a small agricultural and manufacturing community in the northeast corner of the state, where she would visit three installation facilities. It was decided that Catherine would meet with the human resources assistant, who would drive her to the different plants to see operations and to meet with six selected front-line supervisors. The goal of the trip was to gather enough data for the design document. Catherine expressed her concern, "Will one day of interviews be enough?" Pat assured her that the three plants in Oklahoma would provide the best representation of the 66 facilities and that one trip would be adequate for Catherine's analysis. "Use this material. Everything you need is right here." Pat handed Catherine the two large binders of current instructor-led training that she referred to in their first meeting at the IMS office. Catherine then left the meeting to talk with the technical group responsible for hosting the web-based courses.

Back at IMS, Catherine spoke with the chief technical officer and requested that he follow up with the appropriate technical people at Insulware to confirm server requirements. Catherine also spoke with the art director and assured him that she would take several pictures of the Miami sites to give an idea of the company "look-n-feel." This would provide the basis for the web course interface design and architecture. The next few weeks were spent coordinating with the facilities' schedules to see when Catherine could make a site visit with Pat. When Pat became sick and was unable to fly, it was agreed that Catherine would make the trip alone and meet the human resources assistant at 8 A.M. at the first installation facility.

Early June

Catherine had a positive visit with the supervisors in Oklahoma. "I am here to listen. You are the experts, and I am here to absorb as much as I can about what you know," Catherine explained to the six designated supervisors after her brief demonstration of samples of previous web-based courses. Based on her sincere, enthusiastic approach, Catherine felt accepted. The supervisors, all men, started telling Catherine about their experiences with the current corporate-initiated training.

They explained that the training was infrequent and did not pertain to their everyday operations. In addition, the competency ratings were not practiced at a local level, so they did not feel the evaluations applied to them. Also, the training did not transfer to their real-life situations. "When I go back and try to work with my crew members, they do not respond the same way my peer did during the role plays," stated Ben, one supervisor. "My crew members are 18 years old, with no work ethic. They come in late and just don't care."

Ted, another supervisor, piped in, "I came off the floor after 12 years and, all of a sudden, I have to reprimand men who have been my peers for years. They resent the change in authority." Ted continued, "The training we get doesn't help with these kinds of things."

After the meeting, Catherine incorporated the supervisors' requests into the design document and noted how the current training material did not meet the needs of the supervisors. Catherine also requested several training documents from the plant manager, since he had done a good job addressing the plant's training needs on his own time.

A week later, Pat called to express her approval of the design document—except for the change in curriculum. She didn't want to change any of the training material. She wanted a uniform corporate approach that would benefit all the facilities. She requested that Catherine not use any of the individual facilities' materials gleaned from her interviews with the supervisors. When Catherine asked why they weren't looking at what the facilities were doing on a local level, Pat explained that the politics were different everywhere and that Insulware needed a generic approach. Catherine decided that, if she couldn't change the curricular material, she would at least make the learning as interactive as possible.

Mid-June to Mid-August

After returning from her site visit, Catherine didn't interact very much with Carlos, since he was distracted by other projects. In his haste, he did not read the storyboards and did not calculate enough development time in Dan's schedule. From June until August, there was only one storyboard meeting, in which Dan yelled about the number of interactive components in the modules. When they couldn't calmly discuss the storyboards, Dan and Catherine agreed to meet later, when they were both more relaxed. Catherine continued with her original plan for storyboards, seriously attempting to cut out any unnecessary animation but not eliminating the interactivity altogether, as Dan requested. Dan, however, never responded to the request for meetings. Catherine stopped by his office, frequently reminding him that they needed to meet. Each time, Dan kept his eyes on his computer and muttered something like "I'll get to it." Catherine was counting on Dan to allow enough time in his development schedule to talk with her about the importance of the interactive components.

Meanwhile, Insulware's technical team could not agree on whether or not the web-based courses would be hosted internally or externally. In addition, the technical team confirmed that not all of the installation facilities had web access, and a temporary hybrid solution would need to be implemented. The web-based modules would be placed on CD-ROMs temporarily until web access could be added.

Once Catherine finished the storyboards, Carlos sent them to Pat for her sign-off without consulting Dan first. Unfortunately, Dan had not had time to look through them before they were due to the client. Pat approved of the instructional design, content creativity and clarity, and number of interactive, multimedia components. Throughout the design process, Catherine continually explained to Dan and Carlos the need for the interactivity based on the dry nature of the content and the audience's need for simple, audio-based screens. Catherine double-checked with Dan to make sure he had read through the storyboards and asked for clarification. Catherine remembered stopping by his office several times, trying to be friendly and open.

"Dan," she had politely said, "I'm wondering how far along you are with the development." When he wouldn't respond, she mentioned, "The storyboards were approved by Pat. We are all set to go. If there is anything you do not understand, please let me know."

Despite Catherine's attempts to be a cooperative team player, Dan remained noncommunicative, rarely adding any information to the conversation. As time passed, Catherine learned that Dan had not kept up with the project plan and, rather than asking for an extension, had cut out some of the interactive strategies and feedback elements suggested in her storyboards.

Late August

Catherine had started her final review of the course when she recognized that Dan had made unapproved changes to the practice activities for Module 8. "Dan," she confronted him, "Why did you change the Module 8 practice activities? Pat signed off on those when she approved the storyboards."

Dan started yelling, "There's no way I could put in all the interactivity in those storyboards. Those are completely unrealistic for the time I've been given to develop them. Besides, the practice activities you've designed are worthless."

Catherine felt despair, since it was too late to restore all of the interactive components before the deadline. In a reactive mode, Carlos, the project manager, met with Dan and Catherine to fix the practice activity errors. Dan refused to make any alterations to what he had already developed. "No, I am not going to make any changes until Catherine looks through the module to see the mistakes she has made in designing these activities. This is the only way she can prove to me that she knows what she is doing."

Early September

Pat quickly reviewed a few modules and enthusiastically approved the course design. Her only question concerned the changes to the Module 8 activities that Dan had made. "What happened to the parts where the user gets to pick an appropriate and inappropriate comment?" she asked. "Those practice activities made this really good. Why aren't they here? I'm afraid I can't accept this. These multiple-choice items just aren't cutting it. They aren't realistic, and they are hard to understand." When Dan received Pat's feedback, he made the changes without further protest.

The web training was then implemented in several Insulware facilities where the supervisors took part in using it. IMS conducted a focus group evaluation of these facilities to determine the effectiveness of the training. One supervisor complained about having to take time out of his day to critique the training since he would be retiring soon and didn't like computers anyway. For the most part, the comments were neither positive nor negative. Catherine decided that the supervisors were not used to critiquing instruction and were unfamiliar with the focus group process. She concluded that, as part of a future focus group effort, she would explain in greater detail how to critique web-based instruction.

One Month Later

Catherine remembered how strained the atmosphere was at IMS following the Insulware deliverable. Catherine, Dan, and Carlos attempted to conduct a postmortem meeting, but Catherine and Dan still blamed one another for the mistakes. As a result of the project mismanagement, however, IMS discussed new internal processes to keep the same mistakes from happening again.

Unfortunately, the instructional designers in Catherine's group were nervous around Dan, based on what they had observed during the past months. They were afraid to approach him with any multimedia questions. If IMS were awarded other Insulware projects, how would Dan cooperate with her team?

Preliminary Analysis Questions

1. Given her front-end analysis, critique Catherine's design decisions.
2. If you were the project manager for this project, what would you have done to improve team dynamics?
3. What strategies would you suggest to improve IMS team interactions in the future?
4. Identify the project management challenges in the case as well as intervention strategies applicable in the current economy.

Implications for ID Practice

1. Discuss the challenges of implementing standard ID models in real-world settings.
2. Explain how dynamics within an instructional design team can influence organizational performance.
3. Discuss how a project alignment plan may clarify expectations and mitigate interpersonal problems.
4. Discuss how project management in a start-up company, such at IMS, might present unique challenges.

Andrew Stewart
Managing Consulting Activities
in an Evaluation Context
by Steven M. Ross and Gary R. Morrison

Dr. Andrew Stewart looked forward to his meeting on Tuesday with Dr. Lois Lakewood and her staff at Rainbow Design. Aside from wanting to see Albuquerque again (it had been about 10 years since he had last visited), he viewed his assigned role as program evaluator in Rainbow's design project as something he not only was well prepared to handle, but would enjoy as well. Andrew was a professor of instructional design (ID) at a large university in Boston. He was knowledgeable about many aspects of design theory and practice and was considered a national expert in educational evaluation.

The BTB Global Transport Contract

For Andrew, the professional challenge and opportunity seemed tremendous. Rainbow Design had been awarded a $1 million contract from BTB Global Transport (a large and profitable shipping firm) to develop a user support system for a new computer system, called Galaxy, being developed for BTB. The new system would support nearly all business functions, such as inventory management, accounting, billing, and ordering, and would require substantial changes in employee job functions and specific tasks.

On Tuesday, Andrew arrived early at Logan Airport in an effort to escape some of the office distractions and to gain additional time to review Rainbow Design's plan of work. By the time the airplane boarded, he had become thoroughly reacquainted with the "meat" of the plan. Rainbow Design would need to develop varied types of user supports, using a learner-control-type format. Specifically, for each job task (e.g., accessing a customer's order number), the employee would be able to select online support when needed from a menu of options, including, for example, cue cards (brief definitions, reminders, or directives), computer-based instruction (CBI), wizards (intelligent demonstration/application functions), and coaches (response-sensitive correction/feedback). Andrew's main responsibility would be to conduct a formative evaluation—first of the overall design approach and later of the individual support tools as they were developed.

Engrossed in his reading, Andrew barely noticed the smooth take-off of the plane as it left Boston behind and cruised toward the West and Albuquerque. The effects of his early morning wake-up made him drowsy, but, before allowing himself to drift off, he wanted to study one additional part of the plan—the staffing section. It looked good. Rainbow Design had a project manager, Cecilia Sullivan, who would perform necessary administrative functions but remain removed from ID decisions. Lois Lakewood, a talented and experienced designer with a doctorate from a nationally recognized graduate program, would head a diverse team of seven designers, including experts in text instruction, computer programming, CBI, and technical graphic design. In a vague, semiconscious way (especially in his sleepy state), Andrew experienced some discomfort with the role of a second, external design team housed in St. Louis. Because BTB Global Transport had a large satellite division in St. Louis, Cecilia thought it wise to hire local designers who could interface with the computer programmers in St. Louis to acquire a better understanding of how the Galaxy computer system would work when completed. A formidable challenge in this project was that user support prototypes would need to be developed based solely on impressions and draft models of Galaxy because the real system wouldn't exist for an indeterminate time. The St. Louis team consisted of three young designers, all having master's degrees in instructional design from Davis University in St. Louis. Their leader, Alicia Rosenthal, was in her early thirties, and was completing her dissertation for a doctoral degree there.

The Planning Meeting

After arriving in Albuquerque, Andrew made good time while taxiing to the Rainbow Design office, which was located in a suburban strip mall about 10 miles from the airport. The meeting started as scheduled at 1:00 P.M. All the major participants were there, including the Rainbow team, the St. Louis team, and the BTB project manager, Carlton Grove. Lois did an excellent job briefing the group on the purposes of the project. Carlton described his expectations and, despite his lack of much formal ID training (his background was human factors), displayed an excellent intuitive grasp of how user support should be employed and how to increase attractiveness and utility.

Several times during the discussions, Andrew observed that the St. Louis team, through facial gestures and side comments, was inattentive and disapproving of the orientations being proposed. The team had prepared a set of detailed flow diagrams, which, according to their brief description, established a support selection model based on the works of Gagné, Mager, and other theorists. However, there was little time to study the selection model sufficiently, and, as Andrew observed, the St. Louis team members themselves had little interest in it, since they appeared to be primarily a practitioner-oriented group. Lois, he noted, frowned in response to the antics of the St. Louis team, and, when speaking, seemed somewhat tense and guarded.

Andrew closed the day with a clear and forceful overview of his formative evaluation plan. He described it as involving progressive stages of increasing focus and comprehensiveness, as the support prototypes evolved from early drafts to near-final products. In all phases, the evaluation would include multiple data sources (different instruments from different participant groups) to provide triangulation and increase the amount of feedback regarding the quality of the design and its products.

Project Progress

Over the next two months, the Rainbow staff generated several user support prototypes for various employee job functions. Disappointingly, the St. Louis group, given the same assignment, was slow to produce any materials and still seemed constrained by their strict adherence to textbook models they had studied in their ID courses.

In several conference calls among Andrew, Lois (Rainbow), Alicia (St. Louis), and Carlton (BTB), there was obvious strain in the discussions. Provoked largely by Alicia's frequent resistance to the directions proposed, each stakeholder increasingly pursued an individual agenda for his or her team's work. Andrew's agenda, however, was already clearly defined by the current status of the project. With the first series of user supports developed and substantive costs already incurred (as Carlton frequently reminded the group), it was time to initiate the formative evaluation. Carlton wanted it done "yesterday," but "next week would be ok." Andrew mused that this was exactly the type of real-world situation he had recently warned his graduate students to expect.

Developing an Evaluation Plan

Over the next few days, Andrew drafted questions and rough instrument plans and faxed them to Lois, who turned them—almost magically, it seemed—into a professional, polished set of materials. The final product was an "evaluation manual," consisting of a complete set of instructions, prompts, and instruments for guiding the evaluation step by step. In brief, the basic orientation, as designed by Andrew, was one-on-one trials, in which each participant (interviewee) would: (1) describe his or her background and job activities; (2) walk through a simulation of a computer-based job function in the transportation industry (specifically, scheduling rail shipments); (3) examine sample user support tools made available for specific tasks; (4) rate each tool on various utility, user-interface, and aesthetic dimensions; (5) "reflect aloud" on its possible application; and (6) make recommendations. The manual was directly coordinated with the computer simulation and provided (so Andrew and Lois believed) tight control over the data-collection process, as well as an efficient data-recording system.

The final steps before launching the evaluation were to arrange for interviews and to train the evaluators. Interviewees would be approximately 10 employees at 6 national BTB sites. The evaluators would consist of designers from Rainbow Design and would include, to a more limited extent, Andrew (given time and travel constraints) and St. Louis staff (given Lois's concerns about their commitment and orientation).

Three days before the first set of interviews were to take place in the Minneapolis division, Lois received a call from Alicia, who said, "Given that we've been kind of impeded in our work with the BTB tech types here, I am very interested in taking a lead role in collecting evaluation data from the users. This would give me and my staff a really good feel for who's out there in BTB. User analysis is really our strength." Lois felt a tinge of anxiety about this proposal, but the idea did have some merit. It would occupy the St. Louis group (finally!); it would be good politics with her boss, Cecilia, who had hired the St. Louis team; and it would free the Rainbow staff, who now wouldn't have to travel as much, to work on the design task with their increasing demands. An agreement was reached whereby Alicia and staff would do the bulk of the user interviews (about 40 out of 60). They flew into Albuquerque, met with Andrew and Lois, and, along with the Rainbow crew, received training on the evaluation procedure.

Implementing the Evaluation

Data collection began. Over the next few weeks (through the end of March), Andrew and Lois each administered a few interviews and felt good about the procedures and materials they had designed. Alicia called Lois intermittently to give status reports from the field (they were always positive). Carlton from BTB called Andrew on April 2 to request that an evaluation report be submitted as a "deliverable" on April 15. "This can be done," Andrew thought, but he'd need Alicia to wrap things up in a week or so and get the data to him. Alicia, in a call to Lois, agreed.

On April 10, a large package with a St. Louis return address arrived at Andrew's Boston office. He opened it with anticipation. He would now need to contact his graduate student assistants, who would code and analyze the data. Pulling up the flaps of the box, he immediately saw a cover memo from Alicia ("Here are all of our data forms—42 interviews!!"). He then removed a stack of about 10 evaluation manuals from the top. All seemed to have the top page correctly filled out—interview name, employee name, time, date, and so on. When he turned to the second page, he noticed that it wasn't filled out. There were no user ratings of the first support tool, only the evaluator's handwritten notes. The same was true for the rest of the manuals—no ratings, only brief, often illegible comments. "Perhaps this one just didn't go right," he thought. "Really, can't use it." Looking at the next manual, his pulse increased, and then at the next manual and then two more, while his heart raced even faster. He dug into the middle of the box and grabbed a stack of three manuals—same thing. All were filled out in the same informal way that completely omitted the ratings.

Truth and Consequences

It was the next day by the time his call to Lois produced the call to Alicia that brought Lois's call back to him—with the bad news. Alicia's group had decided on their own that the evaluation manual was really just a "heuristic" (general guide) and that the rating scales and specific comments weren't actually needed. "For doing user analysis," Alicia explained,

"My designers favored a more holistic and qualitative orientation." Thus, they formed global opinions that they were certainly willing to share. (Andrew, too, had some opinions, but "share" would be too gentle a way to present them.)

The aftermath in the next few days was that Alicia and her group were severely reprimanded by Cecilia and put on probation in the project. But Andrew had a report to submit. Carlton, from BTB with his scientific orientation in human factors research, would be expecting at least some quantitative results (bar charts and the like), and Andrew had only about 13 correctly completed evaluation manuals—the ones from him and Rainbow Design. The report was due in three days.

Preliminary Analysis Questions

1. Discuss each issue in the case from the perspective of the four key roles featured: evaluator, design manager, external design team, client project manager.
2. Evaluate the actions taken in the four key roles in terms of making the final product (the evaluation study) successful.
3. Discuss what actions you might have taken in each of the four roles to avoid the problems that occurred.
4. Create a scenario in which the evaluation study is successful and the four key stakeholders are satisfied with the results.

Implications for ID Practice

1. Describe the role of formative evaluation in the instructional design process.
2. Describe how instructional design practices can be impacted by unexpected variables and events in real-life contexts.
3. Differentiate among the roles in a design project of a project business manager, a project design manager, an instructional designer, an evaluator, and a client project manager.
4. Describe the importance of a good management system for coordinating the activities of various consultant groups on a design project.

Case Study 31

Alan Wydell

Addressing Issues on Informed Consent in a Hospital Setting

by Nada Dabbagh

Monday Morning

The administrator of McGee Medical Hospital, Dr. George Troppell, began the Monday morning meeting in his usual robust style. "Good morning everyone!" he shouted, pausing slightly for his administrative team to respond with "Good morning!" Dr. Troppell turned to the person on his right and introduced the young man to the group sitting around a large, elliptical mahogany table. Alan Wydell had been hired by the medical facility to design instruction to improve the hospital's practices in informed consent, the legal term describing a patient's agreement with a physician performing an operation or medical procedure.

Alan had worked for a highly reputable training firm in Chicago after graduating with a master's degree in instructional design but decided to move back to Pennsylvania to start his own consulting firm. This was his first on-site contractual assignment. McGee Hospital, a 453-bed facility serving the Philadelphia area, had 2,800 employees, 1,130 staff physicians, and 106 departments, one of which specialized in gallbladder surgery and related complications.

As people introduced themselves, Alan recognized several people whose pictures he had seen on the hospital's website: Joe Gambrel, McGee's lawyer; Dr. Welch Green, head of medical research; Stephanie Robus, human resources; and Sue Shipman, assistant administrator. When introductions were completed, Dr. Troppell explained to the administrative team how they needed to cooperate with Alan as he began his work at the facility. "Give Alan as much information as you can so it does not take long for him to understand how the medical world of ours works. I want to have something we can use with our gallbladder surgery patients as quickly as possible. Without your help, it won't get done. Right?" he emphasized at the end. "Right," the team responded.

Alan sensed that it wouldn't be easy trying to understand how this medical facility worked but he was determined to do so because informed consent was a serious matter. From the preliminary research he had conducted on the topic, he realized that the issue was one of fully representing the risks of any surgery without misrepresenting those risks or causing undue concern on the part of the patient. Further, because problems may arise even when there is no negligence, patients must be aware of routine safeguards and standard operating procedures taken to reduce those risks.

As the meeting came to a close, Joe Gambrel, McGee's lawyer, leaned over and whispered, "Meet me after this meeting. I have some information to share with you." Alan nodded in response. After the meeting ended, Dr. Troppell explained to Alan that he would be working on the eighth floor—the administrative floor. "Your office will be ready and waiting, but first you need to attend a two-day orientation session to McGee's facility, a requirement of all new hires, including contractual employees like yourself. Stephanie Robus from human resources will contact you soon to inform you of the time and place. In the meantime, feel free to orient yourself to the hospital floor plan and familiarize yourself with some of the personnel." Alan told Dr. Troppell that he would be meeting with Joe Gambrel to gather some information and Dr. Troppell nodded approvingly. As Alan walked toward the door to leave, Dr. Troppell called out, "I will meet with you on Friday at 10:00 A.M. sharp to go over your plan of action. Let's get started!"

Later That Morning

"Hi! Welcome aboard! I'm glad you were able to come by." Joe Gambrel walked confidently from behind his desk and firmly shook Alan's hand with both of his. "I realize you need to get acclimated to our environment, but I did want to tell you how concerned I am about the informed consent issue." "Hi, Joe," Alan replied. "It certainly is a complicated issue and I appreciate your offer to help. What type of information can you share with me from your legal perspective? Has McGee experienced some specific cases as a result of this issue?" "I like how you jump right into the problem," Joe chuckled. He motioned to Alan to take a seat in one of two maroon leather armchairs in front of his desk. "First of all, a review of procedures used by various health care providers reveals a broad range of details and types of descriptions used to inform patients about proposed medical care. The amount of information provided by health care providers prior to obtaining a signature granting consent ranges from a complete counseling session—involving the physician, attending assistants, as well as pertinent photographs, video tapes, and models—to a simple request for signature with virtually no counseling or explanation. Many physicians tell patients that they will answer their questions honestly, but will not force unwanted information on them."

"Am I to understand then," Alan asked, "that currently, no national standard exists for administering informed consent to patients?" Gambrel nodded and continued, "When litigation arises from a difference in pre-operative patient expectations and post-operative reality, the final result of the ensuing trial often stems from the proficiency of the legal counsels involved and not from an unbiased review of the facts associated with the case itself. A review of information provided to the patient prior to the treatment often revealed a deficiency in how the information was imparted to the patient in the area of concern. Simply telling a patient what will be done, or offering a general description of the risks associated with a given treatment, does little to explain those procedures or the exact nature of the associated risks. McGee has not had any specific cases or charges brought against it but given the recent increase in litigations concerning gallbladder surgery malpractices, it could be only a matter of time unless we do something about it quickly."

"Well, I need to get started then. Thank you for the background and the support. I could use some help finding a few legal cases involving informed consent. Do you think you can help me find something?" Alan asked. "That shouldn't be a problem at all," Joe replied. "I have some contacts in the state health department who should have a fairly current list of gallbladder surgery malpractice cases in which patients claimed that they were either misinformed or uninformed about the risks of such surgery. I'll drop you an e-mail as soon as I have something to share." Joe stood and shook Alan's hand, adding, "Some of the people around here will be easy to talk to, and some won't be as open. Let me know if I can help in any way." "I look forward to hearing from you soon," Alan replied with a smile as he left Joe's office.

Alan's Office

When Alan arrived at his office, he was pleasantly surprised to find an up-to-date computer system, complete with a network connection, fax, printer, and scanner. A note on his computer included his e-mail user name and initial password. Alan sat down and began planning his week. With the smooth hum of the computer in the background, he made a list of the individuals he wanted to interview. A chime indicated the arrival of his first e-mail message. It was from Dr. Troppell (see Figure 31–1).

After reading Dr. Troppell's e-mail, Alan thought about how to gather information about McGee's informed consent procedures and practices. Should he develop a survey or questionnaire? Who should his target audiences be? Patients? Physicians? Nurses? What type of questions should he ask? His thoughts were interrupted by the ringing of the phone. "Hello, Alan Wydell speaking." "Hello, this is Stephanie, from human resources. We are going to meet at 2 P.M. in the hospital conference room for our orientation session. We only have eight new employees so we should be able to run through the orientation in one-and-a-half days instead of two, if we start this afternoon." "That sounds terrific," Alan replied. "I'll meet you at 2 P.M. in the lobby." Alan was excited about the orientation session. He knew that it was important for understanding the organization's structure but at the same time he couldn't wait to get back to his office on Wednesday to begin a thorough analysis of the situation.

Subject: Informed consent

Date: Mon, 28th, 10:54:39 - 0400

From: George Troppell <gtroppell@mcgeemedical.com>

Organization: McGee Medical Hospital

To: Alan Wydell <awydell@mcgeemedical.com>

Alan,

In the past two years, there have been 99 incidents of legal litigation involving surgical malpractice in Pennsylvania, 15 stemming from gallbladder surgery. Although none of these cases occurred at McGee, our gallbladder surgery unit physicians are very concerned and would like us to examine current informed consent practices related to surgery within this unit.

The question is: How can our hospital conform to the legal requirement to effectively and efficiently educate gallbladder patients from a broad spectrum of educational backgrounds and cultures about the nature of proposed surgical procedures and the risks routinely associated with those procedures?

I look forward to meeting with you on Friday morning to discuss your plan of action to address this issue.

Talk to you later,
George

****

Dr. George Troppell
Hospital Administrator
McGee Medical Hospital

Your Health Is Our Only Mission

FIGURE 31–1   E-mail from Dr. Troppell.

Wednesday Morning

Alan eagerly entered his office early Wednesday morning. There was so much to do. He felt good about having completed the orientation session. He now had a better idea where to find hospital documents and who was responsible for the different units and procedures. He couldn't wait to get started. He grabbed a fresh cup of coffee from the lounge and then

---

Subject: File

Date: Tues, 29th, 17:25:59 - 0500

From: Joe Gambrel <jgambrel@mcgeemedical.com>

Organization: McGee Medical Hospital

To: Alan Wydell <awydell@mcgeemedical.com>

Attachments: cases.doc

Hey there,

Hope your orientation session went well. My friend at the state health department located three cases for you to examine. I have attached a file containing a description of these cases and where you can find more information about them. If there is any legal information or lingo you need interpreted, just let me know. Have fun.

Joe

****

Joe R. Gambrel
Lawyer, Administrative Staff
McGee Medical Hospital

Your Health Is Our Only Mission

FIGURE 31–2   E-mail from Joe Gambrel.

switched on his computer. The e-mail chime announced what he hoped was the information from Gambrel (see Figure 31–2). "This is it!" he exclaimed.

Alan browsed through the three cases: (1) Broadway vs. St. Paul, (2) Addison vs. Emfinger, and (3) Blackwell vs. Nelson. He learned that only one case specifically mentioned "failure to advise the patient prior to surgery of the risks of surgery" as grounds for the lawsuit filed against the physician and his insurance company. The other two cases charged the physicians and the hospital with negligence in treating the patient's condition. However, given the number of malpractice cases filed against physicians for either misinforming, or not informing, patients about possible risks of gallbladder surgery or alternative procedures to correct the disease (15 in the last two years as Dr. Troppell's e-mail indicated), Alan began to wonder whether this was an insurance issue rather than a medical one. He thought about the huge benefits that could accrue to the insurance companies if there was a legal way to verify or validate that patients were fully informed of pre-operative surgical procedures and related side effects. He decided to do more research on the general issue of informed consent before gathering specific data about McGee's procedures and practices.

Informed consent is the name for a general principle of law that a physician has a duty to disclose what a reasonably prudent physician in the medical community in the exercise of reasonable care would disclose to his patient as to whatever grave risk of injury might be incurred from a proposed course of treatment, so that a patient, exercising ordinary care for his own welfare, and faced with a choice of undergoing the proposed treatment, or alternative treatment, or none at all, may intelligently exercise his judgment by reasonably balancing the probable risks against the probable benefits.

FIGURE 31-3   Definition from *Black's Law Dictionary*, 7th edition, 1999.

Informed Consent

Alan spent the rest of the afternoon researching the topic. He began by finding a good definition of informed consent in *Black's Law Dictionary* (see Figure 31–3). He also compiled notes from the *American Medical Association Encyclopedia of Medicine* (1992) and the *Investigator's Manual for the Protection of Human Subjects*, published by the Office for Protection of Research Subjects at UCLA, October 2004 (see Figure 31–4).

Alan wondered why two of the lawsuits he reviewed were settled in favor of the physician even though under Article 10, physicians can be held liable if they did not disclose a potential treatment hazard at the time consent was given by the patient. Alan decided that it was time to find out what type of informed consent forms McGee medical facility used and how they were administered to patients. He contacted Sue Shipman, assistant administrator, and asked where he could find copies of informed consent forms. Sue told Alan that there were different informed consent forms depending on the type of medical/surgical procedure/treatment (e.g., pre-surgery, general anesthesia, etc.). Alan asked if he could look at all of them. Shortly afterwards, Sue delivered four forms to Alan's office.

Alan thoroughly examined these forms. He noticed that although there were different levels of detail in each, the content was very general. For example, there was nothing specific for gallbladder surgery, its risks, and treatment options. He then focused on the form that was used for surgical operations and related medical procedures. He noticed that three signatures were required on this form: the patient or guardian, the physician, and a witness (see Figure 31–5).

Thursday Morning

When Alan walked into his office on Thursday morning he found an e-mail from Dr. Troppell reminding him of their meeting at 10 A.M. on Friday. Alan began to get anxious. He needed to develop a plan of action by the end of the day to present to Dr. Troppell at the meeting. He started flipping through all the documents that he assembled from Wednesday's research

Things to Remember:
Informed Consent

- *Informed consent implies a degree of instruction provided to the patient prior to treatment so that the patient is capable of granting "informed" consent to a proposed treatment. This process includes informing the patient of several aspects of the treatment including the reason for the proposed treatment, the nature of the procedures involved, the expected outcomes of the procedure, and the possible complications stemming from the procedure.*

- *Even as recently as the 1960s, many physicians in the U.S. believed it necessary to conceal much of the information about an illness and its treatment from the patient and his or her family. At that time, few physicians told the patient that they had cancer even when the illness was at an advanced stage, and fewer doctors told patients that they would die. Similarly, few physicians discussed the risk of death or serious complications—small but unavoidable—in any surgical procedure requiring an anesthetic, or explained the full range of side effects possible from treatment with a particular drug. The medical profession justified such concealment in the paternalistic belief that the physician knew best and that patients were unable to understand technical terms or concepts.*

- *The consumer rights movements of the 1960s and 1970s swept away such ideas and physicians now recognize that patients expect full and frank information about illness and its treatment. As a result of legal action in the late 1970s (U.S. Code Article 10, Section 18.2), the U.S. Department of Health instituted medical/surgical consent forms requiring physicians and/or hospital staff to fully disclose the nature of patient illnesses, available treatment, and risks associated with such treatment. A physician has no defense if the patient suffers harm from a foreseeable hazard of treatment that was not disclosed at the time consent was given.*

FIGURE 31–4 Alan's Notes.

and the orientation session. He decided to conduct additional research to find out more information about the legal and medical aspects of informed consent. He browsed the U.S. Department of Health's website and found five required informed consent forms, all based on U.S. Code Article 10, Section 18.2: (1) Surgical Consent Form for Operations, Anesthetics and Other Procedures (Article 18.21), (2) Consent to Medical/Surgical Treatment Upon Admission to Hospital (Article 18.22), (3) Authorization for Medical and/or Surgical Treatment or Examination (Article 18.23), (4) Authorization for Surgical Operation (Article 18.24), and (5) Operative Permission (Article 18.25).

Alan then began to research online medical journals to find out what research had been done about patients' and physicians' perceptions of informed consent. He found six pertinent articles from the *Journal of the American Medical Association*, *Family Systems Medicine*, the *Journal of Gallbladder Surgery*, and *Trends and Issues in Colon Surgery*. He began by reading an article that examined survey results of six physicians' perceptions of informed consent practices and procedures. He closely examined the results of this survey and noticed that all six physicians had the same responses on questions 2, 8, and 10 through 15. For example, all of the physicians (a) defined informed consent based on *Black's Law Dictionary*;

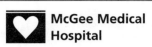

McGee Medical Hospital

Informed Consent Form for Surgical Operations and Related Medical Procedures

Date:_____
Time:_____A.M./P.M.

1. I certify by my signature on this document that I hereby give my consent and authorize Dr._____ , and such other physicans he may designate as his assistants, to perform upon_____ (myself or name of patient), the following operations and procedures, as indicated:

    _____
    _____

2. If any new findings or unforeseen condition arises during the operation or procedure that, in the judgment of my doctor, requires procedures in addition or different from those now contemplated, I further request and authorize him to do what he deems to be advisable and in my best interest.

3. The nature and purpose of this operation or surgical procedure, the possibility and nature of risks and complications, and the alternatives available, have been explained to me by my physician. The physician has answered any questions I have to my satisfaction. I know that the practice of medicine and surgery is not an exact science and I acknowledge that no guarantee has been made about the results that may be obtained.

4. I authorize the hospital to retain or dispose of any tissue or parts, which may be removed.

5. I consent to a blood transfusion if this becomes necessary during my surgery, recovery, or course of hospital treatment. I have been made aware of the risks and benefits of a blood transfusion.

6. I consent to the admittance of authorized observers to the Operating Room and to the taking of photographs deemed appropriate and necessary by my doctor.

_____

CHECK ONE:
___Patient
___Medical Power of Attorney
___Parent
___Legal Guardian

_____
WITNESS

_____
PHYSICIAN OBTAINING CONSENT

FIGURE 31–5 McGee's Informed Consent Form for Surgical Operations.

(b) stated that no set guidelines were imparted to them by their liability insurance as to how much information they should give a patient; (c) agreed that patients only want to know about the risks and complications of surgery and the general procedure involved; and (d) stated that they created an atmosphere that allowed for positive interaction so that patients can feel comfortable asking questions about surgery and related procedures.

In addition, all of the surveyed physicians agreed that hospitals had no means to evaluate the information that patients received prior to signing the informed consent forms and that no post-surgery assessment tools were available to see if the patients felt that the information imparted was helpful or relevant. Furthermore, each of the six physicians felt that he/she was the best judge as to how much information to impart to a patient, that there was no need for standards within the industry for receiving informed consent, and that the health care industry handled the issue very responsibly. However, the physicians' responses differed on the other questions of the survey. These responses are summarized in Table 31–1.

Alan wondered whether these data were representative of McGee's physicians. But even if they weren't, they gave him a place to start his own analysis. He then glanced at the abstracts of two other journal articles (see Figures 31–6 and 31–7).

Alan reflected on what he had just read and wondered what work might be needed with both the patients and physicians. Perhaps it was the patients who needed to be educated to ask the right questions before consenting to a medical procedure, or perhaps a strategy needed to be developed to assist physicians in communicating the information to patients in a more meaningful and structured manner to ensure that patients fully understood what was at stake, thereby enabling them to make an informed decision. Or, perhaps some combination of both was needed.

Alan's thoughts were interrupted by Dr. Welch Green, head of medical research at McGee. "Hello, Alan! We met at the administrative team meeting on Monday. How are things? Would you like to join me for lunch?" Alan glanced at his watch and realized that it was already noon. "Sure, I could really use some help interpreting some research that I have been reading this morning on the issue of informed consent." Alan assembled his papers and walked out with Dr. Green. During lunch, Dr. Green shared his insights on the issue of informed consent. He told Alan that, generally, physicians do not receive formal training in medical school on how to communicate information to patients and that many hospitals delegate the process of obtaining informed consent to nurses because physicians are very busy. Dr. Green also told Alan that although research was beginning to shed light on "best practices" for obtaining informed consent that protect both physicians and patients, he believed every hospital should develop its own practices based on its clientele, administrative structure, and areas of medical specializations.

After lunch, Alan settled in his office to begin writing the action plan that he would present to Dr. Troppell the next morning. He believed he had enough information to draft a plan that would outline the steps needed to examine informed consent procedures and practices at McGee Medical to determine whether they were effective, particularly those involving gallbladder surgery. Alan worked all afternoon and well into the evening. He went home feeling confident that his action plan would please Dr. Troppell and his administrative team.

TABLE 31–1 *Physicians' Survey Results*

Physicians' Survey Results	
Q1: How long have you been in the health care field?	Physician 1: 20 years Physician 2: 15 years Physician 3: 8 years Physician 4: 30 years Physician 5: 10 years Physician 6: 25 years
Q3: In your educational background, were you ever instructed on the communication skills necessary in the policy of informed consent?	Physician 1: No Physician 2: No Physician 3: Yes, through observation of a mentor in residency Physician 4: No Physician 5: Yes, through observation Physician 6: No, learned through trial and error
Q4: What aspects of the proposed treatment should be covered in a discussion with a patient?	Physician 1: Major risks and complications Physician 2: General information on surgery and side effects Physician 3: All aspects of the procedure Physician 3: All information the patient deems necessary Physician 5: Major risks, complications, and alternatives Physician 6: Whatever the physician feels is important to that particular patient
Q5: Do all patients require the same amount of information or should it vary according to the patient? If varied, what characteristics of the patient qualify as determining factors?	Physician 1: No, it depends on the state of mind of the patient Physician 2: No, it depends on the educational background Physician 3: Yes, everyone is entitled to the same information Physician 4: No, it depends on the questions asked by the patient Physician 5: Yes, all patients should get the same information Physician 6: No, it depends on the relationship with the patient
Q6: In a typical patient-physician meeting, what means would you use to tell a patient about the aspects of the procedure (video, reading material, pictures, lecture, etc.)?	Physician 1: One-on-one discussion Physician 2: Video and discussion Physician 3: Video, handout, and discussion Physician 4: Verbal lecture Physician 5: Photographs, handouts, discussion, Q&A session Physician 6: Lecture, followed by whatever the patient requests
Q7: If you were discussing gallbladder surgery with a patient, how long would you estimate the discussion to last?	Physician 1: Half an hour Physician 2: Half an hour Physician 3: All cases are different Physician 4: Quarter of an hour Physician 5: Can't generalize, everyone is different Physician 6: Half an hour
Q9: Are you aware of any disputes regarding informed consent within your organization? If so, what is the basis of the situation?	Physician 1: No Physician 2: No Physician 3: Yes, a patient is suing due to receiving a lack of risk information Physician 4: No Physician 5: Yes, there is a court case in relation to lack of alternatives provided Physician 6: No

Wade, P. D., O'Brien, T., & Manchester, S. (1999). Informed consent: Patients' attitudes towards informed consent. *The Journal of Gallbladder Surgery, 77,* 75–79.

Patients want to know more about their condition and its proposed treatment. Gaining patients' confidence before treatment reduces the chances of their seeking legal redress for an unexpected outcome. As part of a prospective study of informed consent for surgery we have assessed the attitudes of patients towards informed consent when different types of consent interviews are used. We found that most patients are happy to do as their doctor advises but think the informal consent interview is important because it gives them information. They also want to know about most, but not all, complications of the procedure. One-quarter worried about the anesthetic, about one-eighth worried about 'not waking up,' and similar proportions worried about complications and other things such as pain and nausea. Most patients think that the consent form is a legal document. Most patients felt obliged to sign the consent form and thought it had medico-legal implications. However, some patients (17%) felt less obliged to sign the consent form and wanted to be more involved in the decision to operate.

FIGURE 31–6   Abstract from the *Journal of Gallbladder Surgery.*

Smith, J. M., & Murphy, G. L., (1998). What do patients want to know about informed consent? *Trends and Issues in Colon Surgery, 86,* 235–246.

Informed consent has become an increasingly important concern for medical facilities and their patients, yet there has been very little empirical research related to this issue. This paper reports on a study in which the opinions of 80 patients were sought one month after undergoing minimally invasive laparoscopic colon surgery. While approximately 80% of patients were comfortable with their physicians making decisions regarding their treatments, they also expressed a desire to know the details of the treatment and of any possible side effects. Approximately 60% of patients believed that written information about the surgery would be reassuring but about 25% believed that it would increase their anxiety. Almost 90% of patients believed that the consent form they had signed was legally binding and indicated their agreement to undergo the surgery.

FIGURE 31–7   Abstract from *Trends and Issues in Colon Surgery.*

References

Clayman, C. B. (Ed.). (1992). *American Medical Association Encyclopedia of Medicine.* Washington, DC: AMA.

Garner, B. A. (Ed.). (1999). *Black's Law Dictionary* (7th ed.). Washington, DC: West Group, Thompson.

Office for Protection of Research Subjects at UCLA. (1978). *Investigator's manual for the protection of human subjects.* Retrieved June 15, 2006, from http://www.oprs. ucla.edu/human/manual/TOC.

U.S. Department of Health and Human Services. (2004). *Code Article 10, Section 18.2.* Retrieved June 15, 2006, from http://www.hhs.gov/.

Preliminary Analysis Questions

1. List the key stakeholders and their roles and responsibilities relative to the issues in the case.
2. Respond to Alan's uncertainty regarding whether the issues presented in the case are more of a medical concern or an insurance concern.
3. Critique the analysis procedures that Alan has undertaken so far. What else, if anything, needs to be done to complete the analysis process?
4. Develop an appropriate action plan that Alan can present to the administrative team.

Implications for ID Practice

1. What can be done to meet the challenges in designing and delivering solutions that must address the needs of a wide range of users (e.g., different levels of understanding and education, different levels of anxiety)?
2. What can an instructional designer do to optimize the chances that users will implement the proposed solutions in the intended environment?
3. How might an instructional designer handle the potential legal issues that may arise when working in high-stakes environments?

Case Studies

Section 4: Military Audience/Context

Case Study 32

Andrew Brown and Deborah Frye
Evaluating Online Instruction
by Thomas Brush, William Sugar, and Jeannie Brush

Andrew Brown sat in his office staring out the window. He had just reviewed the preliminary data from an evaluation project that his company, *Instructive Technologies,* had just completed for the U.S. military's *Office of Online Learning* (OOL). The project involved a formative evaluation of a new web-based course that focused on gathering information in order to complete a mission analysis—the task of reviewing and assigning available assets to a mission. Although Andrew was not surprised with the results, he realized that OOL would be extremely disappointed. Based on the data, it appeared that there were serious problems. Just by examining some of the key points of the executive summary, he noticed an alarming pattern:

- Only 4 of the 25 individuals participating in the evaluation received passing scores on the final assessment.
- From observation data, it was clear that numerous participants had difficulty navigating through the course, and that several participants stopped going through the course altogether due to issues with the interface.
- Of the 25 participants, 20 stated that they needed more guidance in order to complete the course activities.
- Of the 25 participants, 23 stated that it would have been better to learn about mission analysis by some other method (e.g., a face-to-face course, required readings).

In addition, 15 participants stated that the online course alone did not provide adequate training on mission analysis, and several went so far as to recommend an introductory, face-to-face course *before* using the online course.

As he pondered the best way to discuss these results with OOL, Andrew thought about the approach by which the online course was developed and evaluated. What, if anything, could have been done differently to get better results from the evaluation? What recommendations should he make to OOL?

Mission Analysis

Over the past several years, web-based training (WBT) has become a popular solution for meeting the training requirements of the U.S. military. In the past, funding and staff were not available to support instructor-led training for all military personnel. Rather, instructor-led training focused only on meeting minimal instructional needs. Many of the knowledge-based courses were easily converted to WBT and online testing procedures were developed to confirm that personnel met specific learning objectives. However, courses focusing on procedural tasks were harder to transform into WBT and the development of appropriate online assessment strategies had also been problematic.

The increased need for online training led the military to create the *Office of Online Learning* five years ago. The mission of this office was to oversee the development, evaluation, and implementation of all web-based instruction. Frank Lewis, a civilian professional employee with eight years of experience overseeing training projects for the military, was selected to manage and direct this office. Frank received his master's degree in educational technology from Western Arizona University, and had spent the past three years exploring ways to make training activities more authentic and relevant to participants.

As Frank was reviewing the latest requests coming in to his office for online training materials, one topic caught his attention. The Infantry Support School at Fort Safford, Louisiana, had requested that its lecture-based course on mission analysis be converted to web-based delivery. Frank had spent over a year assisting with the development of that course, and he knew that the concepts and procedures covered in the course were very complex. Successful mission analysis relied upon the use of available resources, accurate analysis of the status of the mission, and the correct alignment of available assets to the needs of the mission. Thus, it did not lend itself to providing a "lock-step" set of procedures because the variables changed based on the situation. In addition, the prerequisite knowledge needed for successful mission analysis was extensive. Military personnel generally did not take the course until the year *after* they had completed their officer's training.

As he looked over the request, Frank thought, "This is a perfect opportunity to really transform this course into a dynamic learning experience! If we can provide learners with multiple types of situations, and allow them to learn mission analysis skills in a variety of contexts, then they'll be able to transfer those skills to different situations." The only potential problem Frank could foresee was the tight time line—the Infantry Support School requested that the course be available within six months.

Frank immediately began working with his design team at OOL to create design documents for the revised version of the instruction. Frank wanted to focus specifically on the use of authentic scenarios in which learners would be placed in a "virtual" mission and provided with tools to collect, analyze, and select appropriate information and resources needed to complete the mission analysis report.

As the team members delved more deeply into the development of this virtual environment, they realized that additional expertise was needed if they were actually going to make this available on the Web and meet the deadline for deployment of the course.

The scenarios they were creating required learners to navigate through various virtual environments, and they wanted to provide realistic scenarios.

Frank decided to contract with *Blumstone Horizons,* a training firm with expertise in online training, to assist with the development of the virtual environment. Frank had worked with Blumstone Horizons and its lead developer, Lichin Chu, on previous projects. Lichin had an undergraduate degree in computer and information science and two years of experience developing online learning environments for several *Fortune 500* companies. In addition, Lichin was a former infantry officer (he spent five years in the military after completing his degree) who had completed the instructor-led version of the mission analysis course only three years ago. Thus, it was decided that he could serve both as the lead developer and subject matter expert. Given the tight time line they were under to complete the course, Frank believed that having Lichin serve dual roles could really save them some time.

Lichin was equally motivated to transform the class from what he believed to be a boring, low-level lecture into a dynamic, engaging experience by using powerful web-based tools to embed simulations within the new online course. He quickly moved this project to the top of his "to-do" list.

Over the next five months, Lichin worked closely with Frank's team on the design and development of the mission analysis course. Frank's OOL team focused on the general design of the instructional activities and assessment procedures, making sure that the objectives, assessment, and proposed activities were in alignment. Lichin focused his efforts on transforming the design documents provided by OOL into the web environment he and Frank had envisioned. He felt that in order to make the simulated activities as realistic as possible, he would need to use a development engine that allowed for the creation of "3-D" environments on the Web. "I haven't seen any online training produced by the military that included 3-D simulations," he thought. "They might be impressed by the added realism the simulations can provide."

Planning the Evaluation

As the deadline for completion of the revised course approached, Frank contacted Andrew Brown at *Instructive Technologies* to discuss the possibilities of his company conducting a final formative evaluation of the course. While *Instructive Technologies* was a relatively small consulting firm (with only three full-time employees), it had extensive experience with evaluation methodologies—particularly with respect to computer-based and online training. Andrew had received his Ph.D. in instructional technology from Northern Indiana University, and had personally conducted several evaluation projects for the U.S. military. His partner/co-owner, Deborah Frye, had a master's in instructional technology from Northern Indiana, and had spent six years as a civilian training specialist with the U.S. military. Andrew explained that he and Deborah would manage the evaluation themselves.

Andrew and Deborah requested a meeting with Frank and Lichin to go over the logistics of the evaluation and discuss the types of data that had already been collected in the earlier, formative evaluation stages of the project. Deborah began the meeting by asking for a status report regarding the completion of the course and the results of the evaluations they had conducted.

"So, how close are you to having the course completed?" Deborah asked.

Frank said, "We should be ready for you to collect evaluation data in about two weeks. We'll assist you with recruiting participants and scheduling a computer lab."

"Sounds good," said Deborah. "I'm assuming your usability testing has been completed and the product is fairly stable. Have you tested it on the Web yet?"

"Well, we've been testing it in my office all during development," Lichin said. "It's still got a couple of bugs, but we're confident that they'll be taken care of by the time you begin testing."

"Can you talk about the results of your usability testing? What do users think about the new 3-D web environment you're using?" asked Andrew.

"The folks we've been working with at OOL think it's awesome!" Lichin said. "They really like the way we've added interactivity to the course." Frank agreed, "Yes, we're very pleased with the way the course looks on the Web. It should be really engaging for the audience."

"But, what did the users think?" Andrew asked. "Did they have any problems navigating through the scenarios? I spent a few hours last week trying to complete several of the activities. Granted, I'm not a content expert, but I had a lot of difficulty figuring out what to do. The navigation tools seemed kind of complicated to me."

"We're planning on having a few soldiers go through the product this week or next," Lichin said. "However, we don't really expect that they'll have any problems."

"You probably want to make sure you do that before we come in and conduct the final formative evaluation," Deborah said.

"We'll take care of it," said Lichin.

"How about subject matter expert review? Did the SMEs approve of the content and the new delivery format?" asked Andrew.

"Lichin had expertise in the content of the mission analysis course, so he was able to serve as both the developer and SME," said Frank. "It really streamlined the design/development process and saved us a lot of time. Overall, we're very pleased with the content and how it's been revised for web delivery."

Deborah looked at Frank and Lichin. "Do you think you might want to have an external SME examine the course?"

"I don't think that will provide much added benefit, and we really need to stick to our schedule," Frank said. "We're planning on making this available to the Infantry Support School within the next 30 days or so."

"OK," said Andrew, although he wasn't convinced that this was a good idea. "One final suggestion. You probably want to make sure you test out the course beforehand on the computers we're going to be using for the evaluation. That way, we minimize the possibility of some wacky glitch occurring during data collection."

"We'll take care of that for you," said Lichin.

Two weeks later, Deborah arrived at the training lab that had been reserved for the evaluation. She brought with her some evaluation forms for collecting attitudinal data, as well as copies of a blank mission analysis report. While the report was supposed to be completed online as part of the final assessment activity for the course, she thought it would be best to bring some copies, just in case. "After all," she thought. "This is probably the most important piece of data we need to evaluate this course."

As she entered the room, she saw Frank and Lichin walking around the room, busily inserting CDs into each of the workstations.

"What's up?" asked Deborah.

"Oh, these computers don't have the browser plug-ins needed for the 3-D engine," Lichin said. "We're installing them on all of the computers right now."

"Did you folks test out the course on these computers?" asked Deborah with some reservation.

"Not these exact computers, but they're the same model as the ones we've used for testing at the Blumstone office, so we should be fine," said Lichin.

Just then, an infantry officer and what appeared to be his platoon of 25 soldiers entered the lab. The officer walked up to Frank.

"Lieutenant Johnson reporting, sir," the officer said. "We've been ordered to report here for some sort of testing."

"That's right, Lieutenant," said Frank. "This is Ms. Frye. She's in charge of the testing."

"Hello, ma'am," said Lieutenant Johnson, "What would you like us to do?"

"Are the workstations ready for the evaluation?" Deborah asked Lichin.

"Just finishing up the last one now," said Lichin. "I've got to head back to the office, but I think everything's ready. Just open up Internet Explorer™, and select 'Mission Analysis' from the 'Favorites' menu. Good luck!"

With that, Lichin hurried out of the lab.

"OK, Lieutenant, have each member of your platoon sit in front of one of the computers. I'm assuming they've been briefed on why they're here?"

"Not really, ma'am," said Johnson. "We were in the middle of some training exercises, and my commanding officer said that we just needed to head over here ASAP. Why are we here, exactly?"

Deborah looked at Frank, then back to the Lieutenant, thinking, "I can't believe they would do this!" However, she held her tongue as she responded politely, "Well, we're conducting an evaluation of the new version of the mission analysis course. It's been redesigned for online delivery, and we want to make sure that individuals can successfully complete mission analysis documentation using the information they learn from the course."

"I took that course," said Johnson. "It sure was boring. I hope this version is a little more engaging. My soldiers get distracted pretty easily!"

"I'm sure they'll do just fine," said Frank.

"OK," said Lieutenant Johnson, "let's get going then. This group is going through some pretty intensive urban combat training, and I need to get them back to their assignments as soon as possible."

As the soldiers took their seats in front of the computers, Deborah motioned to Frank. "Urban combat training?" she whispered. "I requested that you provide junior-level infantry officers for this evaluation. Do these people have the prerequisite knowledge for this course?"

"Well, they're not an exact match to the target population, but they're close," said Frank. "Besides, we have a pretty tight deadline for this evaluation, and you wouldn't believe how difficult it was to get any group released for this evaluation with so many personnel either in training or preparing for deployment overseas."

"Look, I've got another meeting to go to, so I need to head out," said Frank. "Give me a call this afternoon and let me know how things went."

Preliminary Analysis Questions

1. There were differences in how *Instructive Technologies*, *Blumstone Technologies*, and the *Office of Online Learning* viewed formative evaluation. Summarize each of their approaches. Given these approaches, what should Andrew and Deborah have done to optimize the chances of a valid evaluation?
2. Critique Andrew and Deborah's interactions with the main characters in the case, Frank Lewis and Lichin Chu. Should they have done anything differently? If so, what would you recommend? Explain your reasoning.
3. If you were Andrew, how would you discuss the results of the evaluation with Frank Lewis? With Lichin Chu?

Implications for ID Practice

1. Develop a set of principles to guide instructional designers when they are conducting/managing evaluations. Include guidelines for communicating with clients and other stakeholders.
2. What can instructional designers do to present the findings of inadequate or inappropriate evaluation procedures?
3. Describe the relationship between formative evaluation and usability testing of online instruction.